SEVENTH EDITION

The World Today

SEVENTH EDITION

The World Today

CURRENT PROBLEMS
AND THEIR ORIGINS

HENRY BRUN

Amsco School Publications, Inc.
315 Hudson Street, New York, N.Y. 10013

Research by Wilfredo Morales
Cover design by Wanda Kossak

When ordering this book, please specify:
either **R 3080 P** or THE WORLD TODAY

Visit our Web site at **www.amscopub.com**

ISBN: 978-1-56765-648-0
NYC Item: 56765-648-9

PREFACE

This seventh edition of *The World Today: Current Problems and Their Origins* provides information on issues, events, and topics not usually explored in standard textbooks. It will serve classroom needs by providing instructional material usually gleaned from a variety of periodicals. As a supplement to basal texts it will facilitate enrichment of key topics by enabling students and teachers to examine these topics in the light of the most current information.

Rapid and dramatic changes took place in the world in the 1990s and early-to-mid-2000s. This book deals with these changes, focusing upon their causes and immediate effects. Close attention is also given to historical background, providing a combination of readable, concise text and skill-building exercises.

The following features were included:

Comprehensive Coverage. Recent events and the world leaders associated with them are examined in several regions of the globe—Europe, Africa, Asia, the Middle East, and Latin America. A broad survey of global political developments is followed by analysis of such critical topics as nuclear proliferation, human rights, and terrorism. Significant attention is given to new patterns in world business and trade, including corporate enterprise and globalization. Also examined are major innovations and trends in technology and science.

Unit and Chapter Overviews. Each unit and chapter begins with a brief overview that identifies the major developments to be treated.

Maps, Graphs, Charts, and Cartoons. Many maps appear in the text. They provide geographical references. Map exercises reinforce skills development, as do the graph and chart exercises. Students are given the opportunity to analyze and interpret data. Cartoons illustrate key developments and further stimulate critical thinking.

Exercises and Reviews. To enhance the usability of the book as an instructional tool, the text is supplemented by frequent, strategically placed questions and exercises. Additional reviews appear at the conclusion of each chapter and unit. These are designed to require a variety of response efforts—content and data search, reading for factual detail, and the skills of inference, critical thinking, and expository writing.

Reference Section. The index identifies people and topics of current importance.

Henry Brun

CONTENTS

UNIT III   THE GLOBAL ECONOMY   *235*

MAPS AND GRAPHS

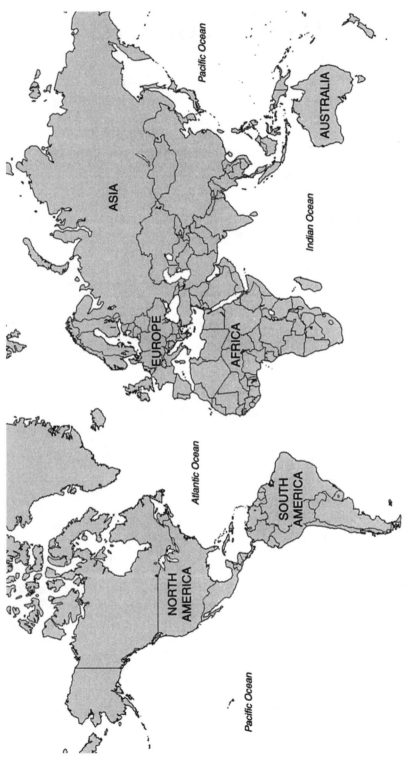

The World Today

Unit I

GLOBAL POLITICAL SURVEY

The end of the 20th century and the early years of the 21st century saw a period of political upheaval. The fall of communism in the Soviet Union and in Eastern Europe and the end of the cold war did not lead to world peace. Although the threat of global thermonuclear war lessened, national and ethnic rivalries sparked regional conflicts in Europe, Africa, the Middle East, and Asia.

Our era has been marked by wars and civil disorders. Ethnic conflicts led to political repression and the movement of refugees across frontiers. International terrorism and drug trafficking remained destructive forces. The struggle for human rights continued.

Chapter 1

The End of the Cold War

Created in 1922, the Soviet Union was the world's largest country. After World War II, it was also a military superpower able to compete with the United States for global supremacy. As the world's first Communist dictatorship, the Soviet Union (the Union of Soviet Socialist Republics, or U.S.S.R.) was distrusted by the capitalist nations of the West. During World War II (1939–1945), the Soviet Union fought on the side of the United States and its Western allies against Nazi Germany, Fascist Italy, and the Japanese Empire. World War II ended with the nuclear bombing of Japan in August 1945. After the war, the Soviet Union made haste to develop nuclear weapons of its own. An *arms race* (a competition to achieve military superiority) developed between the United States and the Soviet Union.

Soviet Expansion and U.S. Response

During World War II, the nations of Eastern Europe were dominated by Nazi Germany. Toward the end of the war, advancing Soviet armies forced the Germans to withdraw from the area. To provide the U.S.S.R. with a buffer zone between itself and the West, the Soviets remained in the countries they liberated and then influenced them to establish Communist governments. Poland, Hungary, Romania, Bulgaria, Albania and later, Czechoslovakia and East Germany became satellites of the Soviet Union. They depended on the Soviet Union for military and economic aid. It was

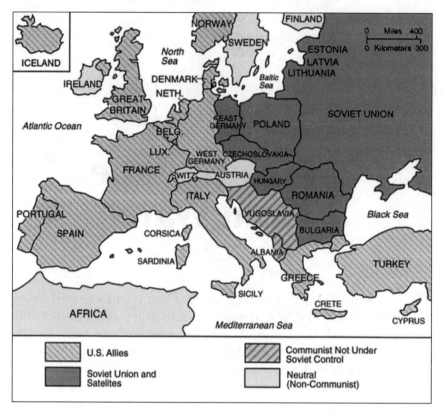

Figure 1.1   The Cold War—Antagonists and Neutrals

said that these nations were behind an *iron curtain.* (Yugoslavia broke away from Soviet control in 1948, and so did Albania in 1961. Each followed an independent Communist course until 1990.)

A civil war began in Greece at the end of World War II. Communist guerrillas, aided by Soviet satellite nations, attempted to overthrow the Greek government. They wished to ally Greece with the Soviet Union. During the same period, the Soviets were pressuring Turkey to give up territory. The Soviet Union also wanted control of the Dardanelles, the passageway between the Black and Mediterranean seas. Turkey asked the United States for help.

♦ *List the nations of Eastern Europe that became Soviet satellites after World War II.*

President Harry S Truman responded in 1947 with a program to give military and economic aid to Greece and Turkey. The program was an outgrowth of the Truman Doctrine, a policy stating that the United States would support free peoples who resist being taken over by outside forces. The Truman Doctrine kept Greece and Turkey from becoming Communist.

The post–World War II period was a time of economic devastation in Europe. To aid recovery and thus prevent the spread of communism, U.S. Secretary of State George Marshall announced, in June 1947, a program to assist Europe. Called the Marshall Plan, it resulted in the flow of $12 billion from the United States to 16 participating Western European nations between 1948 and 1952. Although the Communist countries of Eastern Europe could have participated in the Marshall Plan, they chose not to. Joseph Stalin, the Soviet dictator, accused the United States of using the plan to wage economic warfare on the Soviet Union.

Western Europe recovered and eventually achieved the greatest prosperity it had ever known. Despite the creation of the Council for Mutual Economic Assistance (COMECON) by the Soviets in 1949, to distribute financial aid to their satellite countries, Eastern Europe fell behind the West in economic development.

The series of United States responses to Soviet expansion were part of its *containment policy.* As one diplomat put it, "It is

Cold War Opponents

clear that the main element of any United States policy towards the Soviet Union must be that of a long-term, patient but firm and vigilant containment of Russian expansive tendencies."

The era of hostility and mistrust between the two superpowers that began in the 1940s became known as the *cold war.* Each side took steps just short of a shooting war to advance its own interests. The cold war was a struggle between two political systems—democracy versus totalitarianism—and between two economic systems—the capitalist system of private enterprise versus the Communist system of government-owned and -directed means of production.

♦ *Explain the following terms:*

   a. iron curtain
   b. containment policy
   c. cold war

The Superpowers in Conflict

In 1948, the Soviets tested the will of the United States and its allies to contain the spread of communism in Europe. The test came in Berlin.

After World War II, East Germany was controlled by the Soviet Union, and West Germany by the three Western allies. Although Berlin was located in East Germany, the Soviets occupied and governed only one section of it (East Berlin). Britain, France, and the United States held the rest of the city, called West Berlin.

In an effort to force the British, French, and Americans out of the city, the Soviets shut down all highways and railroad lines to West Berlin from West Germany, a trip that necessitated passage through East Germany. The blockaded city could not receive supplies by land. Instead of trying to break the blockade by sending in troops and possibly starting a war, the United States and its allies decided to airlift supplies to Berlin.

In spite of great difficulties, the Berlin Airlift kept the people of the city from starving. It brought in tons of food, fuel, and clothing every day. After 321 days, the Soviets ended the blockade and reopened the land routes across East Germany. The Berlin Airlift demonstrated Allied determination to oppose Soviet attempts to extend their influence or control.

Fear of Soviet aggression caused 12 Western nations to band together in a mutual defense pact in 1949. The United States,

Canada, Britain, France, Belgium, the Netherlands, Norway, Denmark, Italy, Luxembourg, Iceland, and Portugal formed the North Atlantic Treaty Organization (NATO). The members agreed that an attack on any one member was an attack on all. Later, Greece, Turkey, West Germany, and Spain joined. NATO's forces were stationed in Europe, especially in West Germany.

In 1955, in retaliation, the Soviet Union and the Communist nations of Eastern Europe organized their own military alliance. The purpose of the Warsaw Pact was to protect Eastern Europe from aggression by the NATO countries. The members of the pact were the Soviet Union, Albania, Bulgaria, Czechoslovakia, East Germany, Hungary, Poland, and Romania. Albania withdrew in 1968, when it became more closely allied with Communist China. Yugoslavia never joined. Marshal Tito (Josip Broz), the Yugoslav leader, preferred to remain independent of the Soviet Union.

The Warsaw Pact was dissolved in 1991, but NATO still exists. (See Chapter 8.) East Germany became part of NATO after it reunited with West Germany in 1990.

Meanwhile, the cold war moved beyond Europe to Asia, Africa, Latin America, and the Middle East. As part of its containment policy, the United States established the Point Four Program in 1949 to provide technical assistance to developing nations in these regions.

At times, Soviet–U.S. conflict played a role in actual military combat. Asia was the scene of bloody struggles between anti-Communist nations led by the United States and Communist countries supported by the Soviet Union and China. The most serious of these struggles were the Korean War (1950–1953) and the Vietnam War (1965–1973).

♦ *Describe the organization of alliance systems by the superpowers after World War II.*

Peaceful Coexistence and Détente

After the first crises of the cold war, American and Soviet leaders began to work out ways of easing tensions. In 1959, President Dwight D. Eisenhower invited Nikita Khrushchev to visit the United States. Through friendly talks, they reached some understandings. Hope for *peaceful coexistence* grew. Many people believed that the two powers could compete economically and politically without going to war.

Three international crises in the 1960s delayed progress toward better relations. In 1960, the Soviets shot down an American U-2 spy plane flying over the Soviet Union. It had been photographing Soviet military bases. Soviet anger resulted in the cancellation of meetings with American diplomats in Paris. A visit by Eisenhower to the Soviet Union was also canceled.

Relations between the superpowers became more tense in 1961. During the night of August 13, the East Germans constructed a barrier between East and West Berlin. Within days, a thick wall was built. East Berliners could no longer travel freely to West Berlin. The Berlin Wall remained as a symbol of repression until November 1989, when the borders of East Germany were once again opened, and portions of the Wall were torn down.

The Cuban Missile Crisis of 1962 brought the two powers to the edge of war. In the fall of 1962, the United States learned that the Soviet Union was placing long-range nuclear missiles in Cuba. This island, just 90 miles from Florida, was led by Fidel Castro. He had come to power in 1959 and made the country into a Communist ally of the Soviet Union. President John F. Kennedy demanded that the missiles be removed. After some hesitation, Khrushchev agreed to do so if the United States would promise not to invade Cuba.

In the 1970s, Soviet and U.S. leaders tried harder to lessen tensions. They pursued a policy called *détente,* meaning the relaxation of strained relations. In 1972, President Richard M. Nixon

Berlin—The End of Communist Rule

visited Moscow, the first U.S. president to do so. While in Moscow, he and the Soviet leader, Leonid Brezhnev, signed several agreements. They pledged to cooperate in science and technology, exploration of outer space, and trade relations. The most important agreement the two men signed arose from talks that took place between 1969 and 1972. The Strategic Arms Limitation Talks (SALT I) called for reducing the numbers of certain nuclear weapons, both offensive and defensive.

More meetings took place between 1973 and 1979. The result was a SALT II treaty to place limits on long-range bombers and missiles. When the Soviet Union invaded Afghanistan in late 1979, the U.S. Senate refused to approve SALT II and the treaty died. Relations cooled again. During most of the 1980s, the two countries kept economic, cultural, and diplomatic contacts to a minimum.

1. *Describe three events that caused tension between the super-powers.*

2. *Explain the policies of peaceful coexistence and détente.*

Trouble in the Soviet Empire

In addition to Cuba, the Asian nations of China, North Korea, Mongolia, and North Vietnam became Communist in the post–World War II era. As trade between the cold war antagonists was limited, the Soviet Union and other Communist nations became isolated from the economically advanced West. In the Soviet Union, efforts to compete with the West in the development of military technology and space exploration left little money available for consumer goods and human services.

The Soviet regime was also weakened by a long and disastrous military involvement in Afghanistan. In 1979, the Soviets invaded that country in order to maintain a pro-Soviet Afghan leader in power. Over the next several years, Soviet troops fought a bitter war with Afghan guerrillas. After losing at least 10,000 men, the Soviets finally pulled out in 1989.

The arms race and the space race also prevented the Soviets from giving economic aid to their poorer satellite nations and their allies. In fact, the Soviets depleted the resources of the satellite nations to maintain the military production levels of the Warsaw Pact.

In 1989, the failure of the Communist governments of Eastern

Europe to provide consumer goods, social services, and more freedoms aroused demands for free elections. In East Germany, Hungary, Poland, Czechoslovakia, Albania, and Bulgaria, Communist rule ended peacefully. In Romania, however, the Communist dictator, President Nicolae Ceausescu, was forcibly overthrown.

♦ *Complete each of the following sentences:*
   a. The causes of Soviet economic problems were _____.
   b. Communism fell in Eastern Europe because _____.

Poland Breaks With Communism

Poland was the first country to free itself from communism. The Polish struggle was a long one. Soviet troops put down protests and strikes by Polish workers, students, and intellectuals in 1956, 1968, 1970, and 1976. But the Poles kept struggling. In 1980, workers took to the streets under the banner of Solidarity, a labor organization led by Lech Walesa. They demanded that trade unions be free of Communist control and called for changes in Poland's alliance with the Soviet Union.

Poland's Communist government agreed to some changes, but the workers continued to make demands. Encouraged by the Soviets, Polish authorities outlawed Solidarity in 1981. They arrested Walesa and thousands of others and imposed military rule on Poland. After protests from around the world, Walesa was released in 1982, and martial law was lifted in 1983.

Solidarity won growing support as Poles struggled with rising prices and shortages of consumer goods. Finally, the Polish Communist Party allowed free elections, which Solidarity won in 1989. A Solidarity leader, Thaddeus Mazowiecki, formed the first non-Communist government in a satellite country. In 1990, the Poles elected Solidarity leader Lech Walesa to be the nation's president.

♦ *What was the role of Solidarity in Poland's transition from communism to capitalism?*

The Collapse of the Soviet Union

Mikhail Gorbachev, president of the Soviet Union (1985–1991), abandoned the Brezhnev Doctrine, which stated the right of the

Soviet Union to interfere in any satellite state. Therefore, the Soviet Union took no action to oppose the collapse of communism in Eastern Europe.

Severe economic and political problems had also developed in the Soviet Union. Shortages in food, clothing, consumer goods, and medical services made the Soviet people angry with their government and with the ruling Communist Party. In addition, protests and violence erupted among the Soviet Union's many ethnic groups. Georgians, Ukrainians, Lithuanians, and others demanded independence.

Through reform programs called *perestroika* (restructuring) and *glasnost* (openness), Gorbachev had attempted to make the Soviet economy more efficient and Soviet society more democratic. He also withdrew Soviet forces from Afghanistan and discontinued economic and military aid to other Communist governments. To reduce cold war competition, Gorbachev negotiated an Intermediate Nuclear Forces (INF) Treaty with the United States in 1987. It provided for the elimination of all medium- and short-range nuclear missiles in Europe. In 1991, the United States and the Soviet Union signed the Strategic Arms Reduction Talks (START) Treaty. It called for a 30 percent reduction in offensive nuclear weapons by both powers.

In August 1991, some Communist officials who were opposed to Gorbachev's reforms imprisoned him and seized power. President Boris Yeltsin of Russia and thousands of demonstrators opposed this coup. Unable to gain popular support, the coup leaders were forced to resign. Blaming the Communist Party for the coup attempt, Gorbachev withdrew from the party, and the Soviet Parliament suspended party activities. As a result, the Communist Party lost control of the government, the economy, and the military.

By the end of 1991, the 15 republics that made up the Soviet Union declared their independence. The Soviet Union was no more. Mikhail Gorbachev resigned as president. Most of the republics formed a Commonwealth of Independent States (C.I.S.). These events ended the cold war.

1. *Identify each of the following:*

   a. *Mikhail Gorbachev*
   b. *Boris Yeltsin*
   c. *Commonwealth of Independent States*

2. *Explain why the collapse of the Soviet Union ended the cold war.*

Chapter 1 Review

A. *Choose the item that best completes each sentence.*

1. During World War II, the Soviet Union was a military ally of (a) Nazi Germany and Fascist Italy   (b) the Japanese Empire (c) the United States.

2. After World War II, an arms race developed between the Soviet Union and   (a) Britain   (b) Japan   (c) the United States.

3. The Soviet-dominated bloc of nations was in   (a) Eastern Europe   (b) Western Europe   (c) Africa.

4. NATO was organized as a political and military alliance of (a) the United States and Western Europe   (b) the Soviet Union and Eastern Europe   (c) the Soviet Union and the United States.

5. The Warsaw Pact was a political and military alliance of (a) the Soviet Union and Western Europe   (b) the Soviet Union and Eastern Europe   (c) the Soviet Union and the United States.

6. The cold war was a struggle between   (a) democracy and totalitarianism   (b) private enterprise and government-owned economies   (c) both of these.

7. To assist the economic recovery of Europe after World War II, the United States developed the   (a) COMECON   (b) Marshall Plan   (c) Warsaw Pact.

8. To prevent the expansion of the Soviet Union and the spread of communism, the United States developed the   (a) Truman Doctrine   (b) Warsaw Pact   (c) COMECON.

9. The financial resources of the Soviet Union were strained by competition with the West and by its military involvement in (a) Pakistan   (b) Afghanistan   (c) India.

10. The rule of the Communist governments of Eastern Europe ended in 1989 because of their failure to provide   (a) consumer goods and services   (b) freedom   (c) both of these.

B. *From the list below, select ONE person. Write a two-paragraph essay about that person by answering the following questions:*

HARRY TRUMAN
LECH WALESA
MIKHAIL GORBACHEV

1. *How did this person contribute to the ending of the cold war?*

2. *Why do you admire or not admire this person?*

C. *Explain why the ending of the cold war was a global victory for democracy and free enterprise.*

D. *Reread "The Collapse of the Soviet Union," on pages 10–11. Then do the following:*

1. *Explain how each contributed to the Soviet downfall:*

   economic problems
   nationalism among ethnic minorities
   glasnost and perestroika

2. *PROVE or DISPROVE:*

   a. *There is no difference between the Soviet Union and the Commonwealth of Independent States.*

   b. *The Communist Party played no part in the collapse of the Soviet Union.*

Chapter 2

The Rise of the New Europe

Crisis in Russia

By 1992, Russian President Boris Yeltsin had become the best-known political leader in the new Commonwealth of Independent States (C.I.S.). Agreements reached by Yeltsin and the leaders of the other republics provided for establishing the commonwealth's headquarters in Minsk, the capital of Belarus. The leaders also decided to use the Soviet ruble as a standard currency, to work for nuclear disarmament, and to permit each republic to organize its own military forces. The C.I.S. has remained a loose grouping of independent states with no strong central authority.

The United States and other nations quickly recognized the independence of the post-Soviet republics and opened diplomatic relations with them. Substantial economic and humanitarian aid came from the United States, Germany, France, and other industrialized nations. World leaders especially wanted to support Yeltsin's attempt to develop democracy and private enterprise in Russia, by far the largest of the republics.

Yeltsin's plan for Russia was to turn factories, farms, and other businesses over to private owners who would run them for a profit. This is called *privatization.* Many existing businesses were reorganized, with shares of stock being distributed to private individuals. Each Russian received a certificate, or voucher, that could be traded for stock. To win support for its reforms, the government gave managers and workers free shares of stock in the companies where they worked.

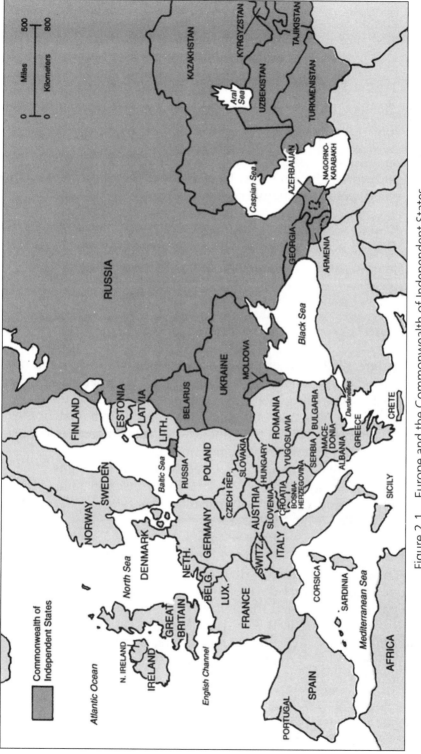

Figure 2.1   Europe and the Commonwealth of Independent States

15

Yeltsin's reforms caused wrenching hardships. Production dropped more drastically than in the United States' Great Depression in the 1930s. Food and consumer goods became hard to get. Prices shot up. Millions lost their jobs. Crime rates rose as racketeers extorted protection money from small businesses, drug dealers found new customers, and armed gangs roamed the streets. What's more, day after day the press carried news of corrupt dealings in business and government.

Many Russians became convinced that democracy and private enterprise did not work. They doubted their president's ability to improve the defective economy.

1. *List the major problems facing President Yeltsin after the Soviet Union broke up.*

2. *State reasons for the support given to Yeltsin by Western nations.*

The Battle for Russia

By late 1992, a bitter power struggle was under way. On one side stood Boris Yeltsin. On the other stood his political enemies in the Russian parliament, elected before the breakup of the Soviet Union. Old-style bureaucrats, former Communist bosses, and supernationalists in parliament were determined to slow privatization and undermine Yeltsin's power.

The anti-Yeltsin deputies pointed to any and all signs of economic trouble as evidence that the reforms had failed. Demonstrations and counterdemonstrations broke out. Would the country collapse into civil war?

With parliament holding round-the-clock sessions in its headquarters, known as the "white house," Yeltsin surrounded it with police and military forces. He threatened to arrest parliamentary leaders. After several days of standoff, civilians who supported the parliament charged the police with clubs and guns. That set off a bloody battle in the heart of Moscow on October 3, 1993. After 26 hours, heavily armed soldiers blasted their way into the parliament. They arrested Ruslan Khasbulatov, the parliament chairman; Vice President Rutskoi; and dozens of their supporters.

1. *Explain how 1993 was a year of crisis for Russia.*

2. *Describe the crisis of September and October 1993.*

Parliamentary Democracy

Russia Struggles On

Despite President Yeltsin's victory, economic problems and crime continued to worsen. At elections in December 1993, Russian voters approved the proposed constitution. However, a large number of seats in the State Duma (the new lower house of parliament) went to extreme nationalists and others opposed to Yeltsin's reforms. Clashes between the president and parliament continued.

Prices spiraled upward at a dizzying pace in the mid-1990s and factory output dwindled. In August 1998, Russia devalued the ruble, allowing it to fall in value rather than propping it up artificially. This meant that the purchasing power of Russians declined and the ranks of the poor increased to more than a third of the population.

There were problems in other areas, too. A rebellion in the southern region of Chechnya flared into all-out warfare in December 1994. Chechnya contains a largely non-Russian population with its own distinct culture and history. Most of the people are Muslims. They have been under Russian rule since the 1860s. When the Chechens declared their independence, Russian leaders responded with force. In an eight-month conflict, the Russian army demolished the Chechen capital, Grozny, and destroyed much of the territory's industry. Casualties included some 1,400

Russian soldiers and 20,000 civilians. A 1995 peace settlement provided that Chechnya would have its own government within the Russian federation. Russia promised Chechnya a large degree of self-rule, but not independence.

At the end of 1999, however, the fighting resumed, and casualties soon exceeded those of the earlier war. Despite a heavy toll among Chechen rebels and the presence of 80,000 Russian troops in Chechnya, rebel forces dug in and continued fighting.

Yeltsin initially played the role of a democratic reformer. Western leaders praised him for his help in ending the cold war. In 1993 he signed a new arms-reduction treaty with U.S. President George Bush. START II, as the treaty was called, provided for the elimination of land-based missiles having more than one warhead. The START II agreement (as later amended) called for destroying two thirds of the nuclear warheads on each side by 2007.

In the presidential election of 1996, Yeltsin emerged victorious. But his abrupt political changes—he carried out four government shake-ups in 17 months—left most Russians disenchanted with his presidency. Many Russians were relieved, therefore, when the ailing Yeltsin suddenly resigned at the end of December 1999. He appointed Prime Minister Vladimir V. Putin, a former KGB officer, as acting president until the March 2000 elections, which Putin easily won.

While preserving Russia's new democratic structure, Putin became known as an authoritarian leader. In a series of steps designed to increase his power, Putin weakened the 89 regional governments and the local strongmen who ran them. He also replaced officials from the Yeltsin regime with his own hand-picked government. Neighboring republics such as Georgia and Moldova were brought into line with Russian policies. In Chechnya, Putin cracked down on separatist rebels.

Credited with gradual improvement in the Russian economy and increased stability, Putin easily won the presidential election of March 2004. Many problems remained to be dealt with during his second term in office. Ending the decade-long conflict in Chechnya was a high priority. Chechen rebels were believed to be responsible for terrorist acts in Russia, including the February 2004 bombing of the Moscow subway, which left 39 dead and more than 100 injured.

To combat government corruption, Putin promised to reduce Russia's bureaucracy, filled with bribe-taking officials. He also ordered the arrest of wealthy businessmen who wielded great political power in Russia. In October 2003, Mikhail Khodorkovsky, the billionaire head of the Yukos oil company, was arrested and charged with fraud, forgery, and tax evasion. Khodorkovsky funded political parties opposed to Putin. Boris Berezovsky, whose financial power also challenged Putin, was accused of fraud in connection with his multimillion-dollar automobile business and fled Russia. Vladimir Gusinsky used his control of television, radio, and newspapers to oppose Putin. Accused of money laundering and fraud, he fled Russia in 2000. By moving against these tycoons, Putin sent Russia's business community a message about interference in politics.

A series of events in 2006 supported the view of Mr. Putin's critics that the Russian president had created an authoritarian, overly centralized political and economic system in which opposition is crushed. The murders of Anna Politkovskaya, a prominent journalist, and Alexander Litvinenko, a former KGB agent in London, demonstrated that those who criticize the Kremlin may be treated harshly.

In December 2006, three major international companies— Royal Dutch Shell, Mitsubishi, and Mitsui—were forced by the Kremlin to give up control of the world's largest oil and gas foreign investment project, Sakhalin II, located in Russia's far east. A majority of shares were sold to Gazprom, Russia's government-owned gas company. Earlier in the year, Russia cut off natural gas supplies to Ukraine in order to force that country to pay higher prices to Gazprom. Belarus was also threatened with the same fate if it did not agree to pay higher prices in 2007.

These tactics reflected President Putin's belief that energy is a weapon with which to restore the lost greatness of the Soviet Union. With oil and gas prices high, Russia has benefited from a flood of revenue. Europe's dependence on Russia for about a quarter of its gas has increased Gazprom's power and influence. The same dependence exists for Japan, the future recipient of most of the gas from the Sakhalin II project. In May 2006, U.S. Vice President Dick Cheney accused the Kremlin of using oil and gas as "tools of intimidation or blackmail."

Under Mr. Putin, the presidency has gained enormous power. Parliament has been weakened, the press muzzled, and television brought under government regulation. Control of Russia's energy resources has increased the Kremlin's influence in world affairs.

The growing power of the "Red Mafiya," or Russian organized crime, has extended from Eastern Europe into Asia and the Americas. Using advanced computer technology and sophisticated techniques, combined with ruthless brutality, the 21st-century Russian mafia engages in a widening range of criminal activities—drug and weapons trafficking, automobile theft, wildlife poaching, bank fraud, money laundering, etc. Their ability to illegally obtain and sell even nuclear and biological weapons has made the mob a threat to international security.

1. *Identify the following:*
   a. *Mikhail Khodorkovsky*
   b. *Chechnya*
   c. *START II*

2. *Describe ways in which Vladimir Putin's rule differed from that of Boris Yeltsin.*

Beyond Russia: Nationalism and Economic Reform

Issues of nationalism and economic disarray also flared up in other republics of the Commonwealth of Independent States. Nations like Ukraine had troubles similar to those that Russia experienced. In addition, leaders of the former Soviet republics cast a wary eye toward Russia, watching for signs of a revived Russian imperialism.

Georgia. Georgia is one of the most troubled C.I.S. republics. Annexed by Russia in 1801 and made part of the Soviet Union in 1922, it gained independence in December 1991. Edward Shevardnadze, former Soviet foreign minister, was elected president in 1992.

Shevardnadze faced a bloody revolt in the Abkhazia region. By late 1993, rebel forces controlled much of the region. Despite the presence of Russian peacekeeping troops, clashes with rebels continued. The South Ossetia region has also tried to cast off control of the central government in Tbilisi. Diplomacy has brought some recent stability to both regions, but tensions continue.

In addition to civil war, Georgians have endured years of poverty, government corruption, and crime. Demands for Shevardnadze to resign grew. His 11-year presidency ended in November 2003, after mass demonstrations over alleged ballot rigging in parliamentary elections. His resignation—a "bloodless revolution," as opposition leaders termed it—prevented violence.

Figure 2.2   Russia and Neighboring C.I.S. Republics

Mikhail Saakashvili, a 35-year-old U.S.-educated lawyer, was elected president with about 96 percent of the vote. He promised to fight government corruption and improve pensions and salaries. Although pro-Western, he wished to improve Georgian-Russian relations.

Saakashvili has also dealt with demands for independence by Ajaria, a region on Georgia's Black Sea coast bordering Turkey. Half the population is Muslim. Led from 1991 to 2004 by Aslan Abashidze, Ajaria is politically stable and prosperous.

In March 2004, Ajarian forces stopped Saakashvili from entering. In response, the Georgian president imposed an economic blockade, halting rail cargoes of oil to the port of Batumi. The blockade was lifted as a result of talks between Saakashvili and Abashidze, who agreed to disarm his army, allow elections, and pay taxes. Saakashvili had won a victory.

Russia has close ties with Ajaria and keeps a military base there. Moscow warned Saakashvili's pro-U.S. government not to interfere in Ajaria. But Russian President Putin seemed to moderate his position in March 2004. He ordered Russian troops in Batumi not to cause trouble. Abashidze fled to Russia in May 2004, enabling more central government control over Ajaria.

With five million inhabitants, Georgia is one of the poorest C.I.S. republics but has great geopolitical importance. The United States wants stability and security there because American companies are invested heavily in an oil pipeline to carry oil from Azerbaijan through Georgia to Turkey. Georgia's armed forces have received U.S. training and equipment. Moscow watches the increasing U.S. influence in Georgia closely.

In 2006, increasing tension between Georgia and Russia led to a Russian embargo on Georgian exports and the suspension by Russia of air, sea, and rail links to Georgia. The suspension of transport service followed the arrest by Georgia of four Russian military officers accused of spying. The Kremlin is opposed to Georgia's pro-Western government.

♦ *Describe the political crises that have troubled Georgia in the late 20th and early 21st centuries.*

Kazakhstan. Oil-rich Kazakhstan—a country four times the size of Texas—is one of the luckier states once part of Soviet Central Asia. It has not only oil but also a modern space-launching facility, at Baikonur. Russia took out a 20-year lease on the facility, providing extra income for Kazakhstan.

Some 17 million people live in Kazakhstan, which borders Russia and China. It produces a lot of cotton and one-third of the grain grown in the former Soviet Union. Besides oil, its resources include gas, iron, gold, silver, copper, and chromium.

The potential for economic growth has attracted Western investors and major American and European firms. Nursultan Nazarbayev, who became president before Kazakhstan claimed independence in 1991, focused on economic reforms rather than political change or democracy. He allowed some state-controlled industries to be sold to private owners. Nazarbayev's authoritarian rule won the seeming support of the people in a 1995 referendum. In the country's first contested presidential election in 1999, Nazarbayev won an easy victory.

Kazakhstan, which came under Russia's control in the 18th century, has two main ethnic groups—Kazakhs (42 percent) and Russians (37 percent). Ethnic Kazakhs speak a Turkic language, follow the Sunni Muslim religion, and resemble Mongols in appearance. Ethnic Russians have dominated the industrial cities for more than 100 years. More than half of the people in Almaty, the capital, are Russians.

Independence brought a surge of Kazakh nationalism after

1991. More Kazakhs moved into major government posts. To avoid ethnic conflict, which would disrupt economic development, President Nazarbayev took steps to protect Russians' rights.

Kazakhstan's economy is closely tied to Russia's. Along with Belarus, Tajikistan, and Kyrgystan, Kazakhstan joined Russia in a free trade zone. In 2000, the five countries formed a "Eurasian Economic Community," planning common policies on many economic issues.

♦ *Why is Kazakhstan considered one of the luckier states in what was Soviet Central Asia?*

Azerbaijan and Armenia. Azerbaijan and Armenia are small countries in the Caucasus region. They are important because of their natural resources and their position at the southeastern tip of Europe. Turkey, Iran, and Russia have long competed for power and influence in this area.

The people of Azerbaijan, known as Azeris, speak a language related to Turkish. They were under Turkish rule for the greater portion of their history. Therefore, their culture and their social institutions are largely Turkish. However, Azeris also were once

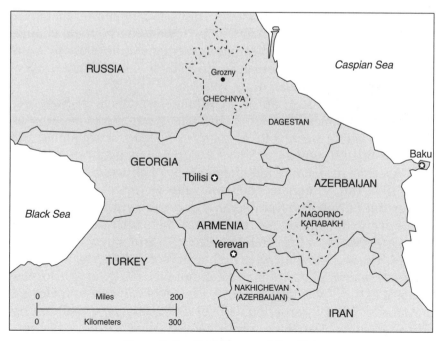

Figure 2.3   C.I.S. Areas of Conflict

under Persian (Iranian) rule. Like today's Iranians, most Azeris belong to the Shia sect of Islam, rather than the Sunni sect that is popular in Turkey.

Russia conquered Azerbaijan in 1813. The oil fields developed by czarist Russia near the capital city, Baku, were among the first in the world. Oil has brought wealth, but also pollution, to the region. As a result of the oil economy, Azerbaijan was the only part of the Soviet Muslim world where the Communist effort to create an urban working class succeeded.

Armenia, the traditional homeland of the Armenian people, is a divided region. Part of it came under Soviet control in 1917 as the Armenian Soviet Socialist Republic. Now it is an independent country in the C.I.S. A larger part of Armenia lies within Turkey. Some Armenians also live in Azerbaijan, in a region known as Nagorno-Karabakh. With their own language and their Christian religion, the Armenians differ from both the Azeris and the Turks. (Part of their national heritage is bitter resentment against the Turks, who were responsible for the deaths of more than a million Armenians during World War I.)

The approaching collapse of the Soviet Union rekindled old quarrels between Azerbaijan and Armenia. Trouble erupted in Nagorno-Karabakh in 1988. The mainly Armenian people of the province resented Azeri rule and wanted Nagorno-Karabakh to become part of Armenia. Armenia's government shared that goal. Mass demonstrations by Armenians demanding political change touched off riots between ethnic Armenians and Azeris in Azerbaijan. Soon, ethnic Armenians from all over Azerbaijan were fleeing to Nagorno-Karabakh or to Armenia.

Outright warfare erupted as ethnic Armenians in Nagorno-Karabakh organized an army and the Azeri government sent troops to quell the revolt. At times Armenia's army joined the fighting. In 1991, when the Soviet Union collapsed, both Armenia and Azerbaijan became independent, but fighting continued. By June 1993, the Armenians had won major victories, pushing Azeri forces out of Nagorno-Karabakh. This resulted in a mutiny in the Azeri army. Rebellious officers, dissatisfied with the conduct of the war, overthrew the Azeri government, and a new leader took power. He was Heydar Aliyev, chairperson of Azerbaijan's parliament, leader of Azerbaijan's Communist Party, and a former general in the Soviet secret police. President Aliyev was reelected in October 1998. International observers questioned the honesty of the election. Declining health caused Aliyev to have his son, Ilham, made prime minister in 2003. While in the United States for medical treatment, Aliyev withdrew from the 2004 presidential election in favor of his son, who was elected. International observers considered this election to be dishonest. The younger Aliyev responded to protests by arresting hundreds of opposition leaders and their followers.

Periodic fighting with Armenia continued, despite a 1994 cease-fire agreement. Slow-moving peace negotiations began in 1998. The administration of U.S. President George W. Bush lifted a ban on weapons sales to Armenia and Azerbaijan in 2002. "Positive developments in Armenia and Azerbaijan" were cited. During the war over Nagorno-Karabakh, 35,000 people had been killed and one million, mainly Azeris, had been forced to flee their homes.

The opening of a new pipeline in 2005 to carry Azerbaijan's huge oil reserves to the outside world is expected to enrich the nation's economy.

1. *Identify each of the following:*

    a. *Heydar Aliyev*
    b. *Armenia*
    c. *Azerbaijan*
    d. *Nagorno-Karabakh*

Figure 2.4   Baltic Republics and Eastern Europe

2. Complete the following sentences.

    a. War broke out between Azeris and Armenians because _____ .

    b. The president of Azerbaijan was ousted when _____ .

The Baltic States. The three countries of Estonia, Latvia, and Lithuania lie along the Baltic Sea. All three were annexed by the Soviet Union during World War II. Since regaining their independence in the early 1990s, they have worked to make the shift from a command to a market economy by privatizing industry and broadening trade relationships with the rest of Europe. All three countries joined NATO in 2002 and the European Union in 2004.

Latvia and Estonia experienced rapid economic growth in 2006. The Estonian growth rate of 11.6 percent and the Latvian rate of 10.9 percent have been attributed to good policies. Both countries are stable and business-friendly and have low costs of living. They are located close to large, rich markets in Western Europe. Both have flat taxes, clean governments, balanced budgets, and stable currencies. All this makes them attractive to foreign businesspeople. Estonia has been Europe's biggest recipient of foreign investment.

Both countries have struggled to integrate Soviet-era immigrants into their economies. Ethnic Estonians make up about 65 percent of that country's population. In Latvia, ethnic Latvians are only about 58 percent of the population. Both countries have large Russian minorities. Therefore, importing more labor from Eastern Europe has been very unpopular. Nevertheless, wages are rising due to labor shortages in the booming construction, retail, and tourism industries. Luring back Latvians and Estonians who emigrated for better paying jobs elsewhere in Europe has been the preferred strategy.

Lithuania has a smaller proportion of Russians and other minorities, and they have been better integrated into the population. This country's main problem is to attain economic well-being, since it has few natural resources.

1. Match the country in Column A with the description in Column B.

       Column A   Column B

    1. Georgia   *a. Oilfields near Baku bring wealth to*
    2. Kazakhstan   *the nation.*
    3. Azerbaijan   *b. It has a modern space launching*
                          facility.

4. Armenia
5. Latvia

c. Suffered under an oil and gas cut-off and a trade embargo.
d. Went to war over Nagorno-Karabakh.
e. Joined NATO in 2002.

2. PROVE or DISPROVE: Nationalism has influenced the actions of the former Soviet republics in the post–cold war era.

Conflict and Change in Eastern Europe

Since the end of the cold war, the former Soviet satellite nations have struggled to develop democratic political systems and free market economies. They have also attempted to negotiate closer relations with the economically stronger nations of Western Europe.

The Czech Republic and Slovakia. Created in 1918 by the uniting of Czech and Slovak lands, Czechoslovakia was occupied and dissolved by the Nazis during World War II. When Soviet armies drove out the Nazis, an elected Czechoslovak government took office in 1946. Communists seized power in 1948 and installed a harsh regime. All dissent was repressed.

In 1968, an invasion of Soviet troops, supported by Polish, East German, Hungarian, and Bulgarian forces, crushed a movement for democracy. Czechoslovak demands for more human rights led to another crackdown in 1977.

In 1989, tens of thousands of people took to the streets of Prague, Czechoslovakia's capital, to demand free elections. Millions went on strike. The Communist Party leadership resigned. Vaclav Havel, a Czech playwright and human rights advocate, was elected president of a non-Communist government.

The Slovaks had been independent during World War II. Their demands for a separate state, in 1992, were opposed unsuccessfully by President Havel. An agreement between political leaders led to a peaceful division of the country. In January 1993, Czechoslovakia split into two independent nations, the Czech Republic and Slovakia. Following separation, the Czech parliament elected Havel to the presidency of the Czech Republic. Vaclav Klaus was elected president in February 2004.

The Czech Republic joined NATO in 1999 and Slovakia entered the alliance in 2004. Voters in both countries approved entry to the European Union (EU) in 2004.

♦ *State an event in the history of Czechoslovakia for each date: 1918, 1948, 1968, 1989, 1993.*

Yugoslavia. Located in the Balkan Mountains of southeastern Europe, Yugoslavia was created in 1918 as a federation of six republics—a mix of ethnic groups living side by side. Serbs made up about a third of the population and were mainly members of the Serbian Orthodox Church. The Croats, a second large group, were Roman Catholics. Other ethnic groups included Muslims (mainly in Bosnia and southern Serbia) and Slovenes, who are Roman Catholics. Generally speaking, neighboring peoples lived in peace and often intermarried.

Yugoslavia was held together by a Communist leader, Marshal Tito, who died in 1980. Communism gave way to ethnic nationalism. In the early 1990s, Croatia, Slovenia, Bosnia-Herzegovina (Bosnia), and Macedonia declared independence. Serbia and Montenegro remained in the Yugoslav federation.

Serbia, the largest and most powerful of the original republics, opposed this breakup. Slovenia and Macedonia were allowed to depart, but not Croatia and Bosnia.

Figure 2.5   The Former Yugoslavia

Ethnic Cleansing

In Croatia, the sizable minority of Serbs resorted to violence against the new government. They were aided by the Serb-dominated Yugoslav army. By 1994, Croatian Serbs controlled some 30 percent of Croatia. In 1995, a lightning offensive by the Croatian army drove Croatian Serb forces out of western Croatia and sent a wave of Croatian Serb refugees into Serbia.

Meanwhile, fighting had also broken out in Bosnia. The world became familiar with a new term, "ethnic cleansing," used to describe a campaign of forced expulsion, often involving beatings, rape, and murder, in order to clear an area of unwanted inhabitants—in this case, most often Bosnian Muslims living in Serb-held territory.

In August 1995, with some 200,000 fighters and civilians having lost their lives, NATO planes launched air strikes against the Bosnian Serbs. That brought a halt to the fighting. At a conference near Dayton, Ohio, in December, the presidents of Serbia, Croatia, and Bosnia signed peace agreements. The Dayton Peace Accords provided that Bosnia was to be divided into a Muslim-Croat federation and a Bosnian Serb republic, joined under a central government in Sarajevo. U.N. troops remained in Bosnia, and U.N. administrators held broad powers over the new federation.

Meanwhile, the United Nations set up a court at The Hague, in the Netherlands, to investigate war crimes in the former Yugoslavia. The court tried and convicted many soldiers and leaders.

Others who were charged included Radovan Karadzic, the former Bosnian Serb president, who remained at large, and Slobodan Milosevic, the former president of Serbia, who went on trial in 2002. While imprisoned at The Hague, Milosevic died in March 2006.

In the late 1990s, new turmoil erupted in southern Serbia, in Kosovo. That Serbian province is inhabited mainly by ethnic Albanians—Muslims who speak Albanian. Kosovo had a measure of self-government until 1989, when the Serbian government revoked it. Ethnic Albanian guerrillas then formed a Kosovo Liberation Army (KLA) and began a campaign for full independence. Among the KLA's methods were terrorist attacks on Serbs in Kosovo.

In 1998, the Yugoslav army began a campaign against the KLA that soon turned into a round of brutal ethnic cleansing. NATO tried to arrange a settlement giving Kosovo self-rule within Serbia, but Yugoslavia's President Milosevic refused. The Yugoslav army stepped up its attacks. In a few months, as many as a million Kosovars were forced out of their homes and whole villages were burned. Many men of military age were killed, and some 700,000 Kosovars took refuge in neighboring countries.

In March 1999, U.S. and other NATO forces began air attacks on Yugoslav troops in Kosovo and on Serbian cities, including the Yugoslav capital, Belgrade. After 72 days, Milosevic gave in. He agreed to pull Yugoslav troops out of Kosovo, while NATO agreed that Kosovo would remain part of Serbia. U.N. administrators and 35,000 NATO-led peacekeepers (including some 5,000 U.S. troops) entered Kosovo, promising to "demilitarize" the KLA.

Refugees began to return. In October 2000, under U.N. supervision, Kosovo voters elected local governments, largely rejecting former KLA leaders in favor of politicians who renounced further violence. Nonetheless, tension remained high. Attacks by ethnic Albanians drove many Serb civilians out of Kosovo. Ethnic Albanian guerrillas launched attacks into nearby areas of Serbia.

Fed up with Milosevic's dictatorial rule and U.N. sanctions aimed at toppling him, millions of Yugoslavs voted for opposition leader Vojislav Kostunica in a presidential election held in September 2000, giving him 49 percent of the vote to Milosevic's 39 percent. When the government scheduled a runoff, it stirred fears that Milosevic was planning to rig the new election and hold onto power. Violent mass protests broke out. In the end, Milosevic resigned, allowing Kostunica to become president.

Several months later, Serbian authorities arrested Milosevic on charges of corruption and abuse of power. Serbia's president then turned Milosevic over for a U.N. war crimes trial, over the opposition of Yugoslav President Kostunica.

Early in 2001, ethnic violence spread to Macedonia, which borders Kosovo and the rest of Serbia on the south. Macedonia has a majority Serb population with an Albanian minority that demanded more freedoms and limited self-rule. Ethnic Albanian guerrillas—the National Liberation Army of Macedonia—launched attacks against government troops. Fearing an upsurge of Balkan violence, NATO helped arrange a cease-fire in August 2001. It sent 3,500 troops to oversee the truce.

In the 21st century, the former Yugoslavia has been overrun by organized crime. This has been especially true in Serbia, where security services allied with gangsters limited the powers of government. As a result, Serbian Prime Minister Zoran Djindjir was murdered in March 2003, after he had appointed a chief investigator to crack down on organized crime. The United States and other Western governments pressured the Serbian government to arrest mafia leaders. In this climate, war criminals fleeing prosecution by The Hague tribunal for murders committed during the wars of the 1990s have found safety in Serbia.

Montenegro ended its union with Serbia and became an independent country in June 2006.

♦ *What roles did the United Nations and NATO play in the crises in the former Yugoslavia?*

Poland. Although Poland welcomed democracy with enthusiasm, it faced immense economic problems. Poland tried what was called "shock therapy." That meant introducing free market capitalism all at once, rather than step by step as in some other countries of Eastern Europe.

Shock therapy brought a rush of Western consumer goods and a sharp rise in foreign trade. However, Polish businesses found it hard to withstand the international competition. At first, industrial production fell, wages dropped, and unemployment soared. Opinion polls showed a sharp drop in the popularity of President Lech Walesa, who had spearheaded the changes.

Despite the pain, shock therapy began to pay off. Poland faced problems, including inflation and high unemployment. Its agriculture, with over 2 million small farmers, was inefficient. Still, it led all the former Communist nations of Eastern Europe in economic growth, with private enterprise accounting for a large share of its output. As the first nation to free itself from communism, Poland found itself a guide for the other former satellites that were pursuing the shift to free market economies. By mid-2006, Poland's economy was booming. Its growth rate was over 5 percent and inflation was the lowest in the European Union.

Poland became a full member of NATO in 1999 and entered the European Union in 2004.

Government corruption and abuse of power, which have flourished in the post-Communist era, have been fought by President Lech Kaczyński, elected in 2005, and his brother Jaroslaw Kaczyński, appointed prime minister in 2006. The center-right coalition they lead has succeeded in reducing the number of parliamentary seats held by former Communists. A powerful new anticorruption agency has been ordered to screen officers of the military intelligence service for abusive or criminal behavior. Poland has become increasingly democratic in the 21st century.

1. *Write the term that best completes each sentence.*
    a. *The Czech Republic has been traditionally oriented toward the _____ for trade.*
    b. *In the former Yugoslavia, the policy of _____ was aimed at creating areas in which only one ethnic group remained.*
    c. *In Poland, the sudden introduction of free market capitalism was known as _____.*

2. *Complete the following sentence: Events in the former Yugoslavia in the 1990s attracted worldwide attention because _____.*

Conflict and Change in Western Europe

Although each Western European nation faced its own special needs and problems, many were affected by two trends that characterized the 1990s. One was a change in political parties. In general, Socialist and social democratic movements became more conservative. They reduced government ownership of industries and called for cutbacks in government spending in order to help balance national budgets. At the same time, new political parties were gaining strength. Environmentalists ("greens") were especially strong in Germany. Ultranationalists also found favor, particularly in France and Austria.

The second trend involved immigration. Western Europe has become home to millions of non-Europeans, some in search of work and others seeking asylum from political conflicts in their homelands. The immigrants provide unskilled labor at low wages

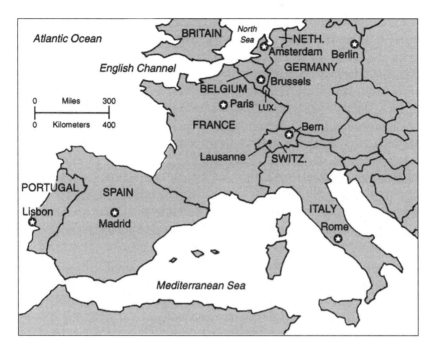

Figure 2.6   Western Europe

and thus keep production costs down. But Europeans have not always welcomed newcomers from Asia, Africa, the Middle East, and the Caribbean. When the host countries have economic problems of their own, resentment toward foreigners has sometimes led to violence.

♦ *PROVE or DISPROVE: Western European political parties have remained unchanged since World War II.*

Germany. At the end of World War II, Nazi Germany surrendered to the Western allies and the Soviet Union. Early in the cold war, Germany split into two nations: East Germany became a Communist satellite of the Soviet Union; West Germany became a democratic, non-Communist ally of the United States. The former German capital, Berlin, was also divided. In 1961, the Communists built a wall across Berlin to prevent East Germans from escaping to a better life in prosperous West Germany.

The fall of communism in Eastern Europe brought down the East German government and the Berlin Wall. In October 1990, the two Germanys reunited. Berlin once more became the capital of a unified Germany.

Reunification brought new problems and tensions. Eastern Germany was far less developed economically than western Germany. To overcome eastern Germany's widespread poverty and unemployment, the German government, led by Chancellor Helmut Kohl, offered far-reaching economic assistance, ranging from business subsidies to welfare payments for families.

Germany had to raise taxes to help finance the aid to eastern Germans. Both western and eastern Germans found much to criticize. Some western Germans thought eastern Germans were "freeloaders." Many eastern Germans resented what they saw as the "high-and-mighty" attitude of the richer westerners. These tensions were made worse by a recession soon after unification.

Although the German economy later recovered, tensions continued, feeding a flare-up of violence against foreigners. During the 1960s and 1970s, West Germany's expanding industries had hired large numbers of "guest workers" from Turkey and other Mediterranean countries. With unemployment rising, resentment of foreigners grew. One result was a surge of activity by neo-Nazis—people who seek to bring back the "Germany-for-Germans" policies of Hitler's time. (See Chapter 9.)

Dissatisfaction with Germany's progress defeated Kohl in the 1998 elections. The new chancellor, Gerhard Schröder, a Social Democrat, advocated a policy called the "new middle"—a compromise between a welfare state, with generous pensions and other benefits, and a free market economy with few benefits. An important new law liberalized strict naturalization procedures, giving citizenship to anyone born in Germany.

Economic problems continued, especially rising unemployment. This enabled Angela Merkel to lead the more conservative Christian Democrats to victory in 2005. Ms. Merkel became Germany's first woman chancellor. She formed a government by establishing a "grand alliance" with the Social Democrats. This coalition came under attack by many critics in 2006 and 2007. The rising cost of health care, an aging population, and continuing high unemployment made the development of a new plan for financing the health system a high priority. This was accomplished by Ms. Merkel in late 2006, but with much political opposition. Another problem for Chancellor Merkel has been the growing power in eastern Germany of the far-right National Democratic Party. Espousing anti-immigration and neo-Nazi views, this party won representation in three of Germany's six eastern states. This threatened Chancellor Merkel's fragile government and raised worries about the future of democracy in Germany.

In 2006, Germany increased its participation in peacekeeping missions by sending warships and troops to patrol the Mediterranean waters off Lebanon. The German ships were part of a maritime force that included ships from Denmark, Norway, Sweden, and the Netherlands. Their mission was to stop the smuggling of weapons to Hezbollah, a terrorist organization operating in Lebanon. German forces have also participated in NATO operations in Afghanistan and peacekeeping missions in central Africa, Bosnia, and Kosovo.

With one of the lowest birthrates in Europe, Germany's population has been declining. It has been estimated that by 2050, the number of Germans over 60 will be twice as high as those under 20. This trend has been worsened by a sharp drop in the number of immigrants entering Germany, while the number of Germans leaving the country has increased. High unemployment and slow economic growth have contributed to the brain drain of doctors, engineers, and other skilled professionals.

♦ *PROVE or DISPROVE: The reunification of Germany in 1990 led to severe problems.*

France. Although France was one of the victors in World War II, postwar political and economic instability made recovery difficult. Problems were made worse by costly colonial wars in Southeast Asia (1946–1954) and Algeria (1954–1962).

General Charles de Gaulle became prime minister in 1958 and president the next year. Under a new constitution, de Gaulle received greatly expanded powers as president. He encouraged economic and technological advances and supported European unity, with the aim of gaining a leadership role for France. Under de Gaulle, France turned away from colonialism in Asia and Africa, negotiating independence for Algeria in 1962. De Gaulle resigned in 1969 after losing a referendum on changes to the constitution—changes that would have further strengthened presidential powers.

De Gaulle's successors, Georges Pompidou (1969–1974) and Valéry Giscard d'Estaing (1974–1981), were conservatives and supporters of Gaullist policies. In 1981, economic problems resulting from a global oil crisis brought a Socialist victory. François Mitterrand became president with backing from French Communists. A Socialist prime minister served with him.

For a time, the Socialists increased government control of the economy. They placed more public services and utilities under government control. They gave workers and unions more power and increased social welfare benefits. But, faced with high inflation and rising unemployment, the Socialists cut taxes and reduced government spending in 1984.

When economic conditions remained poor, voters turned to conservative parties. The conservatives called for privatization of industry and deregulation of the economy. Growing resentment of foreign workers, especially those coming from the former French colonies in North Africa, also strengthened the conservatives. In 1986, the conservative parties won control of the National Assembly. Jacques Chirac, a Gaullist, became prime minister. But the Socialist Mitterrand remained president, and for two years France experienced divided rule.

Elected in 1995, Conservative President Jacques Chirac reduced government spending in order to meet European Union requirements for joining the euro zone, or common European currency. The resulting increase in unemployment angered many French voters, as did a series of government scandals, slow economic growth, and budget cuts in social service entitlement programs. Left-wing parties opposed to Chirac's policies gained votes in the 2004 elections for regional governments and for members of the European Parliament. Despite strong support by the Chirac government, a proposed EU constitution was rejected by French voters in 2005. Chirac's opposition to the U.S.-British-led invasion of Iraq created tension between the French government and the administration of U.S. President George W. Bush.

In November 2005, riots, car bombings, and battles with police broke out across France. Most of the rioters were second-generation Muslims of North or West African origins. Lasting for two weeks, the riots demonstrated the government's failure to integrate Muslim immigrants into French society or to provide opportunities for employment.

In the presidential election of May 2007, Foreign Minister and conservative candidate Nicolas Sarkozy defeated Socialist Party leader Ségolène Royal. Sarkozy promised to "rehabilitate work, authority, respect, and merit." Viewed by many French as pro-American, Sarkozy nevertheless criticized the U.S. for obstructing the fight against global warming, to which he gave a high priority.

♦ *Identify each of the following:*

    a. Charles de Gaulle
    b. François Mitterrand
    c. Jácques Chirac

Sarkozy Becomes French President in 2007

Britain. World War II left Britain weak economically and with diminished influence as a world power. It gave independence to most of its overseas possessions—India in 1947, Ceylon and Burma in 1948, and African colonies from the 1950s on.

In the 1945 elections, Britons turned to the Labour Party. Prime Minister Clement Attlee and his successors, determined on a Socialist welfare state, nationalized 20 percent of industry, and set up a huge social insurance program. Most of it remained in force when Conservatives were in power in ensuing decades.

In 1979, Margaret Thatcher, the first woman elected British prime minister, targeted the "welfare state." Her Conservatives reduced taxes, union power, and social welfare. Forced from office in 1990, she was replaced by Conservative John Major.

In 1997, a restructured Labour Party took control of the government and kept power through the general election (2001) and parliamentary elections (2003). Led by Prime Minister Tony Blair, "New Labour" promised to support business, limit spending, and assist ordinary people to do better financially.

Blair's government faced the opposition of many, including members of his party, for his support of the U.S.-led invasion of Iraq and the involvement of British troops since March 2003.

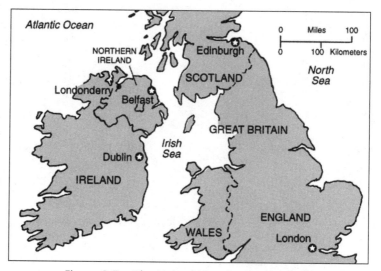

Figure 2.7   The United Kingdom and Ireland

There were also demands for improvements in public services—law enforcement, transportation, education, and health. Blair gave much attention to *devolution*—transfer of political power and control of domestic affairs from Parliament to elected law-making assemblies in Scotland, Wales, and Northern Ireland.

Foreign policy has focused on increasing integration of Britain into the EU, including eventual inclusion in the *eurozone*—countries that have replaced national currencies with the euro. Through stronger ties with France and Germany, Britain hopes to have increased influence on EU policies. With French and German support, Britain has pressed for a European rapid reaction military force to meet terrorist threats. The United States opposes this effort for fear of weakening NATO.

Blair's popularity declined greatly as a result of his decision to join the U.S.-led invasion of Iraq in March 2003. Britons accused the prime minister of lying about Saddam Hussein's weapons of mass destruction and of being too easily led by U.S. President George W. Bush.

By 2006, Blair had become Britain's longest-serving prime minister. However, despite achieving economic reforms and extending them into health and education, critics within his own party forced Blair to leave office in June 2007. (Blair then accepted the post of special envoy to the Middle East representing the U.S., UK, EU, and Russia.) Chancellor of the Exchequer (finance minister) Gordon Brown became the prime minister of Great Britain.

Coping with terrorism at home has been a continuing problem for the British. A terrorist attack in 2005 disrupted the London underground (subway) system. Carried out by suicide bombers who were British-born of Pakistani descent, the action indicated the success of radical groups in recruiting young British Muslims. In August 2006, British authorities prevented a terrorist attack on American airplanes flying between Britain and the U.S. Had the plot succeeded, British police foresaw "mass murder on an unimaginable scale." At least 24 people, mainly British-born Muslims, were arrested. They were believed to be acting for Al Qaeda.

World attention was focused on London in late 2006 by the assassination of Alexander Litvinenko. A former KGB agent critical of the Russian government, Mr. Litvinenko was poisoned with polonium, a radioactive material. Radioactive traces were found on two British Airways jets flying between London and Moscow. This established a possible Russian link to the murder and indicated that more than 30,000 people might have been exposed to low-level radiation. The Kremlin denied involvement in the murder.

♦ *Describe the major problems faced by Britain's Labour government from 1997 to 2006.*

Northern Ireland. Ireland has had a long and turbulent history. Ruled for centuries by England, most of the island has been a self-governing nation (now called the Republic of Ireland) since the 1920s. But six of the nine counties of the northern province of Ulster make up Northern Ireland, which has remained under British rule as part of the United Kingdom.

Northern Ireland has been troubled by internal conflicts for decades. Religious differences are a major factor. While Roman Catholics are a majority in the Republic of Ireland, they are outnumbered two to one by Protestants in Northern Ireland. Tensions in Northern Ireland have often boiled over. Catholics accuse the Protestants there of discriminating against them in politics, employment, and housing. For their part, Protestants fear that union with the Irish Republic—a goal of many Catholics—would subject them to religious discrimination.

Violent troubles began in Northern Ireland in 1969. Catholic groups staged demonstrations demanding an end to property qualifications for voting in local elections. Protestant extremists attacked the demonstrators. Soon, rival terrorist groups were carrying out murderous attacks. On the Catholic side, the Irish

Republican Army (IRA) battled to unite Northern Ireland with Ireland. On the Protestant side, a group called the Ulster Defense Association (UDA) bombed Catholic targets and carried out assassinations. The Protestants were loyalists who wanted to maintain ties with Britain.

Bombings and murders brought danger to Northern Ireland's chief cities, Belfast and Londonderry. In an attempt to influence public opinion, IRA terrorists also carried out bombings in England, often killing innocent bystanders. Britain sent troops to Northern Ireland to try to restore order. It suspended the parliament of Northern Ireland and imposed direct British rule.

The British put IRA terrorists and suspected terrorists in prison. "Imprisoned nationalists," as they called themselves, used hunger strikes to dramatize their plight. In 1981, ten such protesters starved themselves to death in an attempt to force the British to treat them as political prisoners.

Human rights groups criticized the terrorists, but also the British government for raids on civilian homes and harsh treatment of IRA suspects. Rights groups said courts in Northern Ireland seemed more concerned with convictions than with justice.

The government of the Irish republic denounced the violence in Northern Ireland. Irish police acted to block IRA gun-running and other activities. Ireland's leaders said Irish unity could not be achieved through violence.

In 1985, Britain and the Irish republic concluded a pact known as the Anglo-Irish Agreement. The agreement gave the republic of Ireland a limited say in decisions about Northern Ireland. Protestant loyalists condemned the agreement as a betrayal of their cause. Catholic extremists rejected it as an empty gesture. However, some moderates welcomed the agreement as a step forward.

During the 1990s, the search for a settlement began to make headway. In 1992, Northern Ireland's four moderate political parties began talks about the future of the province. Their main concern was the transfer of political power from Britain to Northern Ireland. Soon after, moderate Catholic leaders made overtures to the IRA's political wing, known as Sinn Fein. Behind the scenes, the British began secret contacts with IRA agents.

A breakthrough came in August 1994, when the IRA declared a cease-fire. Militant Protestant groups responded with a cease-fire of their own. For the first time in 25 years, people felt safe in the streets of Belfast and Londonderry. From 1969 to 1994, more than 3,100 people had died in "the troubles."

In April 1998, talks between Britain and Ireland and all the political parties in Northern Ireland brought an agreement, the Good Friday peace accord. It committed all sides to determining Northern Ireland's future by democratic and peaceful means.

Voters in Northern Ireland elected an assembly later in 1998 in which moderate Protestants and Catholics shared power. But snags remained, as Protestants pressed for the IRA to commit itself to full disarmament and Catholics accused Britain of dragging its feet in creating a new police service to replace the mainly Protestant Royal Ulster Constabulary. In the assembly election of November 2003, the Democratic Unionist Party (DUP), led by Ian Paisley, won the largest number of seats. Opposed to the Good Friday agreement, its victory raised fears about continuation of the peace process.

DUP allegations of illegal activities by the IRA, including breaking into police offices to steal confidential files, led to a four-year suspension of the power-sharing agreement. By 2006, however, an independent monitoring commission concluded that the IRA had disarmed and renounced terrorism and criminal activity in favor of political means to achieve its goal of a united Ireland. In December 2006, Gerry Adams, chief spokesman for Sinn Fein, announced his party's intention to withdraw its long-standing objection to the new Northern Ireland Police Service. This raised the hope that the resumption of power sharing would make possible new elections for the Northern Irish Assembly, the alternative to a return to direct rule of the province by Britain.

In a historic event in May 2007, Reverend Ian Paisley, leader of the DUP, was sworn in as first minister of a self-governing Northern

Peace Process

Ireland. Martin McGuiness, an IRA officer and Sinn Fein spokesperson, became deputy first minister. The agreement of these men from bitterly opposed political parties to serve in the same government represented the triumph of negotiation and compromise over violence.

1. List the causes of violence in Northern Ireland.
2. Describe efforts to bring peace to the province.

Chapter 2 Review

A. Choose the item that best completes each sentence.

1. A high priority for Russian President Vladimir Putin has been (a) retaining the loyalty of officials from the Yeltsin government (b) ending the conflict in Chechnya (c) supporting the U.S. invasion of Iraq.

2. Political violence in Georgia has resulted from (a) regional revolts (b) conflicts with other republics (c) poor relations with Russia.

3. Among the most important resources of Kazakhstan are (a) rubber and bamboo (b) oil and gas (c) timber and manganese.

4. Two former Communist nations that divided into smaller republics in the 1990s were (a) Hungary and Poland (b) Bulgaria and Romania (c) Czechoslovakia and Yugoslavia.

5. A struggle for territory among Muslims, Serbs, and Croatians developed in (a) Bosnia-Herzegovina (b) Moldova (c) Latvia.

6. Solidarity played a major role in the political development of (a) Romania (b) Hungary (c) Poland.

7. A major factor in shaping the new Europe was (a) immigration of non-Europeans (b) emigration of Europeans to other areas (c) a revival of militarism.

8. A major problem facing the German government at the start of the 21st century was (a) Soviet aggression (b) revolts in east Germany (c) emigration of Germans to other countries.

9. President Vladimir Putin increased Russian influence in 21st-century European affairs by (a) using gas and oil supplies as economic weapons (b) sending troops into Western Europe (c) refusing to join the European Union.

10. In 1998, a peace agreement created a new elected governing assembly in   (a) Northern Ireland   (b) Chechnya   (c) Nagorno-Karabakh.

B. Reread "Conflict and Change in Western Europe," on pages 32–42, and examine the maps of that region. Which of the following are correct statements? How can the incorrect statement be corrected?

1. Immigrants have encountered hostility in many countries of Western Europe.

2. Germany has shown little interest in European integration.

3. France has experienced several years of divided government since the 1980s.

4. Scotland and Wales have gained more control over local affairs.

5. Politically, six counties of Ulster have been part of the United Kingdom. Geographically, they are part of Ireland.

C. Review the maps in Chapter 2 and complete the following:

1. The largest republics of the former Soviet Union are _____ , _____ , and _____ .

2. Kiev is the capital of _____ .

3. _____ is the capital of Armenia.

4. _____ and _____ quarreled over Nagorno-Karabakh.

5. Three former Soviet republics bordering the Baltic Sea are _____ , _____ , and _____ .

6. Prior to January 1993, the Czech Republic and Slovakia were united as _____ .

7. Sarajevo is the capital of _____ and _____ .

8. The large country on Poland's western border is _____ .

9. From the 1940s to 1990, Berlin was in the Communist nation of _____ .

10. Luxembourg is a tiny nation bordered by _____ , _____ , and _____ .

Chapter 3

Africa in Crisis

Africa is a continent in crisis. It faces not one but many challenges. One is the struggle to build stable, democratic political systems. Often, the end of colonialism brought dictatorship and one-party rule. A second major problem is ethnic and religious violence. Vicious wars have devastated Rwanda, Sudan, Somalia, and Congo in recent years. Third is hunger. Many parts of Africa have suffered from a severe and prolonged water shortage, or *drought*, brought on by insufficient rainfall. The continent's deserts have expanded, and its food-growing areas have shrunk. Almost one-fifth of the African population has faced sustained hunger in recent years. This problem is aggravated by severe economic underdevelopment and rapid population growth.

Democratic Republic of the Congo

In 1885, Belgium extended its control over a large area of south-central Africa, which became known as the Belgian Congo. The Belgian authorities did little to prepare the country's people to govern themselves. As a result, when Belgium granted independence in 1960, the new nation (called Congo-Kinshasa) plunged into political chaos.

Almost at once, the mineral-rich province of Katanga (now called Shaba) attempted to secede. The Congo-Kinshasa government asked the United Nations to help it keep the country united. When the U.N. sent troops to help end the provincial rebellion, fighting broke out between U.N. forces and the Katangan army. Not until 1963 did Katanga finally come under the control of the

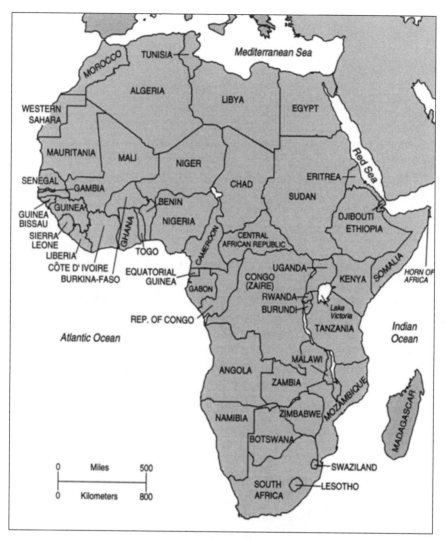

Figure 3.1   Africa

Congolese central government. (It tried unsuccessfully to break away again in the 1970s.)

♦ *Identify each of the following.*

 a. *Belgian Congo*
 b. *Congo-Kinshasa*
 c. *Katanga*

While the civil war was raging, political rivalries resulted in the imprisonment and murder of the prime minister, Patrice

Lumumba. Although a new government was formed in 1964, continuing civil strife made this country one of Africa's bloodiest battlegrounds. Taking advantage of the disorder, an ambitious young army general named Joseph Mobutu seized power in 1965. (He later Africanized his name to Mobutu Sese Seko.) Mobutu changed the country's name to Zaire in 1971.

Zaire was once one of the world's major producers of diamonds, copper, and cobalt. It has soil and rainfall suitable for growing a variety of crops, as well as the potential for hydroelectric power and a logging industry. But Mobutu drained off much of the wealth from the country's natural resources. While the people grew poorer and poorer, Mobutu grew rich. During the cold war, Western powers tended to leave Mobutu's corrupt and inefficient government alone, finding it a useful tool against communism. After the cold war ended, they began pressuring him to make reforms, but he did little.

By the 1990s, Zaire had become a case study in disintegration. Sewage flowed in open ditches through the streets of the capital, Kinshasa. Highways were so full of potholes that trucks could only creep. Hospitals lacked medicines.

In the countryside, a leader named Laurent Kabila gathered a force of anti-Mobutu rebels. In May 1997, the rebels entered Kinshasa and declared Kabila president. Mobutu fled and died soon

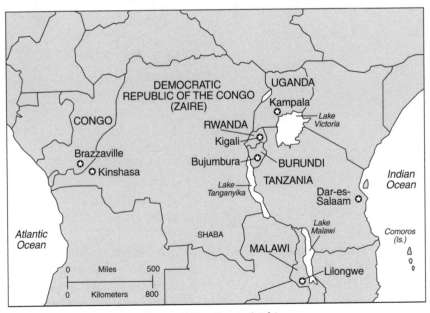

Figure 3.2   Central Africa

afterward. Kabila changed the name of the country to the Democratic Republic of the Congo and, shortly afterward, banned all political parties and public demonstrations.

A revolt began in 1998 and became "Africa's first world war." Rwanda and Uganda supported the Congolese rebels. Angola, Zimbabwe, and Namibia aided Kabila's government. By 2003, Central Africa had been destabilized, and four million lives had been lost.

After Kabila's assassination in January 2001, his son, Joseph Kabila, became president. In 2002, Congo, Rwanda, Uganda, and the rebel militias reached a series of peace agreements. U.N. peacekeepers upheld the cease-fire, as foreign troops went home. In April 2003, President Kabila signed a new constitution, establishing an interim government; four rebel leaders became vice presidents, sharing power with Kabila's supporters. Nevertheless, fighting between the Congolese government and local militias continued.

In December 2006, Joseph Kabila took office as Congo's first democratically elected president in more than four decades. He pledged to fight the corruption and violence that have crippled his resource-rich nation. The U.N. spent hundreds of millions of dollars to maintain the world's largest peacekeeping force in Congo and organize the elections.

♦ *Summarize events in Zaire/Congo between 1964 and 2006.*

The Struggle for Democracy: South Africa

South Africa was settled by three main streams of population. Its first inhabitants were blacks of various ethnic groups, among them Bushmen, Hottentots, and Zulus.

A second group, whites from the Netherlands, France, and Germany, began arriving in the 17th century. They became known as Afrikaners. In order to acquire the rich farmlands of the veld, or plains, the Afrikaners fought long wars against the Zulus and other black Africans. In the process, they developed a strong feeling of enmity toward the blacks and a determination to regard them as inferior people.

The Afrikaners also conflicted with the third stream of population, the English, who began arriving in the 19th century. Attracted by the diamond and gold deposits of the country, powerful empire builders such as Cecil Rhodes wanted to strengthen British control over the colony. Differences in culture and lifestyle resulted

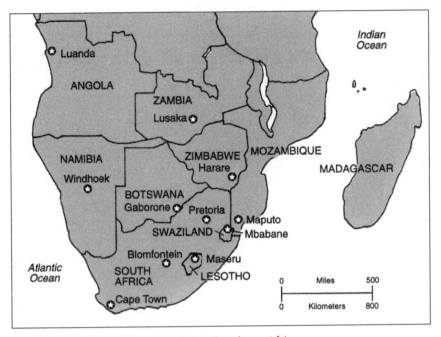

Figure 3.3   Southern Africa

in the Boer War of 1899–1902. The Afrikaners failed in their attempt to break away from British rule. But their resentment of the English persisted, and they vowed to run South Africa in their own way. They had a chance to do so after their National Party, led by Daniel F. Malan, won election in 1948.

The National Party instituted a system of rigid racial separation called *apartheid.* It was designed to ensure the continued rule of the country by a white minority that was only 13 percent of the population. Apartheid deprived blacks of political rights, education, and economic opportunity. It also involved the creation of ten black "homelands," in which blacks could live and develop separately, but under despotic governments and without any economic resources or capabilities. From 1953 to 1989, the National Party held power in ten consecutive parliamentary elections. In response to British criticism of South Africa's racial policies, the National Party withdrew the country from the British Commonwealth of Nations in 1960.

Blacks and some whites organized resistance to apartheid. The largest mainly black group fighting to end white minority rule was the African National Congress (ANC), which set up an underground army. ANC leader Nelson Mandela became an international symbol of resistance during the 27 years he spent in South Africa's prisons.

The white government put a new constitution into effect in 1984. It allowed some representation for "coloreds" (people of mixed racial descent) and Asians. Blacks, however, were still denied political rights.

The ANC's war against the white-dominated government kept South Africa in a continuous state of violence. To express disapproval of apartheid and the disorder it bred, the Western nations agreed, in 1986, to impose limited economic sanctions on South Africa. (*Sanctions* are measures designed to force a nation or region to obey international law; they may, for example, forbid buying its goods.) The economic consequences, and a desire to end internal violence, led some white South Africans to demand change and reconciliation with blacks.

The pace of change picked up in 1990. F. W. De Klerk had become president of South Africa and leader of the National Party. Under his leadership, the government lifted a ban on the ANC and freed Nelson Mandela. De Klerk and Mandela began talks to plan a process of political change.

However, ANC leaders criticized De Klerk for moving too slowly. Guerrilla warfare between blacks and South African security forces continued. Conflict between the ANC and the Inkatha Freedom Party was another source of violence. Led by Mangosuthu Buthelezi, Inkatha gained power in rural areas by promoting Zulu tradition and by making allies of Zulu tribal leaders. The Zulus were the largest ethnic group in South Africa. Unlike Buthelezi, the African National Congress rejected tribal authority. It regarded leadership by chiefs and elders as undemocratic. Nelson Mandela and the ANC called for the election of a national government by South Africans of all backgrounds under the principle "one person, one vote."

Finally, the white government agreed to a plan for universal suffrage. In April 1994, South African voters of all races went to the polls together for the first time. They elected a new legislature. Sixty percent of the votes went to Mandela's ANC, 20 percent to De Klerk's National Party, and 10 percent to Buthelezi's group. With his strong backing in parliament, Mandela became president in May 1994. A multiracial "unity government" set to work to convert South Africa into a truly democratic nation.

In 1997, a new constitution aimed to complete transition from white-minority rule to democracy. Another measure, the Truth and Reconciliation Commission, aimed to uncover human rights

Now the Work Begins

abuses during apartheid. It had power to grant *amnesty*—legal pardon—in exchange for full disclosure by perpetrators. Its work helped South Africans bury past antagonisms.

Mandela's government preserved South Africa's free enterprise system. The ending of economic sanctions enabled increased trade with other nations. Despite the country's strong economy, unemployment, poor housing, and crime continued as severe problems into the 21st century.

Fighting the AIDS epidemic has been a major problem. Government statistics indicate that 1,000 South Africans are infected with HIV every day and 800 more are killed by AIDS. In late 2006, government officials announced a new AIDS strategy, which involved the mass distribution of anti-AIDS drugs at major hospitals. Increasing the number of health-care workers and improving the treatment of HIV positive pregnant women have also been proposed.

Following Mandela's retirement in 1999, another ANC leader, Thabo Mbeki, was elected president. Mbeki's leadership has been prominent in peacemaking efforts, such as those that led to the 2002 Congo agreements. In the parliamentary elections of 2004, the ANC won a huge victory. This ensured Mbeki another five-year term as president. By 2007, President Mbeki's foreign policy was directed at improving South Africa's relations with Russia, China, India, and Brazil and defending Iran's nuclear ambitions. To reduce Africa's dependence on Western help and "meddling," Mr. Mbeki has supported the building of the African Union (AU). South African peacekeepers and mediators have been sent to Sudan and other trouble spots. South Africa has become a favorite mediator for addressing Africa's many conflicts.

1. *What were the most important changes that came to the Republic of South Africa in the 1990s?*

2. *Identify each of the following:*
   a. *Daniel F. Malan*
   b. *F. W. De Klerk*
   c. *Nelson Mandela*
   d. *Thabo Mbeki*

Angola: Cold War Battleground

During the cold war, the United States competed with the Soviet Union for influence in Africa. Intervention by the superpowers in the affairs of African nations became common. In military conflicts, governments supported by the Soviet Union were offered the assistance of troops from Communist Cuba. A civil war that broke out in Angola as it prepared to gain independence from Portugal in 1975 evolved into the worst cold war confrontation in Africa.

Agostinho Neto, leader of the Popular Front for the Liberation of Angola (MPLA), was able to take control of most of the country with Soviet aid and the direct support of Cuban troops. Neto was opposed by Jonas Savimbi, leader of the National Union for the Total Independence of Angola (UNITA). Savimbi received aid from the United States and troops from South Africa.

Originally, UNITA and the MPLA had fought side by side to end Portugal's rule of Angola. After they turned on each other, the result was one of the longest and bloodiest of Africa's wars. Between 1975 and 1994, at least 500,000 people were killed. In addition, 3 million Angolans, in a population of 10 million, became refugees. The war also threatened the operation of Angola's oil industry. The country depended on oil for 95 percent of its export earnings, which were used to purchase weapons and food. As the country's agriculture was ruined, most food had to be imported.

Cuban forces departed in 1991. That same year, UNITA signed

a peace agreement with the MPLA government, now led by Jose Eduardo Dos Santos. The following year, national elections were held under the supervision of a United Nations peacekeeping force. Dos Santos won, but Savimbi refused to accept the results. Once again, he and his 40,000 guerrillas took up arms. As before, violence spread across the country. Capture of the country's diamond and oil-producing regions provided UNITA with substantial wealth so that it could acquire large stores of weapons, including tanks, artillery, and antiaircraft guns. In 1993, however, the United States officially granted diplomatic recognition to Dos Santos' government.

The U.N. arranged a new cease-fire between the government and Savimbi's UNITA in 1994. This held for a few years, but in 1998 UNITA launched a new offensive. Early in 1999, the U.N. peacekeeping mission withdrew in frustration.

In February 2002, Savimbi was killed by government troops. UNITA agreed to a truce soon after. However, fighting between government troops and separatist rebels continued in oil-rich Cabinda province. The rebels agreed to a cease-fire in July 2006.

1. *Explain why the civil war in Angola was at first regarded as a cold war conflict.*

2. *State two actions taken by the United Nations to restore peace in Angola.*

Tribal Rivalries in Kenya

A country of 31 million people, Kenya is an agrarian nation. Its leading exports are coffee and tea. Tourism is a major industry. Kenya has been one of Africa's most stable and prosperous countries. It has been under authoritarian rule since 1964, when the Kenya African National Union (KANU) became its sole political party. Until 1978, KANU was headed by Jomo Kenyatta, who had led the struggle for independence from Britain. Kenyatta was prime minister and then president. Upon his death in 1978, Daniel arap Moi became KANU leader and president of Kenya.

As in many African countries, tribalism has played a major role in Kenyan politics. Moi is a member of the Kalenjin, a minority tribe. This caused resentment among other tribal groups—the majority Kikuyu tribe (which had governed Kenya during Kenyatta's presidency), the Luo, and the Luyha.

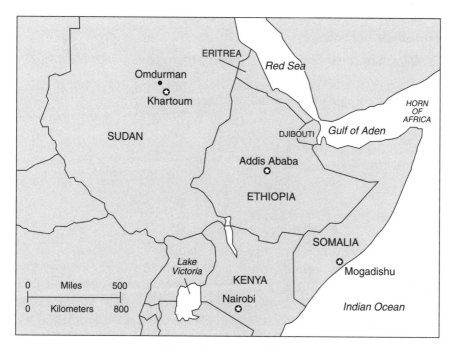

Figure 3.4   East Africa

During the cold war, Kenya's pro-Western political orientation and its strategic location on the Indian Ocean earned it large amounts of Western aid. By the early 1990s, the cold war was over and Kenya owed money to Western nations. They threatened to withhold aid—which provided nearly half of Kenya's annual budget—unless President Moi allowed the formation of other political parties and agreed to hold elections.

Several parties took shape, and voting was held in December 1992. Although Daniel arap Moi won the presidency, parties in opposition to KANU took many seats in parliament. In 1997 voters elected Moi to another five-year term, which by law was his last.

Government corruption, mismanagement, and big economic problems caused the World Bank and International Monetary Fund to end financial aid to Kenya in 1997. The election of President Mwai Kibaki, a respected economist, in December 2002, gave Kenyans new hope. A member of the Kikuyu tribe, Kibaki founded the Democratic Party to oppose KANU. He also served as Kenya's finance minister and vice president. His greatest challenge is to improve the struggling economy.

1. *PROVE or DISPROVE: Tribalism has played a major role in the political life of Kenya.*

2. *Which of the following statements are true and which are false?*
   a. *Jomo Kenyatta led Kenya to independence from Britain.*
   b. *The Kikuyu are the smallest tribe in Kenya.*
   c. *KANU was the only political party allowed by law in Kenya until 1991.*
   d. *The world community has had little influence on the decisions of the Kenyan government.*

Chad: A New Petrostate

A former French colony, Chad gained its independence in 1960. From 1966, French troops assisted Chad's Christian government against Muslim rebels. More French troops were sent in 1983 to oppose Libyan-backed rebels. Libya's long-standing claim to a mineral-rich area on its border with Chad was dismissed by the World Court in 1994. However, continued fighting between rebels and government forces led to the withdrawal from Chad of the U.S. Peace Corps in 1998.

Chad's first multiparty presidential election was held in 1996,

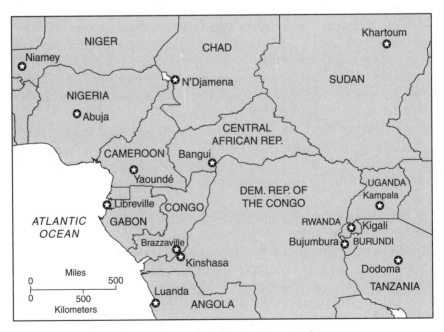

Figure 3.5   Sub-Saharan Central Africa

following approval by voters of a new constitution. Idriss Déby was elected president and was reelected in 2001. Déby is a military leader whose government is known for its corruption. In 2004, he pressed for a constitutional amendment that would remove the bar to a third presidential term.

Chad has been one of the poorest countries in the world. Electricity and water are unavailable to the majority of the country's 9 million people. In 2004, the average Chadian earned approximately $1,000 a year and may die before reaching age 45. Thirty years of civil war have added to the misery.

Nevertheless, in the early 21st century, Chad took the first steps toward becoming a *petrostate*. Under the supervision of the World Bank, a group of U.S., Canadian, and Asian oil companies built a $3.7 billion underground pipeline, stretching 670 miles, to bring crude oil pumped in Chad through neighboring Cameroon to the Atlantic coast. The government of Chad received a $25 million bonus for signing a contract with the oil companies in 2000. In 2004, Chad received an additional $100 million in first oil royalties. This sum enlarged the government treasury by approximately 40 percent.

The World Bank has insisted that the new oil money be used to benefit the people of Chad. A nine-member Revenue Management College of Chadians from civil society, parliament, the Supreme Court, and the government must approve the spending of *petrodollars*.

An oil company spokesperson stated, in March 2004, that $6.5 million had been contributed for health, education, HIV-prevention ads, and environmental projects in Chad. The government, however, used its first oil revenues to buy weapons. Nevertheless, parliament passed a law requiring that 80 percent of the petrodollars be spent on education, health programs, water management, and rural development.

The building of oil fields in Chad was accompanied by the arrival of skilled American oil workers, who live in secure compounds. Oil has not yet improved the lives of most Chadians. Few jobs have been created, but several hundred Chadians were brought to the United States and Canada to be trained for key oil industry positions. One oil company estimated that, in ten years, 90 percent of its staff would be Chadians.

Sudanese Arabs began attacking Chadian villages in 2006. The spillover from the ethnic violence in the Darfur region of Sudan caused more than 50,000 Chadians in villages near the border to flee their homes. In late 2006, however, non-Arab villages in the interior of Chad were attacked by Chadian Arabs. This created fears that conflict between nomadic Arab tribes and settled non-Arab tribes might spread throughout the broad sub-Saharan region.

♦ *How might petrodollars change the lives of the people of Chad?*

Genocide in Rwanda

In 1994, the small African country of Rwanda was the scene of one of Africa's most vicious civil wars. At least 500,000 people lost their lives in massacres sparked by animosities between two rival ethnic groups, Tutsis and Hutus. The killing occurred on such a large scale that it was referred to as genocide. (*Genocide* is the deliberate, systematic killing of a group of people because of their race, religion, or ethnic background.)

The Tutsis are a minority (one-seventh of the population) in Rwanda and neighboring Burundi. Under Belgian rule before 1959, a Tutsi king and his nobles ruled over a Hutu majority. Then Belgian colonial authorities supported a Hutu revolt. In doing so, the Belgians hoped to gain greater control over the Tutsis, who demanded independence. During the uprising, Hutu peasants killed hundreds of thousands of Tutsis. Surviving Tutsis fled to neighboring countries.

After Rwanda became independent in 1962, Tutsi exiles staged guerrilla attacks into Rwanda. Finally, in 1990, an exile army known as the Rwandan Patriotic Front (RPF) managed to get a foothold on Rwandan soil. It waged a guerrilla war against the Hutu-dominated

What Now?

government of President Juvénal Habyarimana, a dictator who had come to power in a military coup in 1973. Rwanda was the most densely populated nation in Africa, with 94 percent of its arable land under cultivation. President Habyarimana argued that there was no room in Rwanda for the exiles.

Nonetheless, his government signed a cease-fire with the rebels in 1993. United Nations peacekeeping troops arrived. But in April 1994, a missile blew up a plane carrying President Habyarimana and the president of neighboring Burundi. Had extremist Hutus killed Habyarimana to block his plans for peace with the Tutsis? That was a common belief—seemingly confirmed when Rwandan government soldiers and Hutu militia immediately began slaughtering Tutsis and moderate Hutus.

As the killing spread, swarms of refugees fled to neighboring countries. In one 24-hour period, 250,000 people poured into Tanzania. More than a million fled to Zaire, where tens of thousands died of cholera. (See map, page 46.) In Rwanda, U.N. peacekeepers found scenes of carnage—headless bodies, rotting corpses, mainly of Tutsis. Even though most of the killing had been carried out by Hutus, the refugees were mostly Hutu.

Amid the chaos, the RPF took control of Rwanda's capital, Kigali. It established a new government that included both Tutsis and Hutus. The last U.N. peacekeeping troops left the country early in 1996. Later that year, hundreds of thousands of refugees returned from Tanzania and Zaire.

But Rwanda's troubles were far from over. Armed Hutus used Zaire (or Congo, as it was called after 1997) as a base for attacks into Rwanda. Accusing the Congo government of supporting the Hutus, Rwanda sent its own troops into Congo, where they became entangled in a widening war. (See page 47.) Eventually, Hutu attacks into Rwanda began to die down. In elections held in April 2000, RPF leader Paul Kagame, a Tutsi, was elected president of Rwanda.

Kagame was reelected by a landslide in 2003. Since then, his government has focused on education, family planning, and attracting foreign investors. Rwanda's entry to the East African Community in 2007 is part of a plan to make the country a bilingual trade center linking French-speaking central Africa with English-speaking east Africa.

♦ *Explain why you AGREE or DISAGREE with the following statement: The civil war in Rwanda differed from other African conflicts of the 1990s.*

Liberia

Like other African nations, Liberia was colonized by Western-ers in the 19th century. In Liberia's case, however, the colonists were freed black slaves and their freeborn children and grand-children from the United States. Later called Americo-Liberians, these American colonists began arriving in the area in 1822. They bought land from native chiefs and settled on the coast. They built Monrovia, the capital, and other coastal cities.

Cultural differences soon caused tension between the Ameri-can colonists and the original inhabitants. The native Africans were treated badly, forced into the interior, and at times, enslaved. Eventually, an American form of government was established.

The Americo-Liberians are Western in culture, English-speaking, and Christian. The rest of Liberia's population of 3.3 million are traditionally African in language, culture, and religion. Some are Muslim. Despite the fact that the Americo-Liberians make up less than one-fourth of the population, they controlled the country's government and economy until 1980.

Charging the government with corruption, soldiers from the interior, mainly enlisted men, staged a bloody coup and took con-

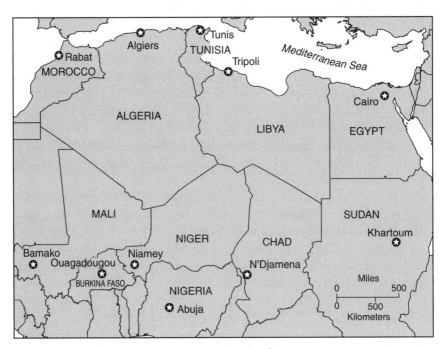

Figure 3.6   North Africa

trol of the government in April 1980. Sergeant Samuel Doe became head of state. Later, he was elected president.

In 1989, when a guerrilla army tried to overthrow President Doe, several tribal militias formed and battled for power. A destructive civil war quickly spread across the country. In September 1990, rebels captured President Samuel Doe and executed him. But the fighting went on. Famine and war made refugees of more than half the population. Desperate Liberians sought shelter in Monrovia, largely destroyed by the fighting. Neighboring countries formed a multinational military force to help restore order.

In August 2003, 14 years of civil war ended when President Charles Taylor resigned and fled. Elected in 1997, he was indicted by the U.N. for war crimes during Sierra Leone's civil war and accused of gunrunning and diamond smuggling. Taylor sought sanctuary in Nigeria. After Nigerian and other West African peacekeeping troops arrived in Monrovia, a cease-fire between government and rebel forces began, and a transition government was established. Ellen Johnson-Sirleaf was elected president in November 2005. She is Africa's first elected female head of state. The rebuilding of Liberia involves providing food and housing for a half million people displaced by the long war.

♦ *Complete the following sentence: Control of Liberia's government and economy by Americo-Liberians ended in 1980 because _____.*

Libya: Rejoining the World Community

Since 1969, when Colonel Muammar al-Qaddafi seized power, oil-rich Libya had been regarded as a rogue state. Qaddafi has been aggressive toward neighboring countries and has supported terrorist groups and activities around the world.

Several land and air battles were fought by Libya and Egypt along their disputed border in July 1977. Libyan troops invaded a uranium-rich region of Chad in 1977 and were finally driven out in 1987.

Violent revolutionary groups in Egypt and Sudan were given weapons by Libya, as were terrorist groups of various nationalities, including the Irish Republican Army. Libya was blamed for aiding terrorist attacks on the Rome and Vienna airports in December 1985. Disagreements between the United States and Libya arose in early 1986 over access to the Gulf of Sidra, claimed by Libya as territorial waters. Colonel Qaddafi was accused of ordering the 1986 bombing of a Berlin discothèque, which caused the death of a U.S. serviceman. The United States retaliated with air strikes on terrorist bases in Libya.

World attention was riveted on Libya in December 1988, when Pan Am Flight 103 exploded over Lockerbie, Scotland, killing 270 people. Libyan agents were suspected of placing the bombs aboard the aircraft. The Qaddafi regime was also accused of causing the explosion of French UTA Flight 772 over Niger in 1989, killing 170 people. When the Libyan government refused to cooperate in the investigations of these tragedies, the U.N. imposed economic sanctions on the country. These restricted the purchase by other countries of Libya's oil and gas and the sale of oil equipment to Libya.

The U.N. sanctions were suspended in 1999, when Libya surrendered two suspects in the Lockerbie crash for trial at the international court in The Hague. Scottish judges convicted a Libyan intelligence officer of murder in 2001. Qaddaffi's government took responsibility for the UTA and Lockerbie bombings and agreed to compensate relatives of the victims. In 2003, Libya agreed to renounce terrorism. U.N. sanctions were permanently lifted.

By late 2003, Libya had serious economic problems and a desire for full diplomatic and trade relations with the United States and the European Union. Qaddafi announced that Libya would scrap its weapons of mass destruction and end all efforts to develop nuclear weapons. In early 2004, hundreds of tons of Libyan weapons and equipment were shipped to the United States for destruction. In addition, Libya signed agreements to permit international inspections.

These developments were followed by a letter of commendation from U.S. President Bush to Qaddafi, a visit to Libya by British Prime Minister Blair in March 2004, and a meeting in Brussels between Qaddafi and Romano Prodi, president of the European Commission, in April 2004. These were regarded as major steps toward Libya's return to the international community.

1. *Why was Libya considered to be a "rogue state" after 1969?*

2. *Explain why you AGREE or DISAGREE with the lifting of economic sanctions against Libya by the U.N., the United States, and Britain by 2004.*

Sudan: A Divided Country

Sudan has the largest area of any country in Africa. Its population is more than 32 million. Much of the country is desert or receives limited rainfall. Cotton and livestock have been Sudan's chief exports. The country is deeply split between Arab northerners, who are mostly Muslims, and black African southerners, who are mostly Christians or *animists* (people who believe in the spirits of animals, vegetation, or natural forces).

For decades, Sudan was administered by Britain and Egypt. After it gained independence in 1956, a parliamentary coalition government ruled. A military coup deposed the government in 1958. All political parties were banned. A Supreme Council of the Armed Forces ruled the country until riots in 1964 forced a change. A brief period of civilian rule ended in another military coup in 1968.

Despite the granting of autonomy to the southern Sudan, a civil war broke out in 1983. Tensions between the Muslim north and the non-Muslim south had been intensified by a government decision to impose Islamic law on civil courts throughout the country. The country's severe economic problems were compounded by a devastating drought that affected much of Africa in the mid-1980s. Another drought struck Sudan in the late 1990s.

By the start of the 21st century, the combined effects of civil war and famine had cost the lives of almost 2 million Sudanese. By then, the war between the Muslim north and the non-Muslim south had become the longest-running war in Africa.

In January 2004, Sudan's government and the southern rebels agreed to share the oil-producing nation's wealth, estimated at $2 billion a year. It was also agreed to establish a monetary system allowing for Islamic banking in the north and Western banking in the south. Most of Sudan's oil is in the south. The United States and other Western governments want peace in order to enable oil companies to have access to the area. They also wish to prevent Sudan from again being used as a base for global terrorists, as it was in the 1990s.

In May 2004, however, fighting between government troops and rebels again flared up, despite an April cease-fire. Since the Sudanese government moved to crush a rebellion in the western Darfur region in 2003, more than 200,000 people have died from hunger and disease. More than 2.5 million have been made homeless. Marauding Arab militias, known as the *janjaweed*, have attacked black African villages, burning homes and killing non-Arab farmers. Despite peacekeeping troops sent by the African Union in 2006, fighting has continued. In late 2006, the Sudanese government gave indications that U.N. peacekeepers might be permitted.

◆ *Which statement is correct?*

  a. *The Sudanese have been the victims of both natural and political disasters.*
  b. *Sudan's oil wealth is a factor in peace negotiations between the government and rebels.*
  c. *Military dictators have played no role in Sudanese political history.*

War and Famine in Somalia

Located on the Indian Ocean, in the mainly desert area known as the Horn of Africa, British Somaliland gained independence in 1960. Shortly after, it joined with the Italian-held portion of Somaliland to form the larger nation of Somalia. In the 1970s and 1980s, the United States and the Soviet Union competed for influence in the Horn of Africa region. When Somalia laid claim to Ogaden, a section of neighboring Ethiopia largely inhabited by Somalis, the Soviet Union sent Cuban troops to assist the Ethiopian government. During the long war that followed (1977–1988), Somali forces were defeated by the Soviet-equipped Cubans. The weapons and military equipment left by the Cubans, and those given by the United States to the Somalis, were later used by rival Somali leaders to arm their personal forces.

Beginning in 1988, these local leaders, or warlords, battled one another and the Somali government. By late 1992, Somalia had almost ceased to exist as a nation. All government had been destroyed. Drought and famine further increased the misery and led to the deaths of several hundred thousand people.

Humanitarian organizations such as the Red Cross worked with the United Nations to bring supplies of food, fuel, and medicine to Somalia. However, distribution of these supplies was disrupted by the rival militias, which attacked the relief workers and looted their convoys and warehouses. With U.N. approval, the United States and other nations sent soldiers to protect relief workers and ensure the distribution of food. U.S. troops also undertook a second task, trying to disarm one of the leading warlords and his followers. However, after 18 U.S. soldiers were killed in October 1993, the United States withdrew its troops. The last U.N. soldiers left Somalia in 1995.

As the fighting between rival militias continued, some Somalis became desperate to end the suffering. After marathon peace talks occurred in Kenya, a transitional government came into being in 2004. As the capital, Mogadishu, was considered unsafe,

President Abdullah Yusuf established his new government in the war-damaged town of Baidoa. Efforts began to repair the town and hold nationwide reconciliation meetings.

Some warlords formed an antiterrorism coalition and battled Islamic militants linked to Al Qaeda. By mid-2006, the Islamists had seized Mogadishu and installed strict religious rule. This raised fears of a regime similar to the Taliban in Afghanistan. In the following months, the Islamists took control of much of Somalia.

Islamist rule was ended by transitional government forces aided by Ethiopian troops supported by U.S. intelligence and bombers. The Islamist forces lost control of Mogadishu and most other parts of the country. The transitional government began to function in Mogadishu in early 2007. A timetable for the departure of the Ethiopian troops and their replacement by African Union peacekeepers remained in question.

1. *Compare the role played by the United States in Somalia during the 1970s and 1980s with its actions in the 1990s.*

2. *Complete the following sentence: U.N. troops withdrew from Somalia because _____.*

3. *Why do you think Ethiopia and the U.S. supported Somalia's transitional government against the Islamist militias in 2006?*

Zimbabwe: Struggle Against Dictatorship

From 1897, when it was named Southern Rhodesia (after empire builder Cecil Rhodes), to 1965, this portion of southern Africa was a British possession. Rich in farmlands and mineral resources, the colony offered a high standard of living to British and European settlers. Internal self-government was granted in 1961. Voting, however, was restricted to ensure that land, resources, and political power remained in the hands of whites.

The demands of the British government for increased voting rights and eventual rule by the black majority were resisted by the white-controlled Rhodesian government. On November 11, 1965, Rhodesian Prime Minister Ian Smith issued a Unilateral Declaration of Independence (UDI) from Britain. This declaration was regarded as illegal by the international community. Following the UDI, the United Nations imposed economic sanctions on Rhodesia, and black nationalist groups began a guerrilla war against the white-controlled government.

A period of bloody civil war continued until a cease-fire agreement in December 1979. Election of a black majority government was followed by legal independence in April 1980. The country was renamed Zimbabwe.

In 1987, Robert Mugabe was elected president. During the civil war, Mugabe had led the largest guerrilla force fighting the Smith government. He also formed the Zimbabwe African National Union (ZANU), later ZANU-PF, which became the country's ruling party.

In the following years, Mugabe gained a reputation as a strongman and dictator. Political opponents have been repressed, often with violence, and journalists critical of Mugabe's government have been imprisoned and tortured.

The United States and Britain have led the international community in condemnation of Mugabe's government, blaming it for economic, political, and social (human rights) abuses. They have also accused Mugabe of cheating his way to reelection in 2002.

Mugabe's determination to drive white commercial farmers from their lands contributed to Zimbabwe's economic collapse in 2002. His confiscation of commercial farms was done, the government claimed, to benefit poor blacks. The country's most productive lands, however, were given to supporters of the ZANU-PF party and military officers rather than to landless peasants. As a result, agricultural production dropped, while unemployment, inflation of prices, and critical shortages of food, fuel, and other necessities soared.

Public medical care in Zimbabwe was crippled in early 2007 by a strike by doctors and nurses. The medical personnel were protesting their pay, which has been eroded by inflation attributed to Mugabe's policies. At more than 1,200 percent, Zimbabwe's inflation rate is the highest in the world. The drop in real purchasing power, therefore, makes low wages even lower. Trade unions have warned of more job boycotts and street protests. Shortages of critical drugs and a huge patient load due to HIV and AIDS have strained Zimbabwe's struggling public health services.

1. *Explain why independence in Zimbabwe was not accompanied by democracy.*

2. *Why has President Robert Mugabe been criticized by the United States and Britain?*

Africa: General Observations

In addition to civil wars and dictatorships, the people of Africa are burdened by political corruption and economic mismanagement. Their situation has been made more difficult by an AIDS epidemic that has swept the continent. Africa today has the highest infant mortality rate, the lowest literacy rate, and the most rapid population growth in the developing world. Less than half the people living south of the Sahara have basic health care. Nearly two-thirds lack safe drinking water. African life expectancy is 52 years compared to the world average of 63 years.

Nevertheless, progress is being made. The number of Africans immunized against serious diseases has increased. Average life expectancy has risen, as has primary school enrollment. The technology revolution has come to Africa in the form of a surge in mobile phone use. This increases business networking and deals. Of great importance are Africa's rich human and natural resources. This was reflected in China's 2007 announcement of a $3 billion loan plan for Africa. Chinese President Hu Jintao toured Africa in 2006 and 2007 to boost ties with a continent that has many of the oil and other resource reserves China needs for its rapidly expanding economy. Trade between China and Africa jumped 40 percent to $55.5 billion in 2006, with the balance of trade $2.1 billion in Africa's favor. (Africa exported more to China than it imported.)

Chapter 3 Review

A. *Choose the item that best completes each sentence.*

1. *The Democratic Republic of the Congo was once ruled by (a) France (b) Belgium (c) Britain.*

2. *In the Republic of South Africa, a long struggle succeeded in (a) ending apartheid (b) establishing a multiracial government (c) both of these.*

3. *Civil war in Angola resumed in 1992 because the results of a national election were not accepted by (a) MPLA (b) UNITA (c) RPF.*

4. *The Kikuyu and Luo peoples are important groups in (a) Kenya (b) Ghana (c) Morocco.*

5. The genocide in Rwanda in 1994 was committed mainly by (a) Hutus against Tutsis (b) Zulus against Hutus and Tutsis (c) whites against blacks.

6. In the 21st century, Chad began its development as a petrostate with the aid of the (a) European Union (b) World Bank (c) Commonwealth of Independent States.

7. Control of Liberia's government and economy by the descendants of American colonists was ended in 1980 by (a) religious dissidents (b) minority tribes (c) military rebels.

8. The nation blamed for terrorist acts, including the 1988 bombing of Pan Am Flight 103, was (a) Libya (b) Kenya (c) the Democratic Republic of the Congo.

9. Fighting between the Muslim-dominated north and the non-Muslim south caused economic collapse and a huge refugee problem in (a) Zaire (b) Sudan (c) Angola.

10. Widespread starvation and continuing violence in Somalia was caused by (a) the breakdown of all government (b) a border war with Ethiopia (c) an influx of refugees from Sudan.

B. Compose a brief essay on contemporary African problems by writing one or two paragraphs in response to each of the following questions:

1. What difficulties have Africans encountered in attempting to establish democratic governments?

2. Why has famine become so critical a problem in certain African nations?

C. Complete the table.

Leader	Nation	Major Problem
Joseph Kabila Thabo Mbeki Eduardo Dos Santos Daniel arap Moi Charles Taylor		

D. *Examine the maps of Africa in Chapter 3 and indicate whether each of the following statements is* true *or* false.

1. *Shaba is a country north of Uganda.*

2. *Pretoria is the capital of the Republic of South Africa.*

3. *Angola and Namibia have Atlantic Ocean coastlines.*

4. *Lake Victoria is located in Somalia.*

5. *Chad is one of the nations of southern Africa.*

6. *Forces opposing the government of Rwanda can cross that nation's border from Tanzania.*

7. *Liberia and Sierra Leone border the Indian Ocean.*

8. *Two nations that share borders with Libya are Chad and Egypt.*

9. *Refugees from the civil war in Sudan might seek refuge in Egypt and Uganda.*

10. *The easternmost part of Somalia is called the Horn of Africa.*

Chapter 4

War and Peace in the Middle East

O ften called "the crossroads of the world," the Middle East has historically been an arena of conflict. Nations, empires, and superpowers have struggled for victory in religious, ethnic, and territorial disputes. In the 20th century, Middle Eastern oil reserves increased the importance of the region to the rest of the world. The era of colonialism has ended, but outside nations continue to attempt to exercise influence within the Middle East.

Poverty, overpopulation, inadequate housing, and government corruption have contributed to the spread of radicalism and unrest in the Middle East. The growth of *Islamic fundamentalism* has added a new element to the volatile mix. Islamic fundamentalists reject many elements of modern life as disruptive of family and society. They seek to "purify" Middle Eastern societies by enforcing a strict interpretation of Muslim law and tradition.

The Sword of Islam

In 1979, Muslim fundamentalists led a successful rebellion against the United States-backed Shah (king) of Iran and took control of that country. Since then, Islamic fundamentalism has grown as a political and religious force. It has spread from the Middle East to North Africa, the Muslim republics of the former Soviet Union, and elsewhere.

Many Muslim fundamentalists focus on trying to live up to the ideals of Islam in their daily lives. They live peacefully with their neighbors. Other fundamentalists have resorted to violence. They

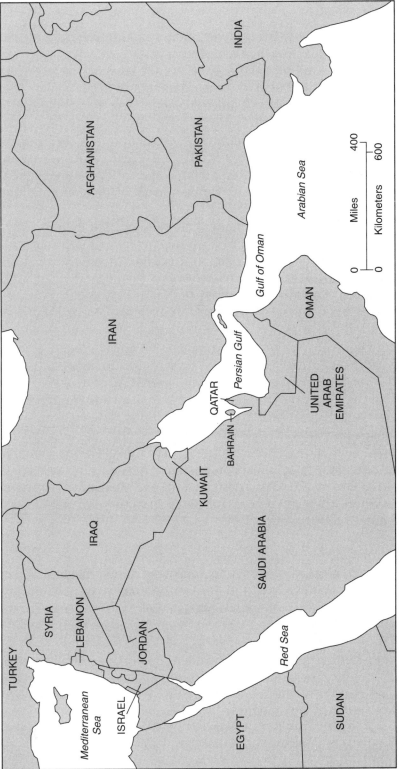

Figure 4.1   The Middle East

seek to overthrow existing governments and impose their ideal of Islamic society by any means necessary.

The most militant fundamentalists, or *Islamists,* reject Western culture and political ideas as remnants of imperialism. They seek to establish Islamic regimes run according to the rules of the Prophet Muhammad, the founder of Islam, and his immediate successors. They also preach the destruction of Israel and the replacement of the Jewish state by an Islamic Palestine. Many Islamists consider the United States a special enemy because of its close ties to Israel and its support for secular moderate Muslim governments.

Militant Islamists have made their presence felt in many ways. The Islamist leader of Iran in 1989 issued a *fatwa* (death sentence) against the Muslim writer Salman Rushdie. Rushdie's novel *The Satanic Verses* was judged *blasphemous* (insulting to God). For many years, Rushdie was forced to live in hiding. Furthermore, Islamists have seized Westerners as hostages. And they have committed terrorist acts. The worst attack blamed on them was the crashing of hijacked airliners into the World Trade Center in New York and the Pentagon in Washington on September 11, 2001. (For more on terrorism, see Chapter 10.)

How to respond to militant fundamentalists has troubled both moderate Muslims and the Western world. One reason some Islamists turn to violence is that most Middle Eastern governments do not allow peaceful opposition or free elections. Islamists have gained many followers in Muslim countries such as Tunisia, Algeria, Jordan, Turkey, Aden, Yemen, and Pakistan. Two countries where they have been particularly active are Afghanistan and Iraq.

Afghanistan. In 1996, a Muslim fundamentalist group, the Taliban, seized most of Afghanistan, including Kabul, the capital, and declared it an Islamist state, ruled by *sharia,* or Islamic law. Banned were television, nonreligious music, jobs for women, and female education beyond age ten. Away from the home, women had to be veiled from head to foot.

Anti-Taliban groups still controlled the north and still received outside help. The civil war continued. Misery and hunger were widespread. After the terrorist assaults on New York and Washington in 2001, Afghanistan's problems grew worse. The nation became the focus of U.S. military action. U.S. leaders targeted Afghanistan because it was the base of Osama bin Laden, suspected leader of those attacks. The Taliban had refused the U.S.

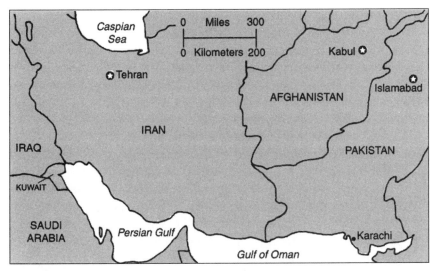

Figure 4.2   Eastern Islamic Nations

demand to surrender bin Laden after the attacks. By late 2001, the Taliban had been defeated. An interim government representing all Afghan political groups was established.

With U.S. support, Hamid Karzai became interim president. His authority was challenged by local warlords, whose militias controlled areas outside Kabul. While NATO troops continued to battle Taliban holdouts and terrorists, a U.N.-sponsored presidential election in October 2004 was won by Karzai. Subsequently, Afghanistan became a major producer of illegal narcotics.

1. *Define Islamic fundamentalism.*

2. *Explain why militant fundamentalism is seen as a threat by governments in the Middle East and elsewhere.*

Egypt. President Hosni Mubarak of Egypt has been a special target of several fundamentalist organizations active in Egypt. The Islamists have many reasons for disliking Mubarak. (1) Egypt has maintained a separate peace with Israel, a nation hated by the Islamists. (2) Mubarak works closely with the United States, and thus Islamists consider him a puppet of "imperialism." (3) Mubarak maintains a semblance of democracy but allows no real opposition. (4) Corruption is widespread within government circles.

The objective of radical fundamentalist organizations like Islamic Jihad and the Islamic Group is to overthrow President Mubarak and establish a purely Islamic government. A less radical group, the Muslim Brotherhood, has been more willing to work within the system. A major figure in the Islamic Group is Sheik Omar Abdel Rahman, an Egyptian cleric who has preached against the Mubarak government from mosques in the United States. (In 1995, a federal court jury in New York convicted the sheik and nine other Islamists of conspiring to carry out terrorist bombings and assassinations in the New York area.)

The Islamic Group launched a campaign of violence in 1992. Terrorists set off bombs in cities along the Nile River, seeking to intimidate tourists, foreign residents, and Egyptian Christians (who make up 10 percent of Egypt's population). In June 1995, the Islamic Group tried to assassinate Mubarak as he arrived in Ethiopia for an international conference. One of the worst attacks by the Islamic Group occurred in November 1997, when 64 tourists were slain at Luxor, in the Valley of the Kings. The violent campaign killed more than 1,200 people before the Islamic Group declared in 1999 that it was renouncing violence.

Egypt, which has been under martial law since 1981 (when President Anwar Sadat was assassinated), has responded to Islamist attacks with harsh measures. Security forces have arrested thousands. (Human rights organizations accuse the regime of torturing many of those it detains.)

Because widespread poverty and government repression have helped to build support for radicalism in Egypt, the Mubarak administration has sought to supplement police action with political and economic reforms. Mubarak's supporters want him to find ways to keep the fundamentalists from convincing Egyptians that life under an Islamic government would be better.

The struggle between fundamentalism and secularism in Egypt, a nation whose 68 million people comprise one-third of the Arab world's population, has worried the United States government. Egypt's support of U.S. interests and its peace with Israel are considered critical to the success of American policies in the Middle East. The U.S. Embassy in Cairo has been a vital center for intelligence gathering in the region and for maintaining contact with a number of organizations. A fundamentalist victory in Egypt would limit U.S. activities and change the balance of power in the Middle East.

♦ *Identify each of the following:*

    a. Hosni Mubarak
    b. Islamic Group
    c. Omar Abdel Rahman

Israel and the Arabs

A state of war has existed between Israel and almost all its Arab neighbors since 1948, when Israel became a nation. Refusing to accept the Jewish state in their midst, the Muslim Arab nations went to war with Israel in 1948, 1956, 1967, and 1973. Before the 1990s, only Egypt had signed a peace treaty with Israel (in 1979).

Palestine, the ancient region along the eastern coast of the Mediterranean Sea, is regarded by the Jews as their biblical homeland. After the defeat of the Ottoman Empire in World War I, Britain administered Palestine as a League of Nations mandate. With Hitler's rise to power in Germany, Jews seeking a haven from persecution in Europe returned to their ancestral land in large numbers. Palestinian Arabs resented the influx of new settlers and feared that the newcomers would displace them. Relations between Arabs and Jews became increasingly hostile, with riots and acts of terrorism. Unable to stop the violence, Britain decided to surrender its mandate and turn over the problem to the United Nations.

In a historic 1947 vote, the U.N. partitioned Palestine into separate Jewish and Arab states. The Palestinian Jews accepted the

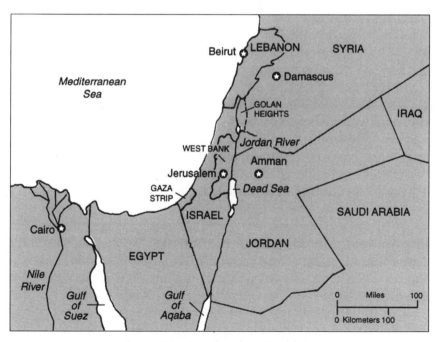

Figure 4.3   Israel and Its Neighbors

U.N. decision and proclaimed the independent state of Israel in May 1948. The Palestinian Arabs, however, rejected the plan. So did the neighboring Arab countries. Seeking to destroy the new Jewish state, they launched a joint attack against Israel. The Israelis fought off the invading armies.

The 1948 war led to a massive flight of Palestinian Arabs to neighboring countries. To escape the fighting, about 75 percent of the Arab population of Israel abandoned their homes. They expected to return after the war but were unable to do so. Although the host countries permitted the Palestinians to remain, they kept them apart from their own people. The Palestinians settled in refugee camps and had little opportunity to obtain jobs, provide for their families, or lead normal lives. For their survival, Palestinian refugees had to depend on aid provided by international agencies and charities.

For decades, the refugees' condition was a major obstacle to peace in the Middle East. Another obstacle was disagreement over arrangements for the West Bank (of the Jordan River) and Gaza, a strip of land along the coast. These territories, inhabited by Arabs, were occupied by the Israeli army in 1967, when the Jewish state defeated Egypt, Syria, and Jordan in the Six-Day War. In 1987, the Palestinians of the West Bank began street protests and riots against Israeli authority. They called their actions an *intifada,* or uprising.

♦ *Describe the growth of the Palestinian refugee crisis.*

Efforts to negotiate a peace settlement were complicated by disagreements within Israel itself. The two leading political parties took sharply contrasting stands. The rightist Likud Party opposed concessions to the Palestinians. The leftist Labor Party was more open to peace talks and bargaining. The two parties took turns controlling the government through shaky coalitions.

Under a coalition led by Likud leader Yitzhak Shamir, Israel's government in the early 1990s encouraged Jewish settlements in the occupied territories. The Shamir government also announced its intention to annex those territories, making them a permanent part of Israel. Shamir's policies infuriated the Arab inhabitants of the conquered territories, who stepped up their *intifada.* Violent clashes broke out with Israeli police and military forces.

Palestinian demands for independence and the fate of Gaza and the West Bank were among the emotional issues that figured in an elaborate peace process arranged by the United States, beginning in 1991. Peace talks involved delegations from Israel, Syria, Lebanon, and Jordan, as well as Palestinian representatives.

♦ *Summarize the differences between Likud and Labor.*

A 1992 election brought to power a new Israeli coalition, with Labor Party leader Yitzhak Rabin as prime minister. One of Rabin's first moves was to commit his government to cut back Jewish settlements in the occupied territories. That policy brought a positive response from the leading Palestinian group, the Palestine Liberation Organization (PLO).

For years, Israeli leaders had depicted the PLO as a terrorist group dedicated to the destruction of Israel. Yasir Arafat, the PLO leader, was widely hated by Israelis. Since the late 1980s, however, the PLO had changed its policies. Arafat had renounced terrorism and accepted the partition of Palestine.

In 1993, Israel and the PLO held secret talks in Oslo, Norway. The PLO agreed that Israel had a "right to exist in peace and security." Israeli negotiators accepted the PLO as "the representative of the Palestinian people." In September 1993, Israel and the PLO signed a historic accord in Washington, D.C.

The agreement was called a Declaration of Principles. It provided for Palestinian self-government in two places to be turned over by Israelis—Gaza, along the Mediterranean coast, and Jericho, a town in the West Bank. Later, the Israelis would turn over more of the West Bank. The PLO would run a new Palestinian National Authority (PNA) that would act as an interim government. Most of the details were left to be worked out in later negotiations over a five-year period.

World leaders hailed the Israeli-PLO pact as a major step toward peace, as did many Israelis and Palestinians. However, many others criticized the accord. Palestinian militants said it created an empty shell that would leave Israelis in control of most of the West Bank for many years. Israeli critics said the pact would undermine the security of Israeli settlements in the West Bank and expose more Israelis to terrorist attacks.

As the two sides began to implement the accord, serious problems emerged. In February 1994, an Israeli settler murdered 29 Muslims at prayer in a mosque at the West Bank town of Hebron. Then Palestinian extremists staged a number of suicide bombings. Dozens of Israelis were killed or maimed as they rode to work on buses or passed along busy streets. An Islamist group called Hamas took responsibility, saying war with Israel would

Reaching Out

go on until an independent and powerful Palestine was created.

The peace process continued haltingly, as both sides sought a solution acceptable to their peace advocates and hard-liners. Arafat remained head of the Palestinian governing council, but changes in Israeli leadership caused policy shifts and delays.

In November 1995, a Jewish extremist shot and killed Rabin as he left a peace rally. May 1996 elections brought to power Likud leader Benjamin Netanyahu, who took a hard line by demanding that Arafat suppress terrorism. Netanyahu also allowed construction of more Israeli settlements on the West Bank.

Talks produced no agreement. In September 2000, a second *intifada* began—street clashes, terrorism, military reactions.

In another election, in February 2001, hard-line Likud leader Ariel Sharon became prime minister. He stepped up military measures and accused Arafat of allowing terrorism. In succeeding months, Islamists made suicide bombings within Israel, and the Israeli military targeted leading Palestinians.

Israel had signed a peace treaty with Jordan in 1994. It was the second Arab nation (after Egypt) to accept Israel's existence. A third, Syria, held 1999 peace talks with Israel. It hoped for return of the Golan Heights, occupied by Israel since 1967.

Israel refused to deal further with Arafat, who it believed supported terrorism. The appointment, in November 2003, of Ahmed Qurei as Palestinian prime minister raised hopes of renewed peace talks. Qurei called for a cease-fire with Israel and an international peace conference. In January 2004, however, Israel began building a concrete barrier around Jerusalem, separating it from Palestinian villages in the West Bank. This wall will be linked to a longer barrier of concrete, ditches, and security posts that Israel is building along its border with the West Bank, as protection from Palestinian suicide bombers. Following Arafat's death in November 2004, Mahmoud Abbas, a veteran peace negotiator, was elected chairman of the Palestine Liberation Organization. Abbas has been a critic of the armed Palestinian uprising.

Hamas, the radical Islamic group, won parliamentary elections in 2006. Fatah, the dominant Palestinian political party for decades, was unseated. Hamas took control of the legislature and the cabinet. As Palestinian president and leader of Fatah, Mamoud Abbas retained many powers and the loyalty of many members of the security forces. A bitter feud between Hamas and Fatah exploded into bloody street fighting in Gaza. In early 2007, King Abdullah of Saudi Arabia joined the efforts of Egypt, Syria, and other Arab nations to stop the violence between the Palestinian factions. At a conference in Mecca in February 2007, President Abbas and the Hamas leaders agreed to form a unity government. Nevertheless, the bloodshed in Gaza continued.

By June 2007, Hamas had driven Fatah forces out of Gaza and taken complete control of the area. This left President Abbas with authority over only the West Bank, where he established a new Palestinian emergency government. To support this government, the U.S. resumed economic aid to the Palestinian Authority. The EU pledged to do the same, and Israel agreed to release to President Abbas tax revenues withheld by Israel since Hamas took control of the Palestinian parliament.

In 2005, Israeli Prime Minister Ariel Sharon decided to pull Israeli troops and settlers out of Gaza and leave the territory to the control of the Palestinian Authority. Sharon suffered a massive stroke in January 2006, and Ehud Olmert became prime minister. When border clashes with Hamas militants from Gaza and Hezbollah—an Iranian-supported terrorist group—fighters from Lebanon led to the kidnapping of Israeli soldiers, Olmert ordered Israeli ground and air forces to attack Lebanon. The brief war that followed ended with a U.N.-sponsored cease-fire in August 2006.

1. *Explain why you AGREE or DISAGREE with the following statements:*

    - *The Six-Day War of 1967 was a great victory for Israel. Gaza, the West Bank, and the old city portion of Jerusalem were brought under Israeli control. However, the next 40 years of continuing military occupation and settlement building in the conquered territories was a mistake, leading to two Palestinian intifadas, the rise of Hamas, and endless bloodshed.*
    - *For peace to come between Israelis and Palestinians, Israel must give up the West Bank and share Jerusalem; the Palestinians must agree to Israel's right to exist as a secure Jewish state.*

2. *Upon leaving office in June 2007, British Prime Minister Tony Blair became special envoy to the Middle East for the United States, UN, EU, and Russia. Blair's mission was to focus on Palestinian economic and political reform. Write a letter to Mr. Blair in which you provide answers to the following questions:*

    - *Should the western powers and Russia support the Fatah or Hamas government?*
    - *How will aiding the Palestinian Authority to develop strong government increase the chances for peace in the Middle East?*
    - *What steps might be taken to improve relations between the Palestinians and the Israelis?*

The Persian Gulf War

In August 1990, Iraq invaded its tiny neighbor Kuwait and annexed it. The Iraqi dictator, Saddam Hussein, wanted Kuwait for its rich oil fields and as a seaport on the Persian Gulf. Hussein then moved his forces to the border of Saudi Arabia. He seemed poised for an invasion of that oil-rich nation also.

U.S. President George H. Bush led worldwide opposition to the Iraqi aggression. He sent troops to Saudi Arabia, a pro-Western nation and an ally of the United States, to protect it. The United Nations demanded Iraq's withdrawal from Kuwait.

Operation Desert Storm began on January 17, 1991. A U.N. coalition of 28 nations used overwhelming military power (mostly that of the United States) to drive Iraq out of Kuwait. U.S. General H. Norman Schwarzkopf commanded the coalition forces. The victory, however, neither ended Saddam Hussein's control of Iraq nor brought peace to the region. U.N. forces stayed to protect the Kurds, a minority group within Iraq, from Hussein's troops. And U.N. inspection teams made periodic visits to ensure that Iraq was dismantling its nuclear, chemical, and biological weapons factories.

Figure 4.4   Persian Gulf States

♦ *Identify each of the following:*

a. Saddam Hussein
b. H. Norman Schwarzkopf

Significant changes occurred in the Middle East as a result of the Persian Gulf War. The Arab nations that had been part of the U.N. coalition demonstrated a greater willingness to engage in U.S.-sponsored peace talks with Israel. That helped lead to direct peace talks between Israeli and Syrian diplomats.

A continuing U.S. military presence in the Persian Gulf region was another result of the war. To block future aggression by Hussein and to keep him from seizing control of the region's oil resources, the Gulf nations agreed to permit the United States to store military equipment in the area and to engage in joint military exercises with them. After the war, U.S. and British planes helped to enforce "no-fly" zones in southern and northern Iraq, from which all Iraqi planes and missiles were excluded.

The war left Kuwait with many serious problems. Kuwait spent huge sums to repair its badly damaged oil fields, which did not return to prewar levels of production until the mid-1990s. Hundreds of thousands of Palestinians who had worked in Kuwait before the war were not permitted to return after the war. They were perceived as Iraqi sympathizers.

Economic damage to Iraq was immense. Industries, roads, bridges, and telecommunications facilities all had to be rebuilt.

Desert Storm

The United Nations continued its sanctions as a way of forcing Hussein to comply with the terms of the cease-fire. One of those terms required him to end all programs to develop nuclear, chemical, or biological weapons. For years after the war ended, U.N. inspectors conducted careful inspections of Iraq's factories and military facilities.

The U.N. sanctions caused much suffering among the Iraqi people. Government food rations were inadequate to meet basic needs. People who tried to buy extra food often found they could not afford it. Middle-class people sold their furniture and even the bricks of their houses in order to buy food. Poor nutrition contributed to diseases that hit children and old people especially. Although U.N. sanctions were designed to allow humanitarian aid to reach Iraq, aid workers said there was too little aid to meet the people's needs.

The Iraq War

In December 1998, Hussein refused to allow U.N. weapons inspections to continue, and U.N. inspectors withdrew. To ensure that the Iraqi dictator was not developing weapons of mass destruction, the United States and Britain demanded the continuation of U.N. economic sanctions. However, when American and British troops invaded Iraq in 2003, no weapons of mass destruction were found. A 15-month investigation by the U.S.-led Iraq Survey Group concluded, in 2004, that Saddam Hussein had destroyed his WMDs in 1991 following the Persian Gulf War.

The regime of Saddam Hussein was swept away by the U.S. and British invasion. The dictator went into hiding but was eventually captured by American forces. He was convicted of crimes against humanity by an Iraqi court and executed. U.S. authorities transferred power to a transitional Iraqi government in June 2004. Following national elections in December 2005, a new government, headed by Shiite leader Nouri al-Maliki, took office in May 2006.

The new government and its security forces have been unable to stop the rising level of sectarian violence between the militias, or private armies, of the majority Shiites and minority Sunnis. The largest of these militias is the Mahdi Army, led by Shiite cleric Moktada al Sadr. Daily attacks, suicide bombings, kidnappings, and executions caused the deaths of 3,086 U.S. military personnel by February 2007 and more than 60,000 Iraqi civilians since the 2003 invasion.

The dissatisfaction of many Americans with the conduct of the Iraq war by the administration of President George W. Bush caused a severe drop in the president's approval rating and defeat for Republicans in the congressional elections of November 2006. As Democrats took control of the House and Senate in early 2007, a great debate began on the Iraq war. Many in Congress demanded the withdrawal of U.S. forces. President Bush proposed sending more U.S. troops to support the Iraqi government and its security forces. Meanwhile, Iran began to strengthen its diplomatic and military relations with the Iraqi government and offered to take responsibility for reconstruction in Iraq. Fearing the growth of Iranian influence in the Middle East, the Bush administration opposed these efforts.

◆ *Prepare a table as shown below and enter the required information.*

PERSIAN GULF WAR (1991) & IRAQ WAR (2003)

Dates	Cause(s)	Leaders	Major Results

Mediterranean Neighbors

By 2004, Syria was benefiting from increased investments from Europe and elsewhere. This brought some economic progress. Neighboring Lebanon, nearly destroyed by 16 years of civil war, continued to rebuild.

Syria. Syria was once the center of a Muslim empire. Under French rule after World War I, it regained its independence in 1946. Syria participated in the Arab attempt to destroy Israel in 1948 and remained at war with the Jewish state.

In 1963, military officers and political leaders of the Socialist Baath Party, dedicated to pan-Arab unity, seized power. It became the only legal party and controlled the Syrian government. President Hafez al-Assad came to power in 1971.

During the Six-Day War of 1967, Syria tried once again to defeat Israel, but it failed. A result of the war was Syria's loss of the Golan Heights, a high point of land from which Syria often shelled settlements in Israel. Syria's loss was Israel's gain, as Israeli settlers moved into the area. In 1973, Syria joined Egypt in still another attack on Israel but gained nothing from its participation in this Yom Kippur War. The following year, several oil-rich Arab nations agreed to provide Syria with funds to continue its anti-Israel activities. In addition, Syria received billions of dollars in military aid from the Soviet Union during the cold war. The aid helped the Syrians build one of the most powerful armies in the Middle East.

♦ *Describe how Syria became a major power in the Middle East.*

Its military power enabled Syria to dominate Lebanon after civil war broke out there in 1975. The war involved numerous Muslim and Christian factions, as well as the Palestine Liberation Organization. Most government functions collapsed and the once-prosperous Lebanese economy crumbled.

Eager to limit the power of Lebanese-based Palestinian guerrillas who operated near its border, Syria sent troops into Lebanon in 1976 as part of an Arab peacekeeping force. Syria's troops battled Muslim forces and Christian militias and even took on the Israeli army, which invaded Lebanon in 1982. Syrian troops eventually helped to restore order in Lebanon in 1991.

During the Persian Gulf War, Syria's Assad condemned Iraqi aggression against Kuwait and sent troops to the U.S.-led coalition. In return, Kuwait contributed to a Syrian development fund. Assad made a few economic reforms, but Syrian industry improved little over the years. Oil revenues soared, but Western investors and businesspeople from the Gulf states were wary of investing much in a police state whose policies might change overnight. However, Syria's food production boomed, and the importation of consumer goods increased significantly.

Syrian security forces brutally suppressed a rebellion by local Muslim extremists in the early 1980s. In the 1990s, Assad, who recognized the growing power of Islamic fundamentalism, became a patron of religious revival. But his efficient security forces prevented any Islamic political party from forming.

Syria opened peace negotiations with Israel in 1991 as part of a U.S.-sponsored advancement in the "peace process." The discussions continued off and on for years but without positive results. With Syria insisting on a return of the entire Golan Heights region, negotiators have so far failed to come close to an agreement.

In June 2000, Hafez al-Assad died. His 34-year-old son, Bashar al-Assad, then assumed power, with the support of the Baath Party and the army. While the new president was quick to call for political and economic reforms, change seemed likely to come only slowly.

U.S. President George W. Bush imposed economic sanctions on Syria in May 2004. He charged Syria with failing to take action against terrorist groups fighting Israel or to halt the flow of foreign fighters into Iraq. All American exports to Syria, except for food and medicine, were banned. During the mid-2006 conflict between Israel and Hezbollah, the terrorist organization based in Lebanon, Syria assisted Iran in sending weapons to Hezbollah.

♦ *Explain how Syria benefited from the Gulf War.*

Lebanon. After receiving independence from France in 1943, Lebanon prospered. Beirut, the capital, became the banking and intellectual center of the Middle East. Lebanon was a showcase of free enterprise in a region largely dominated by socialism.

Under the terms of the National Covenant of 1943, government offices were divided among the main religious communities—Christians, Sunni Muslims, Shiite Muslims, and Druses. At first, the Christians were in the majority. In the 1970s, Muslims became the majority and demanded a larger political and economic role. Tensions increased when the Palestine Liberation Organization decided to make Lebanon its base of operations, after being expelled from Jordan because of Jordanian distrust of the PLO's political ambitions.

Lebanon's problems exploded into full-scale civil war in 1975, with widespread destruction. Under a mandate from the Arab League, Syria sent a peacekeeping force that assumed control of much of the country. Meanwhile, Israeli troops and their Lebanese Christian allies occupied a "security zone" in southern Lebanon to protect Israel's northern settlements from guerrilla attacks. Syria helped to broker the peace accord that ended the Lebanese civil war in 1990. Its troops remained in Lebanon to enforce the peace.

With the civil war over, Lebanese leaders began working to restore Lebanon's economy. They took steps to reorganize the civil service and restore law and order. The army raided criminal havens in several parts of the country, seizing quantities of drugs, weapons, and stolen vehicles. Government troops also entered areas controlled for years by terrorists who had taken Westerners hostage during the 1980s. These steps were made possible with Syria's support.

Tension continued in Lebanon's south, along the border of Israel's "security zone." Here, guerrillas from an Islamist group called Hezbollah launched air and artillery attacks against Israeli settlements in northern Israel. In retaliation, Israeli and South Lebanese forces often attacked camps in southern Lebanon.

In May 2000, in fulfillment of a campaign pledge he had made to Israel's voters, Israeli Prime Minister Ehud Barak withdrew Israeli troops from southern Lebanon. Thousands of Lebanese Christian militia members also moved out of the abandoned "security zone" and into Israel. This left southern Lebanon under Hezbollah's control.

Rafik al-Hariri, a popular former prime minister, was killed by a truck bomb in February 2005. Many Lebanese blamed Syria. As anti-Syrian street protests increased, Syria withdrew its remaining troops from Lebanon. Parliamentary elections brought a new anti-Syrian government, led by Fouad Siniora, into office in July 2005.

Hezbollah's rocket attack on Israel in July 2006—and the capture of two Israeli soldiers in a border raid—resulted in a heavy military response by Israel. Israeli air and ground forces attacked suspected Hezbollah bases in southern Lebanon. In response, Hezbollah fired nearly 4,000 rockets into northern Israel. Nearly 1,150 Lebanese were killed. Roads and bridges were destroyed.

A U.N.-sponsored cease-fire ended the conflict in August 2006. Lebanese troops moved into southern Lebanon, and the U.N. force already there was expanded.

Led by Sheik Hassan Nasrollah, Hezbollah began demanding more political power in late 2006 and early 2007. In January 2007, a violent strike organized by Hezbollah brought Lebanon to a standstill. Saudi Arabia, which supports the government of Prime Minister Fouad Siniora, moved to prevent a civil war in Lebanon by opening talks with Hezbollah and Iran, which supports Hezbollah.

1. *Identify each of the following:*
   a. *Socialist Baath Party*
   b. *Bashar al-Assad*
   c. *Hezbollah*

2. *Complete the following sentences:*
   a. *Syria and Lebanon have been strongly linked because _____.*
   b. *After the Persian Gulf War, Syrian economic progress was stimulated by _____.*
   c. *Islamic fundamentalism did not cause political upheavals in Syria because _____.*
   d. *Two consequences of Israel's withdrawal from southern Lebanon in 2000 were _____ and _____.*

Jordan

Putting an end to 46 years of hostility, the prime ministers of Jordan and Israel met at a desert outpost on the two nations' border and signed a treaty of peace in October 1994. Jordan thus became the third Arab entity, after Egypt and the Palestine Liberation Organization, to make peace with the Jewish state.

Jordan is a latecomer among Arab states. The British carved it out of Palestine in 1921, to reward the Hashemite family for its aid to Britain against the Ottoman Turks during World War I. Jordan received its independence in 1946. Its first king was Abdullah. His grandson, Hussein, reigned over Jordan as king from 1952 until his death in 1999. He was succeeded by his oldest son, Abdullah. Theoretically, the Jordanian king rules as a constitutional monarch, but his broad powers leave little room for democratic government.

Jordan participated in the Arab nations' attack on Israel in 1948. The Arab Legion, Jordan's British-trained and British-led army, was one of the best in the Middle East at that time. In the

1948 war, Jordan gained control of part of Jerusalem and the West Bank. But it lost those territories to Israel in the Six-Day War of 1967 and has since transferred its rights over them to the PLO.

During the Arab-Israeli wars, Palestinian refugees flooded into Jordan. Following Iraq's invasion of Kuwait in August 1990, approximately 700,000 more Palestinians from Kuwait fled to Jordan. The Jordanian economy was already deteriorating, with unemployment between 20 and 25 percent. The Persian Gulf War brought Jordan's economic life to a standstill. After the war, hundreds of thousands of the new refugees remained in Jordan, unable to return to Kuwait and the jobs they had held there. Palestinians now make up about half of Jordan's population of 5 million.

The refugee problem strained transportation and communication systems, health and education services, and water supplies. Consequently, the government had to revise its economic development program, changing its focus from growth and prosperity to maintenance of minimal living standards. Jordan's problems were compounded by the loss of foreign aid from countries embittered by Jordan's support for Iraq in the Persian Gulf War.

Jordan's assistance to Iraq took the form of shipments of food and other goods. Maintaining good relations with its larger, more powerful neighbor, and its dictator, Saddam Hussein, was considered a wise policy by Jordan's rulers. King Hussein's grandfather had been murdered by Islamic militants in the 1940s for his moderate views toward Israel.

♦ *How did the Arab-Israeli conflict and the Persian Gulf War affect Jordan?*

Saudi Arabia

The mission of the U.S.-led coalition during the Persian Gulf War was not only to liberate Kuwait but also to protect Saudi Arabia. With an estimated one-fourth of the world's oil reserves, the Saudi kingdom has been a vital source of energy for the world. Saudi Arabia is a longtime ally of the United States and has received much military and technical assistance. In return, the Saudis often use their influence to encourage moderation among other Arab nations and oil producers.

After liberation from Turkey at the time of World War I, much of the Arabian peninsula was united by a desert warrior named

Saudi Arabia and Al Qaeda

Abdul Aziz Ibn Saud. Ibn Saud became Saudi Arabia's first king and the founder of its ruling family. Although Saudi Arabia covers a large area, only 2 percent of its land is arable. The discovery of oil transformed the Saudi economy in the 1930s. Oil provided the kingdom with a source of enormous wealth and gave it global importance.

Since 2005, Saudi Arabia has been ruled by King Abdullah, an absolute monarch. Saudi Arabia allows no political parties and has no legislature. The Islamic religious code, the *sharia*, is the law of the land. The use of alcohol and Western forms of public entertainment are banned or limited. Women have inferior legal status. In municipal council elections held in 2005, Islamist candidates placed on a "golden list" by conservative religious leaders were successful. These were the first elections since 1963. Women were (and still are) not permitted to vote.

Saudi Arabia has opposed Israel since 1948, sending troops to fight against the Jewish state in that year and in 1973. The Saudis extended aid to the PLO and other militant groups, as well as to Egypt, Syria, Jordan, and other Muslim countries. In an attempt to force the United States and other Western nations to abandon their support of Israel, the Saudi government participated in an oil embargo in 1973. The withholding of oil from the West produced severe fuel shortages and high prices there but failed to achieve its political objective. Saudi Arabia joined most of the other Arab nations in condemning Egypt in 1979 when it negotiated a peace treaty with Israel.

Using its vast oil wealth, Saudi Arabia created what has been called "the world's most extravagant welfare state." The government offered Saudi citizens free health care, free college education, interest-free home loans, and subsidized gasoline. Since those programs were financed from oil revenues, Saudis paid almost no taxes.

Rising oil prices have since given a boost to Saudi Arabia's economy. However, political tensions have remained high. Resentment of U.S. support of Israel and the presence of U.S. troops in Saudi Arabia led to the participation of 15 Saudis in the September 11, 2001, terrorist attacks on the United States. Many Saudis admire Al Qaeda and Osama bin Laden. Wealthy Saudis, including members of the royal family, have been suspected of giving funds to Al Qaeda and other terrorist organizations. This support was shaken by the killing of 52 Saudis by terrorist suicide bombs in 2003. Another suicide bombing took place outside a police building in 2004. Saudi security forces began to hunt down suspected terrorists. Suicide bombers were prevented from blowing up the Abqaiq oil and gas facility in February 2006.

By early 2007, Saudi diplomacy took a more aggressive approach to the main conflicts of the Mid-East: the Sunni insurgency in Iraq, Hezbollah's opposition to the Lebanese government, and the Palestinian rivalry between Hamas and Fatah. A key Saudi goal is to counter attempts by Iran, with its Shiite majority, to increase its influence in the region. The Saudi royal family is Sunni, as are the majority of Saudis. (Shiites and Sunnis are the largest Muslim sects. Their differing religious views and practices have led to widespread conflict and repression of one group by the other.)

The U.S. seeks establishment of an American-backed alliance of Sunni Arab states, including Saudi Arabia, Jordan, Lebanon, and Egypt, and a Fatah-led Palestine. With Israel, such an alliance would be expected to oppose Iran, Syria, and the radical groups they support, such as Hezbollah, a Shiite militia. King Abdullah has played host to meetings of Sunni and Shiite leaders, offered to mediate the Lebanese conflict, and brought Hamas and Fatah to reconciliation talks in the holy city of Mecca.

The Saudi government fears that a withdrawal of U.S. troops from Iraq would be followed by an alliance between Iran and the Shiite-led government of Iraq. This would provide Iran an opportunity to fulfill its ambition to be a regional superpower.

1. *Explain the importance of Saudi Arabia to the West.*

2. *What role did Saudi Arabia play during the Persian Gulf War?*

3. *What problems and fears caused an increase in Saudi diplomatic activity in 2007?*

The Tragedy of the Kurds

Another post–Gulf War problem was the ongoing plight of the Kurds. For centuries, the Kurdish peoples of Turkey, Iraq, Syria, and Iran have struggled to establish a nation of their own. Hostile governments and rivalries among Kurdish factions have prevented the creation of an independent Kurdistan.

The Kurds are an ancient people, known for their military traditions and for so often being subjected to others. They have rarely been independent. Now numbering 26 million, the Kurds are the largest ethnic group in the Middle East without their own government.

World attention turned to the Kurds in 1991. Encouraged by the Gulf War victory of the U.S.-led coalition, Iraqi Kurds revolted against Saddam Hussein. Iraqi troops quickly crushed the uprising and drove thousands of Kurdish rebels and civilians to the borders of Iran and Turkey. Many refugees died of starvation and exposure in the snowbound mountains.

The military forces of the United States and its allies responded by establishing safe havens for the Kurds. Operation Provide Comfort protected the Kurds from their Iraqi attackers and distributed food and medical supplies to them. A Kurdish-controlled zone for 4 to 5 million refugees was established in northern Iraq. Kurds hoped that the zone could eventually become the core of a self-governing Kurdistan.

Within the zone, approximately one million Kurds held an

election in May 1992, to choose a 105-seat assembly. Thousands of armed guerrillas temporarily abandoned their positions opposite the Iraqi army in order to vote. Traditionally, tribal chiefs and Muslim sheikhs had held power among the Kurds, whose loyalties were further divided among eight political parties. The Kurdistan Democratic Party (KDP), the largest and oldest of the political groups, held strong appeal for the mountain Kurds, who were the backbone of the Kurdish military forces. Since its founding in Iran in 1945, the KDP had been under the control of the Barzani family.

Among the other Kurdish political parties was the Patriotic Union of Kurdistan (PUK), led by Jalal Talabani and Ibrahim Ahmad and backed by Iran. They were nationalists who sought to shape a political organization that could bypass tribal loyalties. There was also a Kurdish Communist Party and an Islamic Movement of Kurdistan. The latter group believed that Iraq should become an Islamic state.

By 1994, the Kurdish areas of northern Iraq had fractured into warring districts. As had happened so often before, the Kurds were at one another's throats.

Another Kurdish organization, the Kurdistan Workers Party (PKK), had bases in Iraq but operated mainly within Turkey. The PKK is a Marxist group that demands self-rule and basic rights for Turkey's 12 million Kurds. Under Turkish law, however, Kurds must go to Turkish-language schools and are discouraged from speaking the Kurdish language. Since 1984, the Turkish army has conducted a fierce campaign against PKK guerrillas in southeastern Turkey.

Turkey maintained good relations with the largest Iraqi Kurdish groups. They promised to help stop the PKK from using Iraq as a base for attacks on Turkey. In return, the Turks gave aid to the Iraqi groups. In 1998, the Iraqi Kurds signed a peace agreement in Washington, D.C., and began driving PKK guerrillas out of areas they controlled.

The U.S.-led invasion of Iraq in 2003, followed by the overthrow of Saddam Hussein's government, encouraged Iraqi Kurds to once more demand self-government. Many called for an independent Kurdistan. Others were willing to accept more governmental powers within a united Iraq. The interim constitution signed by the Iraqi Governing Council in March 2004 gave three Kurdish provinces veto power over approval of a permanent constitution. In April 2005, the transitional national assembly of Iraq elected Jalal Talabani as president.

1. Define or identify each of the following:

    a. Operation Provide Comfort
    b. KDP, PUK, and PKK
    c. Jalal Talabani

2. Explain why you AGREE or DISAGREE with the following statement: The United States and its allies should not be involved in the Kurdish effort to achieve self-government.

Chapter 4 Review

A. Choose the item that best completes each sentence.

1. A goal of militant Islamic fundamentalists has been (a) peace with Israel (b) alliance with the United States (c) the overthrow of pro-Western Arab governments.

2. Efforts to make peace between Israel and its Arab neighbors have been hindered by (a) disagreements among Israelis (b) disagreements among Arabs (c) both of these.

3. The Persian Gulf War was caused by (a) the Israeli conquest of the West Bank and Gaza areas (b) the Iraqi invasion of Kuwait (c) U.S. weapons sales to Saudi Arabia.

4. A result of the Persian Gulf War was (a) greater Arab willingness to engage in U.S.-sponsored peace talks with Israel (b) the fall from power of Saddam Hussein (c) an independent Kurdish state.

5. A post–Gulf War problem was (a) Iranian aggression (b) an Israeli refusal to negotiate with its Arab neighbors (c) the eviction of Palestinians from Kuwait.

6. By 1990, Syria had become the dominant power in (a) Iraq (b) Kuwait (c) Lebanon.

7. Arab countries that have signed peace treaties with Israel are (a) Syria and Saudi Arabia (b) Egypt and Jordan (c) Lebanon and Iraq.

8. A country that spent billions of dollars to finance the coalition campaign in the Persian Gulf War was (a) Syria (b) Lebanon (c) Saudi Arabia.

9. A Marxist group fighting against Turkish government forces is the (a) PKK (b) PLO (c) Socialist Baath Party.

10. *The largest ethnic group in the Middle East without a homeland are the   (a) Sunni Muslims   (b) Shiite Muslims   (c) Kurds.*

B. *Reread "The Sword of Islam," on pages 68–72. Then write a paragraph to explain why most of the governments of the Middle East fear the militant Islamic fundamentalists.*

C. *Examine the maps of the Middle East in Chapter 4. Which of the following statements are* true *and which are* false?

1. *During the civil war in Afghanistan, weapons for the various warring factions could be slipped across the border from Pakistan.*
2. *In Egypt, the Nile River flows into the Mediterranean Sea.*
3. *The West Bank territory has borders with both Israel and Jordan.*
4. *Kuwait is governed from Baghdad.*
5. *Syria and Lebanon are separated by Israel.*
6. *Iraq can threaten the security of Saudi Arabia's border.*
7. *An independent Kurdish state might include land in northern Iraq.*
8. *The Golan Heights lie between Israel and Jordan.*
9. *Jordan occupies more territory than Israel.*

D. *Reread "Saudi Arabia" on pages 86–89 and do the following:*

1. *List three conflicts that have been of concern to the Saudi government.*
2. *Explain how the Iraq war and Iranian ambitions have changed Saudi diplomacy.*
3. *Describe the rivalry between Sunnis and Shiites and its effect on the Middle East.*

Chapter 5

Conflict and Economic Growth in Asia

In the early 21st century, China remained Asia's largest Communist nation. Strengthened in 1997, when Britain returned its former colony of Hong Kong, China's remarkable economic growth brought many changes. Economic and political problems threatened Japan's financial stability and its role as an economic superpower. While the people of North Korea suffered from famine, their dictatorial government produced missiles and nuclear weapons. Southeast Asia continued to be the scene of ethnic and political conflicts. In India, violence between religious groups occurred amidst economic growth and political change.

The Modernization of China

The leadership of China's Communist Party continued the dictatorship established in 1949 by Mao Zedong. Throughout the 1950s and 1960s, the party combined political repression with rigid application of Mao's Marxist principles in government, industry, and society. The results were economic stagnation and severe human rights abuses.

Following Mao's death in 1976, a new, more practical Communist leadership came to power under the direction of Deng Xiaopeng. Leaders took steps to improve relations with non-Communist nations. Diplomatic relations with the United States, which had fought China during the Korean War (1950–1953), began in 1979. China's leaders also began reforms in education and industry in an attempt to stimulate economic growth.

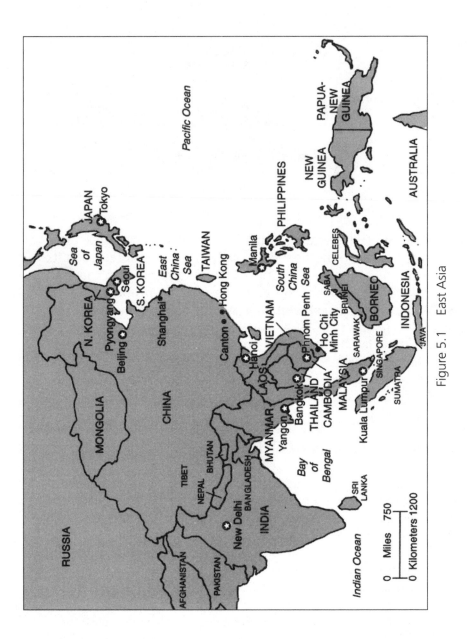

Figure 5.1   East Asia

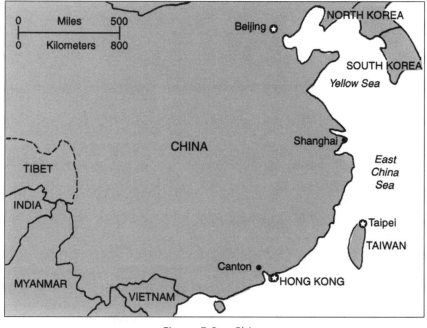

Figure 5.2   China

Economic Reform. By the mid-1980s, China began to abandon rigid central planning and encourage private enterprise. As private business ownership expanded, the Chinese had more consumer goods and enjoyed a rising standard of living.

In the 1990s, China emerged as an economic powerhouse. Industry expanded rapidly, moving from the coastal regions to inland population centers along the Yangtze River. At the national level, once-powerful government ministries lost their monopolistic control of strategic industries, which now had to compete in the marketplace. Foreign investors received a warmer welcome than ever before. Between 2001 and 2004, China accounted for one-third of the world's economic growth. By 2006, the growth rate of China's gross domestic product (GDP)—the total value of goods and services it produced—had risen to nearly 10 percent. Progress in reducing poverty and openness to trade gained China entry into the World Trade Organization in November 2001.

The economies of other nations benefited from China's economic growth. As China's industrial output increased by 50 percent, its need for certain materials skyrocketed. It accounted for one-third of the growth in global oil consumption and 90 percent of the growth in world steel demand in recent years.

Russia, Brazil, and Australia, in particular, gained much from China's economic boom. So did its Asian neighbors, especially Japan. In September 2006, China's trade surplus with the rest of the world had ballooned to $19 billion. The bulk of this trade surplus came from exports to the world's wealthiest regions, particularly the U.S. and Europe. In addition, Chinese companies have invested in Indonesian oil and natural gas fields and shopped for resources in many other countries. Australia's exports to China of iron ore, aluminum, and uranium have produced an economic boom in that country. China has also loaned large amounts of money to Cambodia, Laos, Myanmar, and other poor Asian countries. Trade between China and Africa reached $55.5 billion in 2006. A $3 billion loan plan for Africa was announced by China in 2007.

To modernize its economy, China's government sold many of its unprofitable state-owned businesses to private investors. This *privatization* was regarded by some senior Communist Party members as the undoing of communism in China. Nevertheless, thousands of state businesses were sold to private investors.

Many of the investors were foreigners, including overseas Chinese. Businesspeople from Hong Kong, Taiwan, and elsewhere

Hybrid

improved China's economy by bringing to it new capital and advanced management skills. U.S. and other Western corporate giants also moved into China's huge market. They invested billions of dollars in the telecommunications, automobile, and electronics industries. Motorola and AT&T, for example, established research and development, manufacturing, and sales facilities in China. These investments boosted economic activity and contributed to the dramatic rise in Chinese exports.

Another departure from traditional Communist policies was the encouragement of private enterprise among ordinary Chinese. Throughout the country, individuals were urged to engage in business activity for profit, sparking an economic and social revolution.

After Deng died in 1997, his successor, Ziang Zemin, announced plans to sell 10,000 of China's 13,000 medium- and large-size enterprises to shareholders. Also included in the new plans was the privatization of most of the nation's 300,000 smaller companies.

As a result of all these changes, control of the Chinese economy shifted away from Beijing, the capital. Provinces and towns gained new importance. New "economic development zones" sprang up, and construction boomed. Moreover, manufacturing activities moved increasingly into the provinces, where labor costs were lower than in urban centers.

Despite the development of a market economy, however, the Communist Party remained firmly in power. China's new economic managers, more prosperous than ever before, retained membership in the Communist Party.

◆ *Describe the economic changes that have taken place in China since the 1980s.*

Political Freedom and Human Rights. In the areas of political freedom and human rights, the Chinese government clung to tradition. It remained an authoritarian regime with a huge propaganda machine and prison labor camps. Its repressive policies led to conflicts between China's leaders and many of its people.

A crisis occurred in May 1989. One million Chinese had gathered in Beijing to demand democratic reforms. Activists were demonstrating in 20 other cities as well. The Communist leaders imposed martial law and moved troops into Beijing. In and around Tiananmen Square, scene of the main demonstrations, hundreds were killed or injured. Authorities arrested large numbers of students and workers. Despite international outrage, Deng Xiaopeng allowed Communist Party conservatives to tighten control of cultural and media activities in order to discourage further demands for democracy. Repression of those not following Communist Party doctrine has continued in recent years. Beginning in 1999, the government arrested thousands of members of the Falun Gong religious sect, which practices Taoist and Buddhist disciplines. Chinese leaders apparently saw its mass gatherings and spiritual teachings as a threat to Communist power. In 2007, the leaders of a Protestant Christian sect, which the Chinese government regarded as a cult, were executed.

Critics of the government have been jailed and newspapers have been closed. In 2006, the government clamped down on the Internet, closing blogger sites, filtering Web sites and e-mail for banned words, and tightening control on text messages. Determined to remain in power, the Chinese Communist Party has shown little tolerance for freedom of information.

Other disputes center on trade. China sells far more to the United States than it buys. Therefore, U.S. leaders have worked to increase U.S. exports to China, pressing China to lower trade barriers of various kinds. Lengthy negotiations led to a U.S. decision to support China's entry into the World Trade Organization.

Military issues have also divided China and the United States. Determined to be the top military power in East Asia, China has been building up its naval and air forces. The Chinese moved hundreds of short-range missiles to locations near Taiwan. U.S. strategists saw the Chinese buildup as a threat to Taiwan and a challenge to U.S. and Japanese interests in the region. By 2003, China's military spending was reaching levels second only to the U.S. military budget. Accelerated missile production, Chinese-made strike aircraft, and warships purchased from Russia have been priorities. This increased spending has been driven by the belief of Chinese leaders that, while trade and technology exchanges with the United States are beneficial, the United States poses a long-term military threat, especially to Chinese efforts to recover Taiwan. By 2007, China was modernizing its nuclear weapons, expanding the reach of its navy, testing an antisatellite weapon, and sending astronauts into space. These actions signaled China's intention to join Russia and the United States in military space activities.

Other recent developments in Taiwan have also alarmed China's leaders. For years, China insisted that Taiwan was part of China. Then in 1999, Taiwan's President Lee Teng-hui called Taiwan a state equal to China. In 2000, for the first time in 50 years, the Nationalists lost the presidency of Taiwan. Voters there elected Chen Shui-bian of the Democratic-Progressive Party, a one-time supporter of Taiwanese independence. After his election, Chen said Taiwan would not declare independence unless China made a military attack. Chen was reelected in 2004.

One other contentious issue has been China's population-control methods. With about 1.3 billion people, China has the largest population of any country in the world. The government has pursued a policy of only one child per couple, especially in urban areas. The goal is to halt population growth completely by about 2040, when population may start to decline. The United States denounced China's use of harsh methods to enforce birth control, including compulsory sterilization, forced abortions, and fines for unauthorized pregnancies.

1. *Describe the Chinese political crisis of May 1989.*

2. *List the issues that have dominated U.S.-Chinese relations in recent years.*

3. *PROVE or DISPROVE: The United States should not be concerned about China's military buildup.*

Hong Kong

At midnight on June 30, 1997, the British formally relinquished to China their control over Hong Kong, which they had ruled for 156 years. After this peaceful transition, the former crown colony became known as a Special Administrative Region (SAR) of China.

Located at the mouth of the Canton River, Hong Kong includes a main island, 235 smaller islands, and Kowloon Peninsula, which is part of China's mainland. Hong Kong became a British crown colony after the Opium War of 1839–1842, when Britain forced China to give up the island. In 1898, Britain and China negotiated a 99-year lease.

In the 20th century, Hong Kong became one of the great shipping, commercial, and manufacturing centers of Asia. In addition to a major electronics industry, Hong Kong developed shipbuilding, iron and steel, and a highly competitive textile industry. Free trade, low taxes, a large labor force, and extensive communications made the colony prosperous. By the mid-1990s, Hong Kong had 6.5 million inhabitants.

In 1990, Britain and China agreed on a new constitution, the Basic Law. Hong Kong would keep its capitalist economic system and many features of self-rule for 50 years after 1997. China called this arrangement "one country, two systems."

In its final years as a British colony, Hong Kong was ruled by an elected legislative council and a governor-general appointed by Britain. At the time of the turnover, a new 60-member legislature was created. Voters elected 24 of the 60 legislators, the rest appointed by 800 prominent people. China named a Hong Kong businessman, Tung Chee-hwa, chief executive. After Tung resigned in March 2005, Donald Tsang was chosen as chief executive. Hong Kong activists have complained that the new government is business-oriented and undemocratic. Early on, it suspended certain rights of labor unions.

Hong Kong is valuable to China. It is a port through which the Communist giant can trade with Taiwan and other countries with which it has no formal diplomatic relations. In 2002, the Chinese Economic Area (China, Hong Kong, Taiwan) became the world's fourth-largest center of economic growth.

In May 2004, Chinese warships sailed through Victoria Harbor in Hong Kong. This rare show of force was seen as a threat to democratic activists. China has been accused of increasing intimidation of pro-democracy residents of Hong Kong. The timetable for democratic changes in the territory was delayed in 2004 at the request of China's President Hu Jintao.

1. *Explain why Hong Kong is important to the Asian business community.*

2. *Complete the following sentence: In 1997, Hong Kong reverted to _____ control.*

3. *How does political and economic life in Hong Kong differ from that in most of China?*

Japan: An Economic Superpower

Between 1931 and 1945, Japan used military force to conquer an empire in East and Southeast Asia. Japan's aggression, and its alliance with Nazi Germany and Fascist Italy, led to World War II. That conflict ended with the atomic bombing of two Japanese cities by the United States in August 1945.

At the war's end, most of Japan's cities and industries lay in ruins. Having defeated Japan, the United States acted quickly to

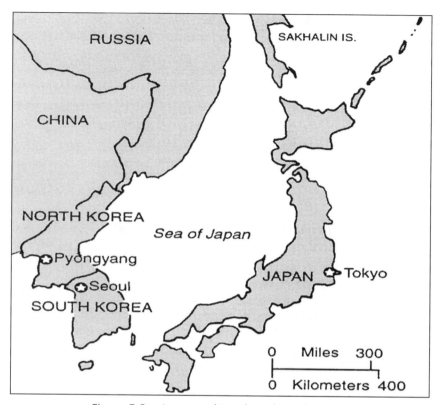

Figure 5.3 Japan and North and South Korea

democratize the country and to help it recover from the ravages of war. With help from American experts, the Japanese wrote a new constitution. It set Japan on a different course, away from the militarism and imperialism that had been such strong forces in its history. A democratic government, led by a prime minister, took office in 1947.

With American aid, Japanese industry grew rapidly. The automobile and electronics industries were especially successful. Japan found willing buyers all over the world for its cars and television sets. It became a leader in the development and manufacture of computer chips and other high-tech products. In addition, Japanese investors became influential in the economies of the United States and other countries.

One reason for Japan's success was its high rate of savings. The savings contributed to heavy investment in new plants and capital equipment—at a rate far exceeding that of the United States. Another factor was Japan's dynamic pursuit of investment opportunities, especially in Asia. In China, Korea, Taiwan, Hong

Kong, Vietnam, Thailand, Malaysia, Singapore, and Indonesia, Japanese firms invested and sold far more than did U.S. and European companies.

Japan's economic success drew on a disciplined and educated workforce and on a traditional unity of purpose among industry, labor, and government. In Japan's unique form of capitalism, government and industry cooperated in laying plans for the future and seeing that they were carried out.

Tensions and Problems. By the 1980s, Japan had become an economic superpower. It ranked second only to the United States in total output, a position it still holds today. Japan's economy, however, slacked off sharply from 1990 onward. Land prices dropped to less than half their former levels. So did share prices on the Tokyo stock exchange. Prospects for a resumption of pre-1990 growth rates seemed no brighter in recent years than in the 1990s.

The stumbling economy shook Japan's political system. Public exposure of corruption in government, especially within the long-dominant Liberal Democratic Party (LDP), touched off political scandals, adding to the disarray. Struggling to reverse the slump, the LDP clung to power through a series of unpopular leaders. A more popular one, Junichiro Koizumi, became prime minister in 2001 but had no magic answer.

In 1997, several Asian economies faltered. A major problem was that their banks had lent vast sums of money to shaky enterprises. When these began to fail, so did the banks, threatening the collapse of entire national economies. The International Monetary Fund (IMF)—a specialized agency of the United Nations— stepped into the breach. It advanced loans to Thailand, Indonesia, and South Korea. The crisis had a severe impact on Japan, a heavy investor in Pacific Rim enterprises. After its largest securities house failed, Japan began a reform of its financial services. But its economy remained shaky well into the new century.

In mid-2003, the economy began to recover. The economic growth rate neared 4 percent. Deflation—falling prices of consumer goods—eased. Bankruptcies were reduced, and many businesses paid off debts. China's growing need for Japanese goods, especially steel, helped. So did restructuring and cost cutting by many larger businesses. Under new leadership, the Bank of Japan provided a more stimulating monetary policy.

♦ *Describe Japan's economic changes in the late 20th and early 21st centuries.*

Overseas Manufacturing. In the 1980s and 1990s, Japanese companies began to do some manufacturing elsewhere, where their products were in demand and costs were lower than in Japan. Factories arose in the United States, Latin America, and Southeast Asia. By 2004, Japanese capital and jobs were flowing to China. Electronics and other high-tech industries have built large factories and research centers there to make use of the huge, cheaper labor force. From China, advanced Japanese consumer products flow to Europe, North America, and even back to Japan. Despite the shut-down of dozens of factories in Japan and the loss of thousands of jobs for university graduates, technology workers, and others, China is expected to remain the focus of Japan's overseas manufacturing.

Trade surplus. For all its recent problems, Japan remains an economic superpower—one not always loved by competitors. Japan has run up large trade surpluses with the United States and Europe. Its surplus with the United States exceeded $65 billion a year in recent years. That meant that Japan received at least $65 billion more for goods and services sold to the United States than Americans received for what they sold to Japan. Many of Japan's

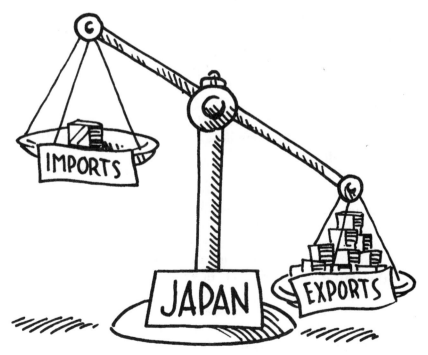

Trade Imbalance

trading partners found Japan's trade and other economic policies unfair. For example, they said that Japanese business practices were designed to freeze out competition from non-Japanese businesses that tried to enter the Japanese market.

In the 1990s, U.S. leaders pressured Japan to open its market to U.S. companies. A series of Japanese concessions included a July 2000 agreement to open its telecommunications industry to more competition. As China's trade with Japan grew to record levels in 2003 and 2004, Chinese manufacturers moved electronic goods and appliances, textiles, and food products into Japan.

♦ *Describe the increased interaction of the Japanese and Chinese economies in the 21st century.*

Foreign Policy. After World War II, Japanese foreign policy was conducted beneath a U.S. nuclear "umbrella." Japan granted the United States valuable military bases. It paid most of the cost of keeping U.S. troops in Japan. Today, despite trade disputes with the United States, Japan permits 45,000 U.S. troops to remain on Japanese soil.

Japan leads Eastern Asia economically but has not attempted to dominate it politically or militarily. Japan's own military forces are strictly limited. After World War II, the United States encouraged Japan to write into its constitution a ban on going to war. The purpose was to avoid a revival of Japanese militarism. In the 1950s, Japan created its own Self-Defense Forces but barred them from going overseas. Japan's military budget is very large—second only to that of the United States. Recently, some Japanese leaders have proposed changing the constitution so Japan can take a stronger role in world affairs.

Japan had a keen interest in the 1991 Persian Gulf War because it depends on oil from the Persian Gulf. But rather than join the coalition fighting Iraq, it gave money. Later, Japan took a noncombat role in a U.N. military mission to Cambodia. It also sent forces to the "war on terror" declared by President Bush in 2001. Parliament approved, on condition that the forces had a noncombat role outside the battle zone. In 2004, however, 1,000 Japanese troops were sent to war-torn Iraq to engage in reconstruction work.

In recent years, Japan has been the world's largest foreign aid donor. It has also been the second largest contributor to the United Nations budget, after the United States.

♦ *Which of the following are correct statements? Revise the incorrect statements.*

a. *After World War II, Japan and the United States cooperated closely on military matters.*
b. *Disputes over Japan's trade surplus in the 1990s led to Japan's asking the United States to remove its troops from Japan.*
c. *Japan's constitution has prevented Japan from maintaining any military forces at all.*
d. *Japan contributed money but not soldiers for the Persian Gulf War.*
e. *Japan spends more on foreign aid than does the United States.*

North and South Korea

Korea was part of the Japanese empire until 1945. After the post–World War II U.S.-Soviet occupations, it became two countries.

In June 1950, Communist North Korea invaded non-Communist South Korea. In the Korean War (1950–1953), U.N. forces, led by the United States, forced North Korea to pull back behind the 38th parallel, the border between the two nations. Fighting ended with a cease-fire but no peace treaty.

North Korea is the most rigidly run Communist state in the world. Despite aid from China (and, in the past, the Soviets), economic development has been limited. Committed to the Communist struggle against the West, its economic resources have been focused on military production. Some 36 percent of the workforce are farmers, with corn and rice as major crops.

In the 1990s, Russia ended much of the foreign aid North Korea needed. A severe fuel shortage reduced industrial and agricultural output, hampered fishing, and caused a serious food shortage. Floods destroyed many crops and left more than 5 million people homeless. North Korea admitted only in 1997 that widespread starvation loomed. International agencies sent emergency supplies that, by 2001, reached 8 of 20 million North Koreans. Some 2.3 million had died.

For 46 years, Communist party leader Kim Il Sung held supreme power. When he died in 1994, his son, Kim Jong Il, took over, making North Korea the first Communist "dynasty."

In the 1990s, the North's nuclear program alarmed Western and Asian governments. In 1993, North Korea rejected international demands to inspect its nuclear facilities. Over U.S. objections, it said it would withdraw from the 1968 Nuclear Nonproliferation Treaty to stop the spread of nuclear weapons.

A prolonged period of tension eased when North Korea agreed, in October 1994, to end its nuclear weapons development. New tensions flared in 1998, when it test-fired a new-model ballistic missile across Japan. The U.S. and Japanese governments feared North Korea's ability to strike their countries with missiles carrying nuclear, chemical, or biological warheads. This concern was heightened by suspicions that North Korea was selling cheap missiles and other weapons to developing nations in the Middle East and elsewhere.

Relations between North Korea, its Asian neighbors, and the United States took a turn for the worse in November 2003, when North Korea announced that it had obtained weapons-grade plutonium and intended to build nuclear weapons. In response, China organized a series of diplomatic negotiations between North Korea, the United States, South Korea, Japan, Russia, and China. The purpose of the six-nation talks has been to persuade North Korea to dismantle its nuclear weapons program in return for more food and energy assistance. These talks continued in 2007, despite a small nuclear test explosion by North Korea in 2006. In February 2007, North Korea agreed to close its main nuclear reactor in exchange for a package of food, fuel, and other aid from the United States and the other nations.

Efforts to improve the economy began in July 2002. In the first steps away from central planning since the Communist government came to power in 1945, state-owned businesses got more freedom to sell manufactured products, farmers' markets became legal, and workers were paid according to productivity. As a result, wages and earnings have risen, more consumer goods are available, and foreign investment has increased. Reflecting Kim Jong Il's interest in modern technology, computers have been made available to those North Koreans who can afford to purchase them. Computer courses have been made compulsory in most schools. Although the World Wide Web is forbidden to most North Koreans, a fiber-optic cable network has made possible a nationwide intranet.

South Korea built a strong capitalist economy, with textiles and cars as major industries. More than 70 percent of the workforce is in manufacturing and services. Since World War II, the economy has been controlled by *chaebol*, family-run businesses with political influence. Companies like Samsung and Hyundai have won a growing share of world markets.

After the Korean War, South Korea became a police state under a military committee. Since 1990, it has evolved into a democracy, with two large parties competing for votes. Roh Moo Hyun, a former human rights activist and self-educated labor lawyer, became president in February 2003. Since the National Assembly attempted to impeach him in March 2004, Roh has led South Korea's first left-wing government. His radical young supporters accuse the *chaebol* of corruption and inequality. They want to compromise with North Korea rather than oppose it. And they are more anti-American than older conservatives.

At one time, Roh asked the United States to withdraw its troops, which defend the country from North Korea. Anti-U.S. demonstrations have strained U.S.–South Korean relations. But news of U.S. plans to reduce its troops in mid-2004 caused fears among South Koreans about their security. As of mid-2006, approximately 30,000 American soldiers were stationed in South Korea. At that time, 3,300 South Korean troops were serving in the U.S.-led coalition in Iraq.

South Korea's exports were valued at $193.8 billion in 2005. China, Japan, and the United States are its main trading partners. More South Korean investments flow into China than elsewhere.

1. *Contrast North and South Korea politically and economically.*

2. *Explain why North Korea has caused concern for Western and Asian governments in recent years.*

3. *Identify:*

   a. *Roh Moo Hyun*   c. *Kim Jong Il*
   b. *Kim Il Sung*   d. *chaebol*

Southeast Asia

Indonesia. Rebelling against Dutch rule at the end of World War II, Indonesia became independent in 1949. It then went through a long period of rule by strict leaders. The first president, Sukarno, was a leftist. He had close ties with Communist China and promoted state ownership of industry. In 1965, military leaders overthrew Sukarno. They said they were saving Indonesia from communism. After the military takeover, bloody riots killed several hundred thousand Indonesians suspected of being Communists. Many of the dead were ethnic Chinese.

For the next thirty years, Indonesia was under the stern rule of a leader named Suharto. He and his ruling party won every election. While the cold war lasted, Suharto's government received strong backing from the United States. Foreign investors helped Indonesia to develop its oil and timber resources. The government continued to own major industries, although there were private businesses too.

Despite its economic progress, Indonesia faced many problems. Most of the people were poor. The islands of Java and Bali were very crowded. To ease crowding, the government encouraged people to move to less developed islands—to Sumatra, to Borneo, to Irian Jaya (western New Guinea). In 1975, Indonesia seized the Portuguese colony of East Timor, and some Indonesians went there. Meanwhile, serious conflicts arose among Indonesia's many ethnic and religious groups—especially between Christians and Muslims. Some 88 percent of Indonesia's 220 million people are Muslims, making it the largest mainly Muslim nation in the world. Other religious groups include Protestants, Catholics (who are a majority in East Timor), Hindus, and Buddhists.

Indonesia was hard hit by the Asian financial crisis of 1997–1998. The government asked the International Monetary Fund for help. The IMF required sharp cuts in government spending,

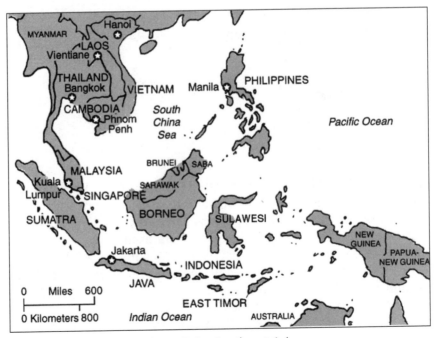

Figure 5.4   Southeast Asia

resulting in rising prices and unemployment. There was great misery among the nation's poor. Consequently, Indonesians began to riot in the streets. Finally, Suharto resigned in May 1998. He and various members of his family were then charged with corruption.

Terrorism has become one of Indonesia's 21st-century problems. In October 2002, terrorists bombed a Bali nightclub and killed 202 people. For this crime, an Indonesian court in 2003 sentenced to death two members of Jamaah Islamiyah, a Muslim terrorist network linked to Al Qaeda and operating in Southeast Asia.

Elected in 2004, President Susilo Bambang Yudihoyno has pursued the growth of democracy despite the opposition of military officers who dominated politics before the downfall of the Suharto regime in 1998. Constitutional amendments introduced direct elections for president and replaced a partially elected parliament, filled with soldiers, with a fully elected lawmaking body. Provincial governors and mayors, previously appointed military officers, are now elected. A large share of tax revenues has been transferred to local authorities, and much money has been misspent or gone unspent. This enables opponents of the president to claim that his democratic regime has done little to solve Indonesia's high unemployment and inflation.

The government is also trying to make the army give up control of the thousands of businesses it owns. Much of the money generated by these businesses finds its way into the pockets of army officers. Also, jobs have been removed from the army that should be done by the police, such as antiterrorism investigation. All of this has provoked military anger. So have proposals that soldiers accused of ordinary crimes be tried in civilian courts.

Retired generals who remain active in politics have demanded the repeal of the constitutional amendments that are the basis of Indonesia's democracy. Observers regard this democracy as a "work in progress." If Indonesians are patient and do not turn back to the military, the new regime may eventually provide solutions to the country's problems.

To add to Indonesia's problems, earthquakes and tsunamis caused destructive flooding and loss of life and property in 2004, 2005, and 2006. Hundreds of thousands of people were killed or made homeless. More floods caused by heavy seasonal rains occurred in February 2007.

1. *Describe the struggle to establish democracy in Indonesia.*
2. *List Indonesia's main problems.*

Cambodia. As a result of the Vietnam War (1965–1973), Communist governments were established in the Southeast Asian nations of Vietnam, Laos, and Cambodia. The most radical of those governments was the Khmer Rouge regime in Cambodia, led by Pol Pot. The Khmer Rouge killed or enslaved more than a million Cambodians suspected of opposition to communism. The regime aroused fierce opposition throughout Southeast Asia.

In 1977, fighting broke out between Vietnam and Cambodia, which had been rivals for centuries. Two years later, Vietnamese forces invaded Cambodia. They ousted the Khmer Rouge and installed a Vietnamese-supported regime of moderate Communists.

Cambodia plunged into civil war. On one side was the new Cambodian government, backed by Vietnamese troops. On the other side were the remnants of the Khmer Rouge, supported by China, plus two non-Communist groups. One of those was headed by Prince Norodom Sihanouk, who had been Cambodia's head of state from 1960 to 1970. The United States helped to arm the non-Communist groups.

In 1989, Vietnam began to withdraw its forces from Cambodia. In 1991, the four rival Cambodian factions declared a cease-fire. They signed a peace agreement drawn up by the United Nations. This accord created a temporary coalition government to serve until a new government was democratically chosen. Despite continuing unrest, elections were held successfully in May 1993 under U.N. supervision. In Phnom Penh, Cambodia's capital, the National Assembly adopted a new constitution in September 1993. It made Cambodia a constitutional monarchy. Prince Sihanouk became King Sihanouk.

Into the Light

In the years that followed, splits developed within the Khmer Rouge and within Cambodia's government. A faction of the Khmer Rouge opposed to Pol Pot captured the aged leader in 1997 and filmed a carefully staged trial in which he was sentenced to life imprisonment. Pol Pot died in 1998. In Phnom Penh, the Cambodian capital, two government factions that had been sharing power had an armed confrontation in 1997. Hun Sen drove the king's son, Prince Ranariddh, into temporary exile. After that, Hun Sen dominated the government as sole prime minister.

By 1999, the Khmer Rouge was defeated and its leaders captured. Cambodia remained poor, with deep political divisions. Hun Sen's party kept power in the July 2003 elections but lacked the votes to form a government without the cooperation of political rivals in the Royalist and Sam Rainsy parties.

By early 2006, Prime Minister Hun Sen had eliminated all political opposition. The rival party leader, Sam Rainsy, fled the country. King Norodom Sihanouk had given up his throne and been replaced as king by his son, Prince Sihamon, in October 2004. The courts, labor unions, and civic groups were subjected to intimidation. Critics and protesters were arrested. Even human rights groups have been attacked. To many observers, Cambodia appeared to be moving away from democracy and toward a one-party state.

In September 2003, Cambodia became the first poor country in deep debt to join the World Trade Organization. WTO membership has had little effect on its economic problems.

1. *Describe the effect of the Vietnam War on Cambodia.*

2. *Summarize the role of the United Nations in Cambodia.*

Vietnam. Vietnam experienced continuous warfare from 1940 to 1975. The Vietnamese fought the Japanese during World War II, French colonialists during the 1950s, and the Americans in the 1960s and 1970s. Since the Vietnam War ended in 1975, all of Vietnam has been under Communist rule.

In 1986, Vietnam's leaders departed from traditional Communist economic control and began to permit privately owned, profit-making enterprises. They called the new program *doi moi*, or renovation. Farmers could now lease land on long-term contracts and pass it on to their children. Family-owned farms replaced some of the nation's farm collectives. Agricultural production increased and incomes rose. Today Vietnam is one of the world's top exporters of rice.

Doi moi made more progress in the southern portion of the country than in the north, which had been under Communist rule for a longer time. A new prosperity arose in Ho Chi Minh City (formerly Saigon), the largest city of the south. In its elegant restaurants, American and other Western businesspeople appeared in increasing numbers. In the north, free market activity led to the emergence of a variety of new businesses in Hanoi.

While Vietnam has started to free its economy, politics is a different matter. The country remains a one-party state with the Communist Party exercising strict control.

The collapse of the Soviet Union deprived Vietnam of the aid it had been receiving from the Soviet Union. Vietnamese leaders tried to improve relations with the United States. They agreed to help U.S. search teams try to account for M.I.A.s—U.S. service personnel listed as missing in action since the Vietnam War.

A U.S. embargo on trade with Vietnam ended in 1994. Formal diplomatic relations between the two countries began in 1995. The visit to Vietnam from Bill Gates, president of Microsoft, in April 2006 symbolized Vietnam's movement toward a new more open version of communism combined with a market economy. The economic development plan of Vietnam's leaders in 2006 was aimed at increasing exports, combating corruption, continuing economic integration with the outside world, maintaining a growth rate of approximately eight percent, and creating eight million jobs. The party seeks to move into a higher level of manufacturing, including electronics.

To attract foreign investors, Vietnam has improved its legal infrastructure and banking system. Its improvement has made the country a safer and more reliable business environment. The United States has become Vietnam's top export market.

The international business community regards Vietnam as a rising economic star. Microsoft and other major companies such as Intel, Canon, and Fujitsu have moved toward investment in Vietnam.

Despite the flurry of interest from U.S., Japanese, and other investors, Vietnam remains a poor country. With 81 million people, its annual production per person was about $1,850 at the start of the 21st century—about one-third that of nearby Thailand. On the other hand, 94 percent of Vietnamese can read and write, tying Thailand for the highest literacy rate in Southeast Asia.

1. *Compare developments in Cambodia and Vietnam since the Vietnam War ended.*

2. *Complete the following sentences:*

   a. *After the collapse of the Soviet Union, Vietnam sought to ____.*
   b. *Signs of improvement in U.S.-Vietnamese relations include ____.*

3. *Identify:*

   a. *M.I.A.s*
   b. *doi moi*

India's Troubles

India, the second most populous country in the world, faced several problems in recent years. Conflict arose in the realm of religion, and in the conduct of foreign affairs. Underlying this strife was the subcontinent's age-old problem of poverty. Dealing with these issues was made more difficult by political instability.

Controversy over religion has split Hindus and Muslims for centuries. When Britain prepared to grant independence to India

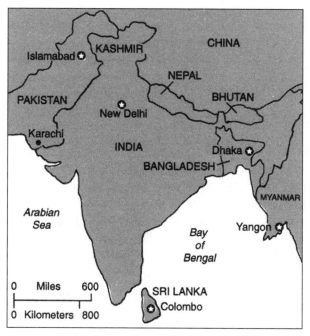

Figure 5.5   The Indian Subcontinent

in 1947, thousands died in violence between Hindus and Muslims. The subcontinent was then divided into Hindu-governed India and Muslim-governed Pakistan. But, with a large Muslim minority remaining in India, religious conflict did not end.

One religious crisis began in December 1992. Hindu extremists in the northern holy city of Ayodhya destroyed an ancient mosque. Hindus believe that the site on which the mosque was built was the birthplace of Lord Ram, a Hindu god. In March 1993, terrorists bombed the Bombay stock exchange. These acts of destruction touched off waves of religious violence, which spread rapidly. Riots in Bombay, Delhi, and other cities resulted in the deaths of more than 1,200. Violence also spread to Pakistan and Bangladesh. More terrorist attacks occurred in March 2006, when homemade bombs tore through a Hindu temple and nearby train station in the city of Varanasi, and in July 2006, when the Mumbai (Bombay) commuter train system was bombed. Mumbai is India's financial capital.

Another source of religious conflict involved Hindus and Sikhs. (Sikhs form a distinct religious community, with beliefs that combine Hindu and Islamic elements.) Violence between the two groups broke out in Punjab state in the 1980s, sparked by Sikh secessionists. Prime Minister Indira Gandhi sent in troops, who, among other actions, stormed the Sikhs' holiest shrine in order to root out terrorists. In revenge, two of Gandhi's Sikh bodyguards assassinated her in 1984. (Her son Rajiv, who succeeded her, was in turn assassinated—by Tamil separatists—in 1991.)

Ever since the partition of 1947, India and Pakistan have been at odds over Kashmir, on India's northwest frontier. The area is inhabited by both Hindus and Muslims. Since 1949, two-thirds of Kashmir has been controlled by India and the rest by Pakistan. Although the U.N. Security Council in 1948 called for a vote of the people of Kashmir to choose which country to join, such a vote was never taken. In Indian-held regions, Muslim guerrillas have been fighting against Indian rule, leading to frequent flare-ups and border wars between Pakistan and India.

Largely because of the Kashmir rivalry, both countries have been eager to build up their military might, including nuclear weapons. In May 1998, first India and then Pakistan tested nuclear devices. (India had already tested such a device in 1974.) The new tests excited pride and patriotism among both Indians and Pakistanis. But the tests alarmed leaders of other countries, who feared a nuclear arms race in the region. Summit meetings between the leaders of India and Pakistan later eased tensions.

Relations between India and Pakistan were further complicated in 1999 when military leaders took over Pakistan's government. The new ruler, General Pervez Musharraf, was seen as a strong supporter of the Muslim rebels in Indian-controlled Kashmir. He called for U.N. mediation to help settle the future of Kashmir. In the past, India has rejected outside mediation, preferring one-on-one talks with Pakistan. Such talks resumed in 2001. Tensions increased, however, when gunmen broke into India's parliament building in December 2001. The gunmen and six other people were killed. Indian leaders blamed Pakistan.

India's huge and growing population, which reached one billion in 1999, is a major cause of the nation's poverty. According to one estimate, almost a third of India's people live on less than $1 a day. Nearly half of India's population cannot read or write. About 60 percent of Indians are engaged in agriculture, much of it involving backbreaking, unmechanized labor.

In spite of difficulties, India has made progress. Food output has soared since the 1970s, reducing need for outside aid. Life expectancy has gone from 39 to 63 years in less than half a century. The fertility rate has declined from 6 to 3.1 births for each woman of childbearing age. In the 21st century, India has grown as a computer technology center. Many U.S. companies have technical assistance "call centers" there to service customers. Information technology jobs have flowed from the United States to India, where they are done at lower cost. From 2002 to 2006, India's average annual economic growth rate increased to 8 percent. While some Indian economists were confident that this strong economic growth would continue, others feared that demand for goods and services would outpace supply. This would slow the rate of economic growth. Obstacles to continued growth are power shortages, especially electricity, highly restrictive labor laws, and the low quality of public services such as education, health, and the provision of water. (In India, half of urban households lack drinking water.)

India is a democracy. The Congress Party led India to independence and ruled for many years after that. By the 1990s, though, corruption and incompetence in the Congress Party gave other parties a chance. The Congress Party leader, Sonia Gandhi (widow of Rajiv Gandhi), was distrusted by many for her Italian birth. A major rival, the Bharatiya Janata Party (BJP), gained popularity on a platform of Hindu nationalism and Hindu self-pride. In 1998, the BJP leader, Atal Vajpayee, became prime minister at the head of a fragile coalition of 19 parties. He retained power in national elections in 1999 with an expanded coalition of 24 parties that held a clear majority of seats in parliament.

In a dramatic 2004 election, the Congress Party regained control of the government from the BJP. Fearing a nationalist backlash, Sonia Gandhi declined the position of prime minister in favor of Manmohan Singh, a Sikh and former finance minister. Peace advocates hoped that he would continue talks with Pakistan about the future of Kashmir.

1. *PROVE or DISPROVE: Religious violence is India's only major problem.*

2. *Which of the following are correct statements? Revise the incorrect statements.*

    a. *India and Pakistan are both Hindu nations.*
    b. *India's government has succeeded in controlling population growth.*
    c. *Kashmir gained independence in 1989.*

Chapter 5 Review

A. *Choose the item that best completes each sentence.*

1. *In the late 20th and early 21st centuries, China's economic policies stressed   (a) rigid state control   (b) privatization and development of a market economy   (c) rejection of foreign investors.*

2. *China's program of population control has   (a) aimed to reduce the birthrate   (b) won international approval   (c) banned all abortions.*

3. *In 1997, China regained control of   (a) Cambodia   (b) Korea   (c) Hong Kong.*

4. *In response to U.S. pressure, Japan   (a) stationed some of its troops overseas   (b) began deregulating businesses   (c) increased exports to the United States.*

5. *By 2004, the focus of Japanese overseas investment and manufacturing was   (a) Eastern Europe   (b) China   (c) Africa.*

6. *In the 1980s, North and South Korea agreed to   (a) hold joint military maneuvers   (b) reunify their two nations   (c) open trade relations.*

7. In 2003, North Korea announced its intention to   (a) build nuclear weapons   (b) send its troops across the 38th parallel   (c) break diplomatic relations with China.

8. Cambodia became the first poor country to   (a) compete in the telecommunications industry   (b) grow genetically modified food crops   (c) join the World Trade Organization.

9. The term doi moi refers to   (a) the Vietnamese program of economic reform   (b) the majority political party in Hanoi   (c) overseas Vietnamese anti-Communists.

10. India has long been troubled by religious strife between (a) Hindus and Jews   (b) Hindus and Christians   (c) Hindus and Muslims.

B. Reread "The Modernization of China," on pages 93–99. Then answer these questions:

1. Describe China's economic growth in the late 20th and early 21st centuries.

2. List the nations that benefited from China's economic boom.

3. Define the following:
   a. privatization
   b. Chinese Economic Area

C. Which of the following statements are true and which are false? Revise the incorrect statements. (Examine maps in this chapter.)

1. Nepal and Mongolia are both part of the People's Republic of China.

2. Yangon, Colombo, and New Delhi are cities in India.

3. Japan is a group of islands.

4. Pyongyang is the capital of South Korea.

5. Hong Kong and Vietnam both have access to the South China Sea.

D. Write a composition on Asia in the 1990s and early 21st century. Include statements about each of the following:

1. the growth of democracy and free market economies

2. political and economic relations with the West

Chapter 6

Drugs and Politics in Latin America

Poverty, inequality, and political repression made revolutions common in Latin America in the 19th and 20th centuries. During the cold war, fear of communism prompted the United States to support a number of right-wing, anti-Communist dictatorships. At the same time, U.S. leaders spoke out in favor of democracy and respect for human rights, as they continue to do. Meanwhile, the United States has been assisting Latin American governments in their struggle against the growing power of drug *traficantes* (dealers). Many Latin American governments have cooperated with their powerful northern neighbor. But resentment of Yankee interference has also been strong.

In the late 20th and early 21st centuries, various Latin American countries made the difficult transition from dictatorship to democracy. They struggled to develop free market economies and form regional free trade zones. Economic and political crises created hardships, especially in Argentina and Venezuela. Widespread poverty was a constant. Increasing opposition to the policies of the United States resulted in the election of socialist presidents in Brazil, Bolivia, and Ecuador, and the reelection of a strongly anti-U.S. socialist in Venezuela. In the Caribbean, extreme weather caused destruction and suffering in Haiti and the Dominican Republic.

The United States and the Drug War

Preventing the shipment of narcotics from Latin American laboratories and processing plants to criminal distributors in North

118

Figure 6.1   Latin America

America has been a major goal of the United States in recent years. To accomplish this aim, the Drug Enforcement Agency (DEA) and other U.S. agencies have sent U.S. officers to Latin American countries to work with local security services. U.S. personnel have coordinated raids on farms growing coca (the source of cocaine), processing factories, and illegal airstrips, and have also participated in the arrest of *traficantes*.

Colombia. One of the world's largest suppliers of illegal narcotics, Colombia leads the world in the production of cocaine. It is the home of the Medellín and Cali drug cartels (named for the cities in which they have headquarters; see map, page 127). Colombian drug lords control private armies, airplanes, ships, laboratories, and processing plants. They have been accused of buying political influence with huge "contributions" to national elections and to important people in the army and the media. Campaigns of violence by the drug cartels against government and civilian targets are known as *narcoterrorism.* Hundreds of political and military officials have been murdered. Such killings reached a peak in 1989 and 1990, when three presidential candidates were assassinated.

Colombia has been racked by warfare waged by left-wing guerrillas since the 1960s—the longest-running civil disorder in Latin America. The two main guerrilla groups are the Revolutionary Armed Forces of Colombia (FARC) and the National Liberation Army (ELN). Both groups claim to be fighting for social and economic reform, but many observers believe that their main goal is simply to win control of the government. The guerrilla groups and the right-wing paramilitary forces (linked to the army) that fight against them are financed in large part by the drug trade. The chief support for all these groups consists of "taxes" levied on drug production in the territories they control.

Buying Influence

The paramilitary groups were originally formed by cattle ranchers in the 1980s to combat extortion and kidnapping by left-wing guerrillas. They later turned into powerful armies that inflicted terror on many areas of the country, killing guerrillas and civilians alike. Like the guerrillas, many were involved in drug trafficking.

Colombia's oil pipelines became targets of antigovernment guerrilla attacks. In the late 20th and early 21st centuries, oil became important to the Colombian economy following the discovery of a large underground sea of crude oil in the foothills of the Andes Mountains. Large foreign investments were attracted. By 2000, oil was Colombia's top export and provided 35 percent of the government's revenue.

A succession of Colombian presidents employed a variety of strategies to put the guerrillas and paramilitary forces out of business. Andres Pastrana (1998–2002) turned over a huge area—about the size of Switzerland—to FARC as a "demilitarized zone." The guerrillas would not be attacked by the army while they negotiated with the government.

Hoping to destroy the coca plantations from which *traficantes* get their raw materials, Pastrana launched "Plan Colombia" in 2000, with strong support from the United States. The $7.5 billion plan called for airplanes to spray chemicals onto the coca plants and thus kill them. It also involved stepped-up negotiations with various rebel groups and a program of efforts to strengthen the economy. Pastrana received from the United States a pledge of $1.3 billion in aid, most of it for military applications, such as to furnish combat helicopters and train Colombian soldiers.

1. *Define narcoterrorism.*

2. *Identify:*
   a. *FARC and ELN*
   b. *paramilitary forces*
   c. *Plan Colombia*

Álvaro Uribe was elected president of Colombia in May 2002. An independent liberal with hard-line views on law and order, he took a tough position on fighting the civil war. In addition to pushing through reforms to help the faltering economy, Uribe has made a massive assault on the drug trade and the Marxist guerrillas and narcoterrorists who support it. As a result, coca cultivation declined 21 percent in 2003.

By 2007, some 30,000 paramilitaries had demobilized under a peace deal with Uribe's government. In exchange for confessing and paying reparations, their leaders are eligible for reduced prison sentences of no more than eight years' confinement. They will also not be extradited to the United States to face drug trafficking charges. Colombia produces an estimated 90 percent of the cocaine reaching the United States. Other rebel groups, such as FARC, have continued to fight.

An amendment to the constitution enabled Uribe to run for a second consecutive presidential term. He easily won reelection in May 2006. To increase Colombia's supply of exportable oil, Uribe's government has intensified efforts to attract more foreign oil companies. This has resulted in $1.5 billion a year of new investment in oil exploration. Experts believe that if recent investment levels continue, Colombia should maintain its oil self-sufficiency until 2015. More than a dozen foreign companies were looking for new sources of oil in Colombia in early 2007.

♦ *Find out what is wrong with each of the following statements. Then rewrite each as a correct statement.*
   a. *Drug trafficking played a minor role in Colombia's history.*
   b. *Antigovernment guerrillas fought to reduce the drug traffic in Colombia.*
   c. *President Pastrana's democratic security policy improved public order and security in Colombia's 40-year civil war.*

Mexico. In 1993, Mexico drew closer to its northern neighbor by entering into the North American Free Trade Agreement (NAFTA). But tension continued between the U.S. Drug Enforcement Agency and Mexican security forces. The operations of *traficantes* in Mexico City and elsewhere, where they lived in open luxury, frustrated U.S. officials trying to intercept drugs being smuggled across the border.

Mexican presidents worked with U.S. officials. In 1997, however, the general heading Mexico's top antidrug agency, accused of taking bribes from a powerful drug lord, had to resign.

Some Mexicans objected to this U.S. involvement. Others worried about the rising power of the military involved in the antidrug campaign. Was local civilian authority being undercut? Some questioned giving more weapons, equipment, and training to the military, with its poor record on human rights.

Figure 6.2   Central America

Vicente Fox was the first president in over 70 years who was not a member of the Institutional Revolutionary Party (PRI in its Spanish initials). Troubled by corruption and scandals, the PRI had been in slow decline. During the 1980s and 1990s, its tight control over state governments and the Congress lessened, as voters turned to opposition parties. Fox, a businessman, was the candidate of the center-right National Action Party and won the presidency in July 2000 with 43 percent of the vote in a three-way race. The change was hailed as a victory for Mexican democracy.

Fox promised continued Mexican-U.S. cooperation in fighting *traficantes*. He offered Zapatista Indian rebels peace, backing their proposed Indian-rights constitutional amendment. Masked Zapatistas marched across Mexico to the capital to urge Congress to pass the amendment. It did, but removed many features the Zapatistas wanted. The amendment took effect in 2001.

On his first day in office, Fox signed a technical cooperation agreement with the office of the U.N. high commissioner for human rights. The result of this agreement was the issuance of a U.N. report, in December 2003, that provided a road map for a national human rights program in Mexico. The report urges Mexico to change its constitution to guarantee the protection of human rights and a defendant's right to be presumed innocent until proven guilty. It also attacks long-standing abuses of the justice system, such as the torture of criminal suspects and the failure to protect vulnerable populations from discrimination and violent crime. A dramatic example of this failure is the unsolved murders of hundreds of young women and girls in the past decade in Ciudad Juárez, a city on the U.S. border.

Fox spent much of his six-year term fighting with a divided Congress, which blocked many of his proposals. The belief of many Mexicans that Fox failed to deliver on a long list of promises caused his National Action Party to lose votes in the 2003 congressional elections.

President Felipe Calderón, elected in July 2006, faces a range of pressing issues, from job creation and poverty relief to a worsening war between drug cartels and violent social conflicts. More than 2,000 people died in 2006 in an underworld war between rival drug traffickers. Many of the dead were police officers and other law enforcement officials.

Since taking office in late 2006, Calderón has called for unity and reconciliation. He has made fighting poverty and reducing crime his top priorities. Tax incentives to encourage investment have been promised. Calderón has also undertaken the task of reorganizing Mexico's fractured and ineffective police forces to combat the drug cartels. A tight monetary policy, aimed at keeping inflation low and avoiding overspending on public programs, has begun.

Among the obstacles faced by Calderón are the followers of Andrés Obrador, a defeated left-wing presidential candidate who does not recognize Calderón as president. He must also deal with the opposition of some of Mexico's business leaders, who have fought efforts to break the dominance of a few big companies. And powerful unions oppose competition in the energy industry and changes to the education system.

At least a quarter of working-age Mexicans labor in an underground economy, selling stolen or smuggled goods in street markets. Each year, some 400,000 Mexicans immigrate to the United States in search of work. This escape valve for the unemployed became more difficult to use as the U.S. tightened border control to stop illegal immigration in 2006 and 2007.

♦ *Describe two major problems faced by Mexican presidents in the late 20th and early 21st centuries.*

Criticisms of U.S. Policy. Peru, like Colombia, has been a center of coca leaf production. To encourage peasant farmers to switch from coca to the cultivation of such legal crops as rice and corn, the Peruvian government has requested additional U.S. aid.

Alternative Development

Such alternative development has been pursued, with limited success, in Bolivia. The peasants of that Andean nation live in grinding poverty. They have the shortest life span in the Americas. Less than half the population of Bolivia has access to safe drinking water. The sale of coca leaves to drug traffickers has kept alive whole communities of farmers.

The drug war led by the United States has aroused resentment in Latin America. Many critics blame the United States for Latin America's drug problems and denounce U.S. "meddling" in local affairs. Critics say that North Americans should focus on reducing the demand for cocaine in their own country.

Political leaders in coca-growing countries point to economic and political problems. Farmers growing coca are often taxpayers and voters. Many employees of *traficantes* have no other income. Spraying chemicals to kill coca stirs concerns about side effects. Governors of four Colombian provinces charged that U.S.-backed spraying threatened the health and food supply of rural residents. Thus, some Latin American leaders negotiate with drug lords rather than fight them.

Human rights groups have denounced the practice of using the military, rather than the police, to fight the drug trade. They claim that the torture of prisoners and other violations of the rights of the accused have resulted, especially in Colombia and Mexico.

Efforts to reduce coca growing in Bolivia were halted after Evo Morales took office as president in 2006. An advocate for coca farmers, Morales acknowledged that the size of Bolivia's coca-growing areas was about double official estimates. As a result, the U.S. reduced drug enforcement aid to Bolivia by 25 percent in 2007.

Elsewhere in Latin America, President Hugo Chávez of Venezuela has joined Ecuador's president, Rafael Correa, in criticizing the U.S.-financed spraying of Colombia's drug crops. Correa has argued that spraying herbicides on illegal Colombian crops along the Ecuadorian border ruins legal crops and harms people's health on Ecuador's side. He has also threatened to refuse to extend the lease on a major U.S. counternarcotics operation in the Ecuadorian port of Manta. From Manta, American air crews have flown missions over Colombia, Peru, and Bolivia.

When the U.S. ambassador to Venezuela said that drug smuggling was soaring in that country, President Chávez accused him of lying. Venezuela severed its cooperation with the U.S. Drug Enforcement Administration in 2006. Chávez has also insisted that the United States is using its antinarcotics drive to gain a military foothold in Latin America.

1. *Define alternative development and explain why it has had limited success.*

2. *Explain why you AGREE or DISAGREE: The drug policy of the United States should be focused on reducing the demand for narcotics in North America rather than on eliminating the sources of supply in Latin America.*

Peru

Peru's troubled history includes: military dictators (1968–1980), food shortages and labor strikes (1970s–1980s), a cholera epidemic (early 1990s), and presidential instability (early 2000s).

Guerrilla Warfare. Beginning in the 1960s, Peru suffered from a brutal guerrilla war against the elected government. A Maoist organization named the Shining Path, led by Abimael Guzman, fought its way from the rural highlands to the streets of Lima, the capital. The rebellion arose out of years of resentment caused by political corruption, unemployment, and racial discrimination. Another issue was inflation, which climbed as high as one million percent in

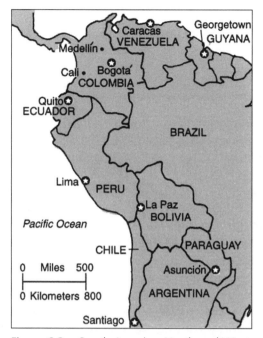

Figure 6.3   South America: North and West

the 1980s. The combined effect of a high rate of population growth and limited farmland also contributed to discontent.

Specializing in political assassinations, kidnappings, and car bombings, the guerrillas killed tens of thousands of Peruvians. At their strongest, the Shining Path guerrillas numbered about 8,000. They financed themselves by charging "landing fees" to drug traffickers who flew coca leaves out of Peru. They also received money from overseas groups.

Alberto Fujimori, an agricultural engineer of Japanese descent, was elected president in 1990 with broad support from the lower and middle classes. Once in office, Fujimori turned to the military for support of his efforts to improve the economy and combat terrorism. Tension developed between him and the Congress, which the president criticized for not doing enough to resolve Peru's political and economic problems.

In April 1992, Fujimori dissolved Congress and the courts, claiming that they were obstructing the fight against terrorism. Fujimori assumed dictatorial powers. For nine months he ruled by decree. The president gave police and military agencies sweeping powers to arrest and interrogate suspected terrorists, without regard for their constitutional rights. Criticizing his actions, the United States reduced its economic aid to Peru.

As more arrests were made, terrorist violence subsided. To many Peruvians, Fujimori became a hero. His popularity soared with the capture of Abimael Guzman, the guerrilla leader, in September 1992. In a 1993 poll, 64 percent of Peruvians approved of Fujimori's policies. Guzman's capture dealt a devastating blow to the Shining Path. In April 1993, the president claimed that 95 percent of the Shining Path's leadership was in prison.

Economic Change. President Fujimori claimed that the stability demonstrated by his successful campaign against the Shining Path would attract foreign investments and help Peru become a strong industrial nation. He gave up his dictatorial powers after the election of a new Peruvian Congress in 1993.

Peru's economy grew briskly for a time. Duly impressed, Peruvian voters gave Fujimori a landslide reelection victory in 1995. Many Peruvians hoped that Fujimori would make headway against the country's immense social problems. But the economy's rapid growth proved short-lived. Half of Peru's people continued to live in poverty, and only one worker in seven held a full-time job.

Fujimori's antiterrorism policy remained troubling to many. Critics accused the president of allowing the police and military to imprison, torture, and kill hundreds of innocent people. In 1995, Congress passed and Fujimori signed a broad amnesty for the military. It meant that soldiers who had tortured or unjustly killed in the war against the Shining Path could never be brought to trial. The United States registered a strong protest, as did human rights groups.

In November 2000, allegations of bribery and blackmail by Fujimori's powerful intelligence chief erupted. As public anger rose and Fujimori's power base crumbled, he flew to Japan "for a visit," announced his resignation, and stayed there.

Hoping to revive their ailing democracy, voters elected Alejandro Toledo president in May 2001. A business professor of Indian parentage, he had little political experience. He vowed to cut the military budget and help the poor and middle classes.

By 2004, critics accused Toledo of promising too much and delivering too little. His efforts to sell government-owned businesses to private investors set off a popular revolt in 2002. More protests by civil service workers led to the resignation of Toledo's entire cabinet in 2003. The revival of the Shining Path guerrilla

Figure 6.4   South America: North and East

movement further damaged Toledo's popularity, as did accusations that a former advisor was bribing judges hearing corruption cases involving the government. In April 2004, Toledo's approval rating was only 10 percent.

In July 2006, Alan Garcia took office as Peru's president for the second time. His first presidency (1985–1990) had ended with the country experiencing guerrilla war and high inflation.

1. *Tell how President Fujimori became a hero to many Peruvians.*

2. *Explain why Fujimori lost public support and resigned.*

3. *Explain why you AGREE or DISAGREE: Suspected terrorists should not be protected by constitutional guarantees.*

Turmoil in Venezuela

A democracy since 1958, Venezuela has the largest oil reserves outside the Persian Gulf. When oil prices soared in the 1970s, Venezuela prospered.

During the 1970s, much of Venezuela's oil revenues were used to underwrite ambitious construction projects and to provide jobs and social services for Venezuelans. Times were not so prosperous in the 1980s, with the result that consumer prices rose and there were cutbacks in public services. By 1992, however, the first Persian Gulf War caused oil prices to rise once again. The resulting increase in revenues caused Venezuela's economy to improve.

From 1993 to 1998, Venezuela experienced a number of troubling political and economic problems. These included a dispute with neighboring Colombia over ownership of the oil-rich Gulf of Venezuela, bank failures, government budget cuts, and concerns about the alarming increase in crime and political corruption. These concerns led to the suspension of certain constitutional rights.

In December 1998, Hugo Chávez was elected president. He was a former army officer and paratrooper, but he also had, as part of his background, involvement as a revolutionary, who had led an unsuccessful attempt to overthrow the government of Venezuela in 1992.

As president, Chávez seemed to take a perverse delight in doing things calculated to annoy the U.S. government. He made friendly overtures to Fidel Castro's government in Cuba. He lobbied other oil-producing nations to raise the prices they charged for oil. He recognized and praised guerrilla movements that were active in neighboring countries. And he was outspoken in denouncing the stepped-up U.S. involvement in Colombia's drug war.

In Venezuela, one of Chávez's first undertakings was to organize several thousands of soldiers, civil servants, jobless people, and national volunteers in an effort to repair the nation's dilapidated public services. At the same time, he sent soldiers into schools in the poorer areas, where they helped supply free meals and after-school care.

Chávez reorganized the structure of Venezuela's central government. In 1999, after calling for a referendum, in which 88 percent of the voters gave their approval, he summoned a special assembly for the task of writing a new constitution. Adopted later in 1999, the new constitution eliminated one of the two legislative bodies that had existed and set a six-year presidential term. In August 2000, Chávez easily won reelection, and voters gave his supporters firm control of the National Assembly. Chávez promptly asked for, and was given, additional powers to govern by decree for specified purposes. In a December 2000 referendum, the voters agreed to merge all of the labor unions in Venezuela into a single federation. Supporters of this new consolidation said that it would "democratize" the country's labor movement, which had been a focus of increasing opposition to Chávez's tactics as president. First, the International Labor Organization was quick to pronounce the proposed change anti-democratic. Then, the U.N.'s high commissioner for human rights, Mary Robinson, voiced her own concern about Chávez's ongoing efforts to concentrate his power over Venezuela's institutions.

Was Chávez taking Venezuela down the road to dictatorship? Some feared that he might be. Venezuelan labor leaders and human rights groups sharply criticized him. So did some officials of the U.S. government. On the other hand, even critics said that Chávez had followed the rules of democracy and that his election victories had been fairly won. By early 2007, Chávez and his "Bolivarian socialism" appeared to be unstoppable. The National Assembly renewed his power to legislate by decree for an additional eighteen months. Constitutional reforms will turn Venezuela into an officially socialist country and will allow the president to stand for reelection indefinitely.

Chávez's program of land reform has been a key element in his march toward socialism. Starting in 2002, when approximately 5 percent of the population owned 80 percent of Venezuela's private land, the government has seized large agricultural estates and turned them over to peasant squatters. The original owners have received no compensation. The goal of the nationwide resettlement has been to make Venezuela less dependent on food imports. Economists warn, however, that demand for food climbed more than 30 percent between 2005 and 2007, while Venezuela's capacity to produce food increased by only 5 percent. Despite the land redistribution, the country may become more dependent on imported food.

By 2007, the government had seized about 3.4 million acres and resettled more than 15,000 families. A program of building communal towns for the peasants has begun. Homes, a school, and a building with high-speed Internet access are standard. Violence has accompanied the transition with peasants killed by gunmen hired by the wealthy owners, and landowners being killed by squatters. This action has been regarded as an unavoidable consequence of the building of a "socialist fatherland."

Chávez has used Venezuela's oil wealth to expand his influence in Latin America and beyond. His friendship with Fidel Castro has ensured Cuba of critical economic support, including 100,000 barrels of oil a day sold at low prices. A booming trade with Venezuela has helped Cuba defy a long-standing U.S. trade embargo. Castro and Chávez are united by what they call a crusade against U.S. dominance of Latin America and the unrestrained capitalism that they believe is driving the world to ruin.

By 2007, Venezuela had come to rival the United States as Bolivia's main source of economic aid. It has provided assistance for Bolivia's army, cattle ranchers, soybean cultivation, urban sanitation, and oil industry. Despite U.S. opposition, Venezuela has helped Bolivia move ahead with plans to increase exports of its industrial production of coca, the main ingredient of cocaine. All this aid has helped Venezuela to accomplish its goal of limiting the regional influence of the United States. Previously, Bolivia was one of the largest recipients of U.S. aid in the world.

The struggle for dominance has also extended to Uruguay. The Bush administration offered Uruguay's left-wing government a free trade agreement. Hugo Chávez countered by offering to invest in a Uruguayan oil refinery and in oil exploration projects. He has also put money into unprofitable businesses that employ large numbers of Uruguayan workers. A free trade agreement with the United States would weaken Mercosur, the regional free trade group that includes Venezuela, Argentina, Brazil, Paraguay, and Uruguay.

Beyond Latin America, Chávez has strengthened Venezuela's ties with Middle Eastern governments, including Syria and Iran. In addition to keeping oil prices high, Chávez has sought to build an alliance to curb U.S. influence in developing countries. Venezuela has defended Iran's nuclear program and has joined Iran in criticism of Israel and the United States.

In August 2006, Chávez visited China, where he signed multibillion-dollar contracts for the delivery of Venezuelan oil badly needed by China's expanding economy. Part of the oil received by China was previously supplied to the United States. The building of a strategic alliance between the two countries has been supported by Russia, which supplies Venezuela with weapons. China also agreed to pay for construction of 20,000 homes for Venezuela's poor and to build railroads and irrigation systems in Venezuela.

1. *PROVE or DISPROVE: Under President Chávez, Venezuela was no longer a democracy.*

2. *State the goal of Hugo Chávez's foreign policy and explain how he has used Venezuela's oil wealth to pursue this goal.*

Changes in Brazil

Like other Latin American nations, Brazil had a tradition of relying on the military to provide strong government. Between 1964 and 1985, military leaders governed Brazil by issuing decrees and by appointing promilitary politicians to key posts. The military rulers concerned themselves chiefly with state-guided economic development. Civilian society was organized to provide support for government economic projects.

A country with a wide gulf between the very rich and the very poor, Brazil discovered that economic progress could not come about without democratic reforms. Such progress was needed to gain the support of foreign governments and investors. During the 1980s, the armed forces began a program of *abertura,* or "political opening." The government offered amnesty to its critics and opponents, increased freedom of the press, and encouraged popular elections of regional and local officials. The military regime ended in 1985, with an electoral college choosing a civilian president. Brazil adopted a new constitution, and in 1989, voters elected a new president. Fernando Collor de Mello became Brazil's first directly elected president in 29 years.

♦   *PROVE or DISPROVE: The military has had a leading role in Brazilian politics.*

Accusations of bribe taking forced Collor to resign in 1992. The Senate impeached him, and the Supreme Court barred his right to hold political office until 2001. The military did not interfere with the peaceful removal of the president. Nor did the government curb freedom of the press when newspapers and magazines reported the impeachment charges. This proved the strength of Brazilian democracy.

During the 1990s, Brazilians worried about severe inflation and rising unemployment. The government reorganized the nation's finances. A new currency, the *real,* was loosely linked to the U.S. dollar. Steps were taken to develop a free market economy while strengthening social welfare programs. Brazil's Congress approved a law allowing private foreign investment in the government-controlled oil industry.

Despite these measures, Brazil's economy went into recession. In return for substantial assistance received from the International Monetary Fund (IMF) in 1998, Brazil had to cut government spending and increase taxes. Over the next few years, the economy returned to health.

Luiz Inacio Lula da Silva, a union leader and reformer, took office as president in January 2003. By that time, Brazil's debt to the IMF and other lenders exceeded $260 billion. To reduce this debt and lower inflation, Lula's economic team tightened the government's budget beyond what the IMF had demanded. The resulting reduction in social services and increased unemployment have been unpopular. To add to Lula's problems, various schemes to help the poor failed in 2003.

With little money available to invest in badly needed factories, roads, and power plants, Brazil has tried to attract more foreign investment, which declined badly in 2003. Investment in energy has been especially important. By 2008, Brazil's present abundance of electricity may be depleted.

Lula has based much of his economic hopes on increased trade with China. By mid-2004, China became Brazil's fourth-largest market. Sales to China of iron ore, steel, and soya beans account for two-thirds of Brazil's exports. Citing the need for a "new geography of world trade," Lula sought to arrange for Chinese investment in Brazil's railways and ports.

Despite corruption scandals in his Workers Party, followed by indictments and arrests of some of the people he relied upon, Lula won reelection as president in October 2006. He then vowed to increase Brazil's economic growth rate to 5 percent a year.

In early 2007, Lula reached an agreement with Bolivian President Evo Morales on the prices Brazil will pay for Bolivia's natural gas. Imported Bolivian natural gas is used for power generation, fuel for cars, and cooking gas. The possibility was also raised that Brazil's state oil company, Petroleo Brasileiro SA, may make new investments in Bolivia, home to South America's second largest natural gas reserves after Venezuela.

Lula has also attempted to improve economic relations with neighboring Uruguay by offering President Tabare Vazquez funding for infrastructure and energy projects. These economic incentives were aimed at preventing Uruguay from signing a free-trade agreement with the United States. Such an agreement would weaken Mercosur, the regional trade organization in which Brazil is a powerful member.

1. *Explain why removing President Fernando Collor de Mello from office in 1992 seemed a triumph for Brazilian democracy.*

2. *Complete the following sentence: In return for financial assistance, the IMF demanded* _____.

3. *List the problems faced by President Luiz Inacio Lula da Silva.*

Argentina: From Economic Growth to Economic Collapse

The photographs and videotapes were starkly dramatic. In late 2001 and early 2002, angry mobs took to the streets of Argentina's capital city. Crowds on Buenos Aires street corners were banging pots and pans. Some were denouncing politicians. Others were storming banks. All were protesting Argentina's economic situation and the government's actions. The people had reason to be angry. Some 44 percent of the city's population were poor (they had incomes under 120 pesos a month). In December 2001, 28 people were killed in these riots. But in the first half of the 1990s, Argentina had been a model of a prosperous, booming economy. What had happened?

People and History. Argentina is a nation of 37 million people. They inhabit the second largest country in South America (see map, page 119). Because of its fertile lands and natural resources, many Europeans immigrated to Argentina in the 19th century. Large landowners dominated Argentine society and government. In the early 20th century, Argentina was one of the ten richest countries in the world.

Military Control. After a period of democratic reform in the 1920s, Argentina fell into the hands of military *juntas* (dictatorships), which ruled from the 1930s into the 1950s. Under General Juan Perón (1946–1956), Argentina practiced economic *protectionism* to aid its economy. Businesses received special favors to help them against foreign competition. Many industries were *nationalized* (the government took over ownership and operation). Perón also had the constitution amended to give himself more power. He established social and economic programs to benefit the working classes. After Perón, Argentine leaders tried to reform its economic policies, but in 1974, the military seized control once more. It committed many human rights violations against its opponents. Thousands were killed or abducted and never seen again. (The latter became known as "the disappeared.")

In 1982, the Argentine army invaded the Falkland Islands in an attempt to take them from Great Britain. But Britain defeated the Argentines.

Return to Democracy. Democratic elections were held in 1983, and the military was turned out of power. But Argentina soon ran into trouble. There were two banking collapses and two periods of very high (or hyper) inflation. In 1989, Carlos Saúl Menem was elected president. Menem and his party made decisive changes in the Argentine economy. They dropped economic protectionism and advocated a free market economy. Most government-owned businesses were *privatized* (sold to private companies).

The Early 1990s: Growth Years. During the first half of the 1990s, there was rapid economic growth and much foreign investment in Argentina. The economy grew at a rate of 6 percent per year from 1991 to 1997. But political corruption and lack of a sound tax structure hurt the economy. Many government supporters received good-paying jobs for which they did little work. The government spent more than it received in income, and borrowed to pay its operating costs. The tax system was badly in need of reform. Many people paid few or no taxes. Argentina's currency—the peso—was linked in value to the U.S. dollar. That is, one peso was equal in value to one U.S. dollar. When it needed money, the government printed more pesos or sold bonds. A large public debt was the result.

Recession and Collapse. A serious recession started in mid-1998. Many of Argentina's industries were inefficient. Many products were too expensive on the international market because of the high value of the peso in relation to other currencies. Large numbers of workers were laid off by newly privatized industries. Unemployment rose sharply. Menem meanwhile was trying to overturn the Argentine constitution's two-term limit on holding the office of president. His bid for a third term was rejected by Argentina's supreme court.

Menem's successor was Fernando de la Rúa, elected in 1999. He increased taxes on high incomes, but conditions worsened. Many well-to-do people were shipping their assets abroad to foreign banks. (An estimated $100 billion of assets left Argentina.) The middle class also began to withdraw its savings from Argentine banks. An estimated $15 billion was withdrawn between July and November 2001. Despite a $14 billion loan from the International Monetary Fund, there was no money in circulation. In December 2001, the government froze savings bank deposits. People no longer could withdraw their savings. The Argentine economy ground to a halt. Government workers were not paid. Unions staged a nationwide one-day strike. Average yearly personal income had fallen nearly 50 percent. The December 2001 riots caused the downfall of de la Rúa's government. In short order, the Congress appointed new presidents who served briefly and then resigned.

In early 2002, Eduardo Duhalde was appointed president. Duhalde took the lead of a nation in which business activity was at a standstill. Imports and exports had almost ceased. Surgeons staged a one-day work stoppage to protest the shortage of needed medicines. Teachers in seven provinces went on strike because they had not been paid in months. The Duhalde government was forced to *default on* (declare it could not pay back) Argentina's public debt. This amounted to $155 billion worth of the government's loans, bonds, and other obligations.

Next, the government took a long-expected step: the devaluation of the peso. In February 2002, the peso was no longer tied in value to the U.S. dollar. It was allowed to *float*—to reach its true value in relation to other nations' money. The value of the peso quickly fell by half. Duhalde eased controls on savings deposits to allow people to withdraw up to $5,000 from their accounts. To raise its revenues, the government imposed taxes on all *exports* (goods sold to customers abroad).

Néstor Kirchner, a provincial governor and Peronist, was elected president in April 2003. Argentine voters wanted a government with enough authority to solve problems. The Peronist Justicialist Party seemed to offer this. Kirchner was successful at reviving Argentina's economy, the third largest (after Brazil and Mexico) in Latin America. In December 2005, Kirchner announced that Argentina had paid its debt to the IMF. By 2006, the country's GDP had grown by 45 percent, an average of 8.6 percent a year. Unemployment had fallen to 10.2 percent. Consumer spending and exports, especially of beef, had increased dramatically.

Fearing that inflation would endanger the renewed prosperity, Kirchner began the use of "voluntary" price controls. The prices of hundreds of consumer goods were frozen. He also prohibited the export of most cuts of beef in order to drive down the price of Argentina's best known product and favorite food.

Economists warned Kirchner of the long-term dangers of his strategy. In recent years, price controls have not been used in Latin America, other than in Hugo Chávez's Venezuela, as most governments shifted to a free market economy in which supply and demand determine prices. Critics claimed that Kirchner's methods would halt investment, which increased to 21 percent of GDP between 2002 and 2006. This has enabled Argentina to sustain an economic growth rate of 4 percent a year.

Energy is Argentina's biggest worry. In this industry, Kirchner's critics have been proved correct. Because of price controls, Argentines pay half as much for energy as do other South Americans. However, although consumption has risen, investment has collapsed. Gas reserves have depleted to less than ten years' worth of production. Fear of blackouts has limited investment in industries that are heavily reliant on energy, such as steel, aluminum, and petrochemicals. Nevertheless, government officials remained confident, in 2007, that Argentina's economic growth would be sustained.

1. *Explain why many citizens of Argentina engaged in protests and riots in late 2001 and early 2002.*

2. *If you lived in Argentina, what steps would you urge President Kirchner to take to maintain the economic recovery?*

The Caribbean

In the late 20th and early 21st centuries, political upheavals and natural disasters in the Caribbean region have been newsworthy. Other Latin American nations, seeking to play an international role, have shown interest in the region's problems.

Haiti. This island nation has a long, proud history. When a slave rebellion won independence for Haiti in 1804, it was hailed as the world's first black republic. Later it fell under military rule and dictatorship. But a path to greater freedom opened in 1986, when unrest provoked by crop failure and famine put an end to 28 years of dictatorship. The dictators were François Duvalier, who died in 1971, and his son, Jean-Claude Duvalier, who fled to Europe in 1986. Four years of military rule followed. In 1990, a left-wing Catholic priest named Jean-Bertrand Aristide became the first democratically elected president to lead Haiti since 1950.

Aristide ruled only briefly. His proposed democratic reforms

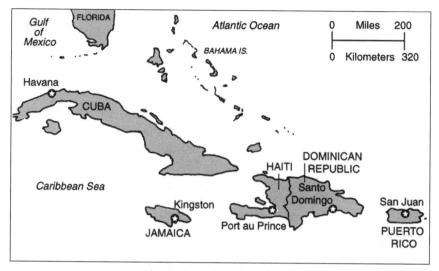

Figure 6.5   The Caribbean

alarmed both the military and Haiti's small educated elite, who saw them as a threat to their power and wealth. In September 1991, the military arrested Aristide and expelled him from Haiti. General Raoul Cédras assumed power at the head of a military junta.

Although some U.S. officials distrusted Aristide for his leftist ideas, the United States and the Organization of American States demanded that he be restored to power as Haiti's rightful leader. They placed an economic embargo on Haiti in October 1991. The embargo caused serious damage to Haiti's economy, the poorest in the Americas. The damage worsened after the United Nations put an embargo on oil and weapons sales to Haiti in June 1993.

Even before the embargoes, the majority of Haitians had lived in poverty. They crowded into urban slums or scratched out meager livings on small farms. An upper class of less than 5 percent of the population controlled Haiti's limited wealth. The embargoes made life even harder for most Haitians. Unemployment and starvation spread. Despite the suffering brought by the embargo, many Haitians supported it, in the hope that it would bring back Aristide.

Fearing rebellion, the army terrorized the slums and country-side. Thousands of Haitians attempted to flee to the United States by boat. However, Presidents George Bush and Bill Clinton refused to admit most of the boat people, saying the Haitians were motivated by hope for economic gain rather than fear of political perse-cution. Some critics claimed that the U.S. policy was racially biased.

In July 1994, the U.N. Security Council authorized the use of force against Haiti. On the eve of an announced U.S. invasion, a

Boat People

team of U.S. negotiators persuaded Cédras to let U.S. troops land peacefully and to step down within 30 days. Some 20,000 U.S. soldiers entered Haiti, without military opposition.

On October 15, 1994, cheering crowds greeted Aristide's return to Haiti on a U.S. government plane. At parliamentary elections in June 1995, a coalition of his supporters won two-thirds of the seats. Six months later, voters elected René Préval, Aristide's close associate, as his successor.

In 1999, Préval dissolved parliament and began ruling by decree. Aristide's opposition caused these former allies to become rivals. Aristide was reelected president in November 2000. Unable to stop government corruption, he attempted a violent crackdown on the growing opposition. In early 2004, a coalition of political groups demanded Aristide's resignation, and armed militias attacked his supporters. To avoid a bloodbath, Aristide resigned and departed in late February, finding eventual asylum in South Africa. Boniface Alexandre, chief justice of the Supreme Court, became leader of a powerless transitional government. Control of the country was seized by the armed militias, including army veterans and former death squad members. American-led U.N. troops moved in to restore order.

In May and September 2004, torrential rains and floods caused great damage and many deaths in Haiti and the neighboring Dominican Republic. As Brazilian-led South American troops replaced the U.S., French, and Canadian peacekeepers, Haiti's future seemed grim. René Préval was reelected president in February 2006.

1. *Why did many Haitians accuse President Aristide of preaching democracy but not practicing it?*

2. *Complete the following sentence: Haiti has had a tragic history because _____ .*

3. *Identify each of the following:*

    a. *Jean-Bertrand Aristide*   c. *François Duvalier*
    b. *Raoul Cédras*   d. *René Préval*

Cuba. Another vivid example of U.S. involvement in the affairs of a Latin American nation is provided by Cuba. For years, Americans owned many businesses there, including most of Cuba's crucial sugar industry. In 1959, a rebel army led by Fidel Castro overthrew the Cuban government. When Castro took control of U.S.-owned businesses, the United States clamped an embargo on trade with Cuba. Castro soon proclaimed himself a Marxist and sought economic help from the Soviet Union.

In 1961, the United States trained an army of anti-Communist Cubans and organized an invasion aimed at overthrowing the Castro dictatorship. The Bay of Pigs invasion failed because the Cuban people did not support the U.S.-trained force. The next year, the United States and the Soviet Union nearly went to war over Cuba. Soviet Premier Nikita Khrushchev had placed nuclear missiles in Cuba. President John F. Kennedy demanded their removal and ordered a naval blockade of Cuba. Finally, the Soviets gave in to Kennedy's demand.

Soviet economic aid to Cuba continued until the collapse of the Soviet Union in 1991. When aid was cut off, the Cuban economy went into a sharp decline. To fight the decline, the Cuban government introduced limited free market reforms modeled after those in China. For example, Cubans were allowed to form small private businesses and set up their own farm cooperatives.

In 1994, the Cuban government allowed more than 30,000 people to leave, sending a flood of Cubans to the United States. President Clinton responded by ending a 35-year-old policy of welcoming all Cuban refugees. Later, the United States agreed to admit 20,000 Cubans yearly, with Cuba's cooperation.

In 1996, Cuba shot down two aircraft owned by U.S. citizens, claiming that the planes were in Cuban air space. In response, Congress passed the Helms-Burton Act, strengthening the U.S. economic embargo by penalizing foreigners who invested in Cuba. That angered U.S. allies like Canada and Mexico. Later, the law was eased to permit U.S. sales of food and medicines to Cuba.

Starting in 2002, the United States used its naval base at Guantánamo Bay to detain Taliban and Al Qaeda prisoners captured in Afghanistan and Iraq.

The Organization of American States (OAS) has urged the United States to end its trade embargo on Cuba, described by its opponents as a relic of the cold war. In 2006, Fidel Castro's declining health caused him to turn over much of his authority to his brother, Raoul Castro. While the world speculated about the future of the Cuban revolution should Castro die, Venezuelan President Hugo Chávez has provided Cuba with massive economic aid. This aid and the expansion of trade between Cuba and Venezuela have limited the effects of the U.S. embargo.

♦ *Explain how the involvement of the United States in Cuba has changed in the post–cold war period.*

Chapter 6 Review

A. *Choose the item that best completes each sentence.*

1. The country that has been the world's largest supplier of illegal narcotics and the home of the Medellín drug cartel is (a) Peru   (b) Bolivia   (c) Colombia.

2. Two other countries that have also been centers of narcotics production and distribution are (a) Peru and Bolivia (b) Cuba and El Salvador   (c) Nicaragua and Haiti.

3. The country that has been trying to get Latin American farmers to stop growing coca is   (a) France   (b) the United States (c) Britain.

4. The country terrorized by the Shining Path guerrillas was (a) Bolivia   (b) Colombia   (c) Peru.

5. The country whose citizens feared their president might be attempting to establish a dictatorship in late 2001 was (a) Venezuela   (b) Argentina   (c) Brazil.

6. Luiz Inacio Lula da Silva was reelected president in 2006 despite corruption scandals in   (a) Cuba   (b) Haiti   (c) Brazil

7. Despite a $14 billion loan from the International Monetary Fund in 2001, an economic crisis threatened   (a) Argentina (b) Colombia   (c) Mexico.

8. In 2004, President Aristide resigned his office in   (a) Haiti   (b) Panama   (c) the Dominican Republic.

9. In the 1990s, the termination of Soviet aid caused a decline in the economy of   (a) Panama   (b) Haiti   (c) Cuba.

10. The United States maintains a trade embargo against   (a) Mexico   (b) Peru   (c) Cuba.

B. Write two or three sentences to further explain each of the following statements. Give specific examples from the chapter to support your information.

1. In recent years, the United States has been concerned about drug trafficking in Latin America.

2. Terrorism has been a major problem in Latin America.

3. In both Brazil and Argentina, 21st century presidents have led economic revival.

C. Examine the maps of Latin America in Chapter 6 and indicate which of the following statements are true and which are false.

1. Caracas, Bogotá, and Lima are South American capitals.

2. Bolivia is a landlocked nation.

3. Cuba and Haiti share the same island.

4. San José is the capital of Mexico.

5. Nicaragua borders Costa Rica and Honduras.

D. Select two Latin American leaders. Describe their problems and policies.

Unit I Review

A. Examine the maps and the list of events below. For each description, write the letter of the region in which the event occurred.

1. Following the abandonment of communism by its satellite nations, the Soviet Union collapsed. These events ended the cold war.

2. Islamic fundamentalism threatened the stability of governments in this oil-rich region.

3. A major breakthrough was made in ending white minority rule and terrorism. However, tribal and clan rivalries, combined with drought and famine, brought misery to millions in this region.

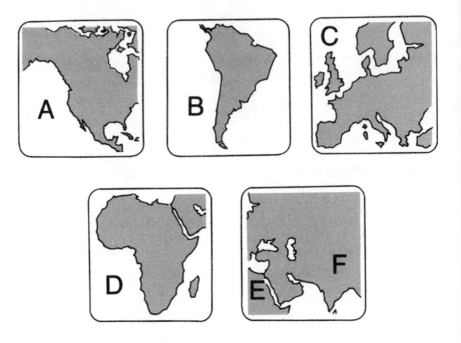

4. While China and India experienced rapid economic growth, Vietnam turned to capitalism, and Cambodia moved closer to dictatorship.

5. The United States attempted to end its trade war with Japan, while bringing food to starving Somalis and seeking ways to end the bloodshed in the Balkans.

6. Increased democracy under civilian governments was pursued in a region in which military leaders have traditionally played a strong role in political affairs.

B. Use information from Unit I to complete the chart below.

National Leader	Nation	Major Problem
Vladimir Putin		
Thabo Mbeki		
Hosni Mubarak		
Ehud Olmert		
Saddam Hussein		
Ziang Zemin		
Ariel Sharon		
Kim Jong Il		
Alberto Fujimori		
Jean-Bertrand Aristide		

C. *Use information from Unit I to explain the significance of each of the following newspaper headlines.*

GERMANY OPPOSES U.S. POLICY IN IRAQ

FIGHTING IN SUDAN HALTS FOOD RELIEF

PLO CRACKS DOWN ON HAMAS TERRORISTS IN GAZA

CAMBODIA'S HUN SEN BECOMES MORE AUTHORITARIAN

ARISTIDE RESIGNS, FLEES HAITI

D. *Review Chapter 2, "The Rise of the New Europe," beginning on page 14. Then select TWO of the statements below. For each, write a paragraph to explain why you agree or disagree with it.*

1. *The Russians were better off economically under communism than they have been under the free market system of the post–cold war period.*

2. *Under communism, consumer goods were available to Russians in greater quantity.*

3. *While the movement toward a free market economy has given some Russians the opportunity to earn more, inflation has placed consumer goods beyond the reach of many Russians.*

4. *Vladimir Putin has increased democracy and human rights in Russia.*

5. *Under communism, most Russians had a higher income.*

Unit II

THE SEARCH FOR INTERNATIONAL SECURITY

Among the global struggles of the late 20th and early 21st centuries were attempts (1) to reduce the threat of atomic disaster by seeking to limit the number of nations possessing nuclear weapons; (2) to keep the peace, especially through regional and international organizations; (3) to prevent human rights abuses by governments, and to bring perpetrators of this type of criminal action to justice; and (4) to curb international terrorism.

In recent years, world leaders and a variety of organizations have labored to attain these objectives. Their fulfillment would strengthen international security and permit nations and people to pursue their political, economic, social, and personal goals without fear of repressive governments, brutal terrorists, or destructive leaders armed with nuclear weapons.

Chapter 7

Nuclear Proliferation

The nuclear age began in August 1945, when the United States ended World War II by dropping atomic bombs on the Japanese cities of Hiroshima and Nagasaki. Horrified by the enormous death and destruction in these cities, the Japanese government surrendered. Since 1945, the United States has sought to limit *nuclear proliferation*—that is, the spread of nuclear weapons.

Cold War Developments

The United States did not enjoy its nuclear monopoly very long. The Soviet Union exploded its first atomic bomb in 1949. In the years that followed, the two superpowers engaged in an arms race that produced thousands of nuclear weapons.

One type of nuclear device, the *strategic weapon* (so-called because it forms part of a nation's overall strategy), travels great distances and aims to destroy key sites in an enemy's homeland. *Ballistic missiles,* which have a high, arching flight, include intercontinental ballistic missiles (ICBMs) that can travel more than 9,000 miles. *Cruise missiles* fly low in order to escape radar detection.

The other type of nuclear device, the *tactical weapon,* is designed for use at close range in a battle or similar situation. Tactical weapons include intermediate-, medium-, and short-range ballistic missiles. Nuclear power is also used in artillery shells, land mines, and depth charges.

Throughout the 1950s, the United States had overwhelming nuclear superiority. By 1960, however, the Soviet Union had built a nuclear stockpile large enough to ensure that any attack upon it would be met with full retaliation. By the late 1960s, the Soviet nuclear arsenal was roughly equal to that of the United States. Out of this balance of power arose the belief in *mutual assured destruction* (MAD). Its proponents reasoned that neither the United States nor the Soviet Union would resort to the use of nuclear weapons if each had the ability to destroy the other. Each nation, therefore, developed and maintained enough nuclear weapons to deter an attack by the other. MAD provided both the United States and the Soviet Union an incentive to maintain the nuclear balance. It was recognized that the development of an imbalance would jeopardize international security.

This interdependence led the United States and the Soviet Union to seek ways to assure stability. Beginning in the 1960s, they negotiated arms control agreements to maintain a balance of nuclear weapons and to curb weapons systems that might upset the balance of power.

Nuclear Arms Control. Nuclear weapons have not been used in warfare since 1945. The Soviet Union did not use them in Afghanistan. The United States did not use them in Vietnam or Iraq. However, the possibility that nations with nuclear arsenals would use them has caused widespread concern.

An early effort at control was the founding of the International Atomic Energy Agency (IAEA) in 1957. The 130 members of this independent United Nations agency work to encourage peaceful uses of atomic energy. They also try to discourage the construction of nuclear weapons and to prevent the conversion of nuclear plants from civilian to military use.

Another step was the Nuclear Nonproliferation Treaty of 1968. This is an agreement signed by 185 nations to halt the spread of nuclear weapons to other countries and to support an international authority for the development of peaceful nuclear technologies. The treaty's signers pledged to allow inspections of their nuclear facilities by the IAEA.

An important treaty between the United States and the Soviet Union was signed by President Richard Nixon and Soviet leader Leonid Brezhnev in 1972. It grew out of Strategic Arms Limitation Talks (SALT) that began in 1969. The SALT I treaty, as it was called, limited each nation's long-range missiles. A SALT II treaty was signed but never ratified.

The London Suppliers Agreement of 1976 is designed to prevent the export of any nuclear materials or technology with military potential to nations that do not possess any nuclear weapons.

Also, EURATOM, the European nuclear authority, has an independent legal responsibility for ensuring that nuclear material in its nonweapons state is not diverted to nuclear weapons or nuclear explosives. The EURATOM Commission can directly penalize any person or organization that violates its rules and bring an offending nation before the European Court of Justice.

In 1987, the United States and the Soviet Union signed the Intermediate Nuclear Forces Treaty, which called for the destruction of missiles with ranges of 300 to 3,400 miles. Moreover, two Strategic Arms Reduction treaties were signed in the 1990s. START I (1991) reduced each nation's long-range missiles by about a third. START II (1993) further reduced the number of U.S. and Russian missiles. Talks on a START III began in 1999.

To remove obstacles to the development of his new missile defense program, President George W. Bush withdrew the United States from the 1972 Anti-Ballistic Missile (ABM) Treaty with Russia in 2002. Over Russia's strong protests, Bush cited the need for the United States to build defenses against the enemies of the 21st century.

In 2004, Libya's dictator, Muammar al-Qaddafi announced his intention to surrender his nuclear weapons and end development of chemical and biological weapons. Qaddafi was motivated by a desire for closer relations with Europe and Libya's critical need for economic development and foreign investment.

1. *Define nuclear proliferation.*

2. *What are the goals of the International Atomic Energy Agency?*

3. *List four measures taken to prevent nuclear proliferation.*

The Spread of Nuclear Weapons. Britain exploded its first atomic weapon in 1952; France followed in 1960. In Asia, China conducted nuclear tests in 1964, India exploded its first "nuclear device" in 1974, and Pakistan tested a bomb in 1998. South Africa's white-minority government built atomic weapons in the 1980s but gave them up voluntarily while negotiating an end to apartheid in 1991.

Nuclear warheads are capable of being deployed by, or are currently being held in reserve stockpiles by, China, France, India, Israel, Pakistan, Russia, Britain, and the United States. North Korea and Iran have begun work on the development of their own nuclear weapons.

♦ *List the nations with known or suspected nuclear arsenals.*

Cause for Worry

The Nuclear Technology Trade. In late 2003, international nuclear inspectors revealed that Pakistan was the source of crucial technology about how to enrich uranium, and that North Korea, Iran, and Libya had used this technology to build nuclear weapons. The focus of their investigation was Dr. Abdul Qadeer Khan. The so-called father of Pakistan's atomic bomb, Dr. Khan is regarded by the Pakistanis as a national hero. Nevertheless, he and other Pakistani scientists have been accused of selling nuclear designs around the globe. Because of Dr. Khan's fame and popularity, the Pakistani government has been reluctant to prosecute him.

The ease with which North Korea, Iran, and Libya obtained nuclear technology from Pakistani scientists prompted President George W. Bush to propose, in February 2004, a U.S. plan to make it more difficult than ever to successfully finalize international black market sales of nuclear designs and equipment. Critics complained that Bush's plan did not call for an end to all trade in fissionable material—for example, enriched uranium or reprocessed plutonium. It would only limit such shipments to countries that do not already possess enrichment and reprocessing plants. This proviso avoided interference with multibillion-dollar fuel reprocessing operations in nonnuclear nations like Japan. Bush also urged a sharing of information among nations about weapons shipments so as to prevent terrorists from getting nuclear weapons.

In December 2006, concerns about Iran's nuclear development program resulted in a U.N. Security Council resolution prohibiting the sale to Iran of goods and technology related to that program. The measure was aimed at stopping Iran's uranium enrichment, which Iran has claimed is for peaceful purposes. The United States and some European countries believe that Iran is intending to make nuclear weapons. In February 2007, top officials from the United States, Britain, China, Russia, Germany, and France agreed to work on a stronger resolution that would increase economic pressure on Iran.

Western fears of an Iran armed with nuclear weapons have focused on President Mahmoud Ahmadinejad, elected in June 2005. Ahmadinejad has claimed that his nation is becoming a superpower and has stated that U.N. sanctions would not prevent it from pursuing its nuclear program. He has also called for the destruction of Israel and has described the Holocaust, the genocide of six million Jews and three million other Europeans during World War II, as a hoax. By early 2007, however, the president had come under increasing criticism from Iranian students, businessmen, and political leaders. Western political and economic pressure on Iran has reduced foreign investment and weakened its energy industry.

Iran has been the world's fourth largest oil exporter. It has the second largest oil and gas reserves. In 2006, oil exports, totaling $47 billion, accounted for half the government's revenue. In recent years, however, domestic demand for oil has increased while production has fallen. Analysts believe that if this trend continues, Iran will have no more oil to export by around 2015. The Iranian leadership has claimed that it needs nuclear power to free its oil for exporting. The United States and other Western countries have said Iran is using its energy program to build weapons.

President Ahmadinejad called the U.N. sanctions ineffective. In Iran, however, conservatives joined moderates to warn that the president's dismissive attitude could have dangerous political and economic consequences. Among these consequences has been a possible U.S.-military strike on Iran.

♦ Explain why you AGREE or DISAGREE:

    1. The United States wishes to maintain a monopoly on nuclear weapons.

2. Nuclear proliferation increases the danger of terrorists obtaining nuclear weapons.

3. The United States should use military action to stop Iran's nuclear development program.

Iraq: A Special Case

The belief, particularly by officials in the United States and Britain, that Iraq was secretly building nuclear, chemical, and biological weapons was a key justification for the U.S.-led invasion in 2003. Support for this belief was increased by Saddam Hussein's reluctance to allow U.N. inspection teams to operate freely in Iraq. These teams attempted to determine whether Hussein was complying with Security Council resolutions formulated after the Persian Gulf War of 1991, which required him to destroy still-existing weapons programs.

However, during the occupation of Iraq by U.S. and other coalition troops, no nuclear weapons or other weapons of mass destruction (WMDs) were found. A 15-month investigation by U.S. weapons experts was concluded in October 2004. Charles A. Duelfer, the top inspector, reported that Iraq had destroyed its WMD stockpiles within months after the Persian Gulf War of 1991. It was concluded that between 1991 and 2003, Saddam Hussein had sacrificed his weapons program to the larger goal of ending U.N. economic sanctions. Hussein attempted to maintain confusion about whether or not Iraq had WMDs, as a deterrent to military action by Iran, its rival.

Although no nuclear, chemical, or biological weapons were found in Iraq, the United States and other nations were determined to continue the effort to prevent such weapons from being developed by hostile "rogue" nations or passing into the hands of terrorist groups.

♦ *Complete the following sentences:*

a. After 1991, a U.N. Security Council resolution required Iraq to _____.

b. During the U.S.-led occupation of Iraq, weapons inspectors found _____.

c. It is believed that Saddam Hussein _____ after the Persian Gulf War of 1991.

Ukraine: No More Missiles

When the Soviet Union broke apart at the end of 1991, 1,800 of the country's nuclear warheads were in Ukraine. Newly independent Ukraine had suddenly turned into the world's third-ranking nuclear power, after Russia and the United States. Russian and U.S. leaders quickly set to work to persuade the Ukrainians to give up the nuclear weapons.

But many Ukrainians had different ideas. For one thing, they were deeply suspicious of Russia. How could Ukraine protect itself if Russia tried to build up a new Russian empire? Moreover, Ukrainian nationalists wanted Ukraine to be a powerful state in its own right. What better way than to keep the weapons the country had inherited from the Soviet Union?

The start of the post-Soviet era was a time of political and economic turmoil in Ukraine. Russia sharply increased the prices of its gas and oil exports, which Ukraine desperately needed. Coal miners went on strike in a region critical to the Ukrainian economy. Prices soared out of sight, rising three times as fast as in Russia. Many Ukrainians blamed Russia, their main energy supplier, for both the strikes and the inflation. Adding further strain was a dispute between Ukraine and Russia over who now owned the Black Sea fleet of the former Soviet navy.

The issue of Ukraine-based nuclear weapons, therefore, was linked to worries about Ukrainian security and to Ukraine's political and economic future. The United States and other Western powers assured Ukrainian leaders of their support for Ukrainian independence. They sweetened the pot with economic aid. Then the United States, Russia, and Britain jointly promised that they would respect Ukraine's borders. They also pledged that they would not use economic means to put pressure on Ukraine. In exchange, they asked Ukraine to give up its nuclear weapons and sign two major disarmament treaties—the START I arms-reduction treaty and the Nuclear Nonproliferation Treaty.

Ukrainian President Leonid Kuchma, a former rocket engineer, accepted the bargain. In November 1994, Kuchma went before his nation's parliament and urged it to ratify the nonproliferation treaty. He suggested that by so doing, Ukraine could win increased respect from the rest of the world. "The process of world disarmament depends on our decision today," Kuchma said. The treaty passed by a vote of 301 to 8.

Ukraine soon started dismantling its nuclear missiles. The

Peace Work

warheads went to Russia to be destroyed. The missiles stayed in Ukraine to be cut apart. Later, the resulting cylinders would be used as farm silos or fuel tanks. The operation was complete by June 1996. In Ukraine, at least, the turning of "swords" into "plowshares" had begun.

1. *Explain how relations between Russia and Ukraine affected the efforts of the United States to reduce the nuclear arsenal of the former Soviet Union.*

2. *Correct each false statement.*
   a. *Ukrainians fear possible aggression by Russia.*
   b. *Russia supplies most of the oil and gas needed by Ukraine.*
   c. *The United States gave economic aid to Ukraine to try to persuade it to give up nuclear weapons.*
   d. *Ukraine's President Kuchma insisted that his country remain a nuclear power.*
   e. *Today, Ukraine has the world's third-largest stockpile of nuclear weapons.*

An End to Nuclear Testing?

Serious efforts to halt nuclear testing began in the 1950s. At the time, a major concern was the health threat posed by radiation that was released into the atmosphere by aboveground nuclear tests. In 1963, the United States, Britain, and the Soviet Union signed the Limited Nuclear Test-Ban Treaty. The treaty pledged those nations not to test nuclear weapons in the atmosphere, under water, or in space. It allowed underground tests to continue. In recent years, the other two declared nuclear powers, China and France, have observed the same restrictions.

In October 1992, a *moratorium* on, or temporary halt in, nuclear weapons testing went into effect. It was the result of an agreement among the United States, Russia, France, and Britain. Meanwhile, representatives of 38 nations began meetings in Geneva, Switzerland, to hammer out an agreement on a comprehensive, or complete, test-ban treaty. Such a treaty would ban all types of tests, including those underground. A key issue at the Geneva talks was whether or not to continue to allow very small underground nuclear tests. The United States and Russia said they needed such tests in order to be sure of the safety and reliability of their weapons. Nonnuclear states strongly opposed any such loopholes. In August 1995, President Clinton dropped the U.S. request for small tests and said a new test ban should be fully comprehensive. That put pressure on Russia to go along.

When the Nuclear Non-Proliferation Treaty came up for renewal in 1995, the nations that had signed the treaty met to discuss what to do. Should they extend the treaty indefinitely? That was what the United States and other nuclear powers wanted. Or should they limit the extension to 25 years? That was what many nonaligned nations proposed. The smaller nations did not want an indefinite extension until they felt confident that the nuclear nations would keep their promise to give up their own nuclear arms. That vague promise was part of the original treaty. After a four-week conference in New York, the signatory nations accepted the U.S. position and extended the treaty indefinitely. In order to win the extension, the nuclear powers had to repeat their old promise. They also made new promises—including a pledge to conclude a comprehensive ban on nuclear testing by the end of 1996.

In 1996, the discussions in Geneva did produce an important new agreement. It was called the Comprehensive Test Ban Treaty (CTBT). The world's five major nuclear powers agreed to sign the CTBT. However, as part of the agreement, the treaty would not go into effect formally until all 44 of the nations with nuclear reactors ratified it.

Although other nations continued to observe a moratorium

on nuclear weapons testing, India and Pakistan each carried out a series of underground nuclear tests in 1998. Neither of the two nations had signed either the Nuclear Non-Proliferation Treaty or the CTBT.

By 2003, 168 nations had signed the test-ban treaty, but only 104 of them had ratified it. Among those who had not were North Korea, Iran, and the United States. Representatives of countries attending a CTBT conference in Vienna, in 2003, were persistent in noting the growing threats of terrorism and further proliferation of nuclear weapons. Referring to the nightmarish scenario of terrorists who might resort to using weapons of mass destruction, supporters of the CTBT stated their belief that the treaty could prevent not only the development of new nuclear weapons but also the improvement of existing ones.

Kim Jong Il's Nuclear Garden

A small nuclear test explosion by North Korea in October 2006 caused world concern about how many bombs the country's dictator, Kim Jong Il, had in stock and how many more tests he would conduct. In February 2007, Kim agreed with the United States and five other nations to close North Korea's main nuclear reactor in exchange for a package of food, fuel, and other aid. To ensure that Kim did what he promised, the agreement provided North Korea with a small amount of fuel in return for freezing its plutonium facilities. More generous aid was to follow more extensive disarmament and abandonment of plutonium and uranium materials. Strong pressure to accept the deal was placed on Kim by China, the main supplier of military and economic assistance to North Korea. Kim's nuclear test angered China, which supported the U.N. resolution imposing economic sanctions on North Korea. China's shift from protector to accuser shocked Kim into joining the six-nation talks. Subsequently, the United States agreed to begin discussion of extending full diplomatic recognition to North Korea.

1. *Explain how the Geneva talks on the Comprehensive Test Ban Treaty were related to the extension of the Nuclear Non-Proliferation Treaty.*

2. *What conditions would have to be fulfilled for the Comprehensive Test Ban Treaty to take effect?*

3. *How did the United States and other nations respond to North Korea's nuclear test in 2006?*

Plans for a U.S. Missile Defense Shield

In late 2002, U.S. intelligence officials confirmed that China had deployed its newest intercontinental missile. The Dong Feng (East Wind) 31 missile can hit targets in the United States and Europe. Armed with a hydrogen bomb, a single DF-31 can destroy any major U.S. city.

The proliferation of Chinese missile technology in Asia and the Middle East has been a growing concern. With extensive Chinese assistance, North Korea developed missiles that can reach the western United States. Iran has pursued the development of a missile force and the possible acquisition of nuclear weapons with the help of North Korean engineers working in Iran and Chinese parts and designs exported from North Korea. All three of these nations regard the United States as a potential military enemy.

Commencing with the presidency of Ronald Reagan, American

leaders have pursued the construction of a missile shield. As a cold war president, Reagan wanted a defense against a full missile attack by the Soviet Union. This could have involved multiple nuclear warheads striking U.S. targets. Reagan's Strategic Defense Initiative (SDI) of 1983 was also called "Star Wars" because it called for space-based weapons such as orbiting mirrors and particle beams. The Defense Department killed the project in 1993. The costs were too high and the technical problems were too great.

Post–cold war presidents have been concerned with protecting the United States from attacks by rogue nations and terrorists. In mid-2004, the administration of George W. Bush announced development of the "great grandson of Star Wars." This new plan provides for ground-based special interceptors to be deployed in silos in Alaska, California, and other sites. Although much smaller in scale than the Reagan plan, the Bush project has sparked skepticism and opposition. Critics have demanded more testing of a system that is being put into the field without an adequate measurement of its capabilities.

Supporters of a missile shield point out that missiles fired by a rogue nation or terrorist group might or might not have nuclear warheads, but even conventional warheads would produce unacceptable damage and loss of life.

A missile shield developed with currently available technology would not protect the United States from an all-out missile attack by a militarily powerful nation. Critics also argue that enforceable arms agreements are a better method of protecting against attack by a rogue nation. There are some who claim that missile assaults are less likely than terrorist bombings or biological or chemical attacks by terrorist or rogue nations.

Nevertheless, the nuclear test explosion conducted by North Korea in 2006, combined with the continuing development of its missile program, has created concern in the United States and elsewhere. Iran's nuclear program has caused similar concerns. For many, such developments reinforce the need for a missile defense shield.

Russia objected to the Bush administration plan. In early 2007, the commanding general of Russia's strategic forces warned Poland and the Czech Republic not to allow the rockets and radars of a U.S. antimissile system to be installed on their territories. Failure to heed this warning would result in Russian forces having the capability to target the Czech and Polish installations. This came as a surprise to many, as Russian president Vladimir Putin is well aware that the bases in Eastern Europe would be part of a defensive shield that NATO had concluded could help defend the United States and Europe from the growing danger of long-range missiles from countries such as Iran and North Korea.

Other governments have come to accept that their security is at risk. Japan and Australia have been cooperating with the United States to fend off the danger from North Korea's missiles.

1. State the main argument for a missile shield project.

2. Describe the weapon being developed by the administration of George W. Bush.

3. Define:

   a. DF-31

   b. Star Wars plan

4. Match each term or person in Column A with the correct identification from Column B.

Column A	Column B
1. interceptor	a. proposed a "Star Wars" defense
2. President Reagan	b. nonnuclear missile
3. conventional weapon	c. considered a possible rogue state
4. North Korea	d. ground-based installation for destroying an incoming missile

Chapter 7 Review

A. Choose the item that best completes each sentence.

1. The nuclear age began in 1945, when   (a) the United States used atomic bombs to end World War II   (b) the Soviet Union used nuclear weapons on Japan   (c) the United States and the Soviet Union fought a nuclear war.

2. During the cold war, the superpowers   (a) scrapped their nuclear weapons   (b) engaged in an arms race   (c) shared their nuclear technology with other countries.

3. The purpose of the International Atomic Energy Agency is to (a) see that nations with nuclear technology use it for civilian, rather than military, purposes   (b) prevent accidents in nuclear power plants   (c) fund the research and development of nuclear weapons.

4. The purpose of the Nuclear Non-Proliferation Treaty is (a) to ensure the destruction of all nuclear weapons (b) to prevent nuclear weapons testing (c) to prevent the development of nuclear weapons by nations that do not possess them.

5. During the 1990s, the START I and II treaties reduced Russian and U.S. (a) missile-launching submarines (b) long-range missiles (c) tactical missiles.

6. After the 2003 U.S.-led invasion of Iraq, occupation forces (a) found and destroyed Saddam Hussein's nuclear weapons (b) were unable to find any nuclear weapons (c) found nuclear, biological, and chemical weapons.

7. In 1994, Ukraine agreed to (a) destroy its nuclear arsenal (b) surrender all of its nuclear weapons to Russia (c) join Russia in a combined nuclear weapons development program.

8. The Comprehensive Test Ban Treaty (a) took full effect in 1996 (b) took full effect when the U.S. Senate ratified it in 1999 (c) will take full effect when all 44 nations known to have nuclear reactors sign and ratify it.

9. The U.S. missile defense shield favored by President Bush is designed to defend the United States against attack by (a) a nation with tactical nuclear weapons (b) a nation like Russia, with many long-range missiles (c) a terrorist group or rogue nation.

10. The global effort to prevent nuclear proliferation is made difficult by (a) the ease with which plutonium can be diverted from civilian to military use (b) a lack of interest by the United Nations (c) U.S. support of the nuclear weapons programs of its Asian allies.

B. Use the information found in the chapter to explain each of the following newspaper headlines.

NORTH KOREAN MISSILES WORRY U.S. LEADERS

PAKISTANI SCIENTISTS SELL NUCLEAR TECHNOLOGY

C. Which statements are supported by the information in the following graph and in the chapter?

1. The decision by Ukraine to give up nuclear weapons will result in the rapid elimination of Russia's nuclear arsenal as well.

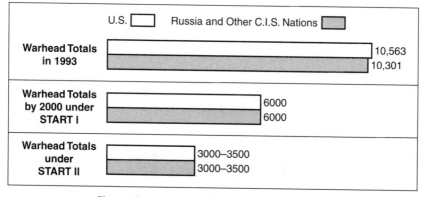

Figure 7.1   Strategic Weapons Reduction

2. At the beginning of the 21st century, the United States and Russia still possessed thousands of nuclear warheads.

3. Under START II, the United States and Russia are entitled to equal numbers of nuclear warheads.

4. Tension between Ukraine and Russia prevented ratification of the START treaties.

5. The United States had little direct role in the negotiations to persuade Ukraine to give up its nuclear weapons.

Chapter 8

The Struggle to Keep the Peace

After World War II, the United Nations was the hope of the world for global peace. That hope was frustrated during the cold war and the struggle against global terrorism.

During those years, the U.N. was unable to prevent destructive wars (in Korea, Vietnam, and Afghanistan) between Communists and anti-Communists. Nor could it prevent violence between Communists and anti-Communists in the so-called Third World (Cuba, El Salvador, Nicaragua, and other developing nations). As the cold war ended in the 1990s, the big powers turned from confrontation to cooperation. New peacekeeping efforts in Latin America, Asia, Africa, and Europe expanded the role and responsibilities of the U.N. But crises in Afghanistan, Iraq, and elsewhere have made the U.N.'s ability to achieve international peace and security doubtful.

Regional organizations have also worked for peace in recent years. After the cold war, the North Atlantic Treaty Organization (NATO) developed a new mission. In Latin America, the Organization of American States (OAS) cooperated with the U.N. in dealing with crises in Haiti and Peru. The African Union (AU) encouraged the independence of Namibia and the building of a multiracial society in South Africa. The Arab League mediated disputes among member nations in the Middle East and North Africa.

In addition to the upheavals caused by nationalistic, religious, and other competing groups, peacekeeping efforts were made more difficult by the growing international trade in weapons and military equipment.

The United Nations After the Cold War

For some decades after World War II, most U.N. peacekeeping forces were positioned between the armies of rival nations—for example, Israel and its Arab neighbors. More recently, the U.N. has also sent peacekeepers into domestic conflicts. Of a string of nine recent peacekeeping operations authorized by the Security Council, seven involved internal wars.

The U.N.'s peacekeeping role expanded greatly in the early 1990s. In 1988, the U.N. had only five active peacekeeping operations; by 1993, it had 28. As a result of the U.N.'s expanding role, the troops under U.N. command increased from 9,500 in 1988 to 70,000 in the mid-1990s. By the year 2006, however, the number of peacekeeping missions had declined to 18. The number of military troops and civilian police serving in peacekeeping operations in that year was approximately 71,840.

Successes and Failures. The U.N. has had some notable successes in recent years. In Asia, U.N. peacekeepers helped put an end to a civil war in Cambodia and helped restore peace to East Timor. In Africa, U.N. forces helped smooth Namibia's transition to independence after a long struggle against South African colonial rule. They also helped Ethiopia and Eritrea to restore peace after a border war. In Latin America, they helped El Salvador restore peace and maintained stability in Haiti after the end of military rule.

These were the successes. In other cases, the U.N.'s peacekeeping efforts stumbled. Examples of such stumbling can be found in Somalia, Bosnia, Rwanda, Sierra Leone, and Congo.

In Somalia, U.N. peacekeepers stepped in early in 1993 when savage fighting among rival warlords threatened the country with chaos and starvation. Once there, U.N. troops became caught in a quarrel with Muhammad Farah Aydid, one of the warlords. In June 1993, Aydid's forces ambushed and killed 24 Pakistani soldiers of the U.N. force. U.N. and separate U.S. forces responded by going after Aydid. Casualties among the U.N. and U.S. forces rose as they played a bigger role in the war. In October 1993, 18 U.S. Rangers died in a battle against Aydid's forces. Four days later, President Clinton announced that he was withdrawing U.S. troops. In March 1995, the U.N. too gave up and withdrew its peacekeepers. The Somali warlords kept on fighting.

The U.N. did do some good in Somalia. One of its goals was to protect food deliveries. In the early 1990s, famine had taken the lives of at least 300,000 Somalis. The arrival of U.N. and U.S. troops in 1992 allowed much more food to be distributed. The intervention also allowed Somali farmers to boost their output and may have saved 100,000 lives.

Bosnia, in the former Yugoslavia, was another big test for the United Nations. At first, in 1992, U.N. troops concentrated on protecting food aid. Soon they were protecting "safe havens" (areas that were supposed to be immune to attack). The U.N. also monitored a "no-fly zone," where all military flights except those approved by the United Nations were barred. U.N. forces in Bosnia were at various times shot at, shelled, arrested, and held hostage. More than 120 died in the first four years of the operation.

In Bosnia, as in Somalia, peacekeepers risked taking sides. Hostility developed between U.N. forces and the Bosnian Serbs, who defied many of the Security Council's orders. At the end of 1995, 60,000 NATO troops (including 20,000 Americans) replaced the U.N. peacekeepers in Bosnia in order to enforce the Dayton Peace Accords. U.N. administrators, not peacekeepers, played a role later in Kosovo, another region of Yugoslavia. After NATO forces had ended Serbia's ethnic cleansing there (see Chapter 2), U.N. personnel operated a temporary civil administration, restoring basic services and establishing courts and a police force.

In Rwanda the U.N. began by sending military observers in 1993 to patrol borders. When rebels and the government agreed on a cease-fire, the U.N. sent 2,200 peacekeepers to monitor compliance. Their task became more complex and dangerous when, in 1994, genocidal slaughter broke out between Rwanda's two major ethnic groups, Tutsis and Hutus. When U.N. troops pulled out in 1996, they left a country still seething with unrest and violence. President Clinton later apologized for the U.S. role in blocking a larger U.N. force that might have limited the genocide.

The U.N. Security Council was unable to keep U.S. and British forces from invading Iraq in 2003. The Anglo-American decision to proceed without U.N. approval brought a storm of criticism from many nations. Britain and the United States were accused of violating the U.N. Charter. By early 2004, failure to find weapons of mass destruction in Iraq or evidence of support for Al Qaeda by the government of Saddam Hussein increased international demands for U.N. involvement. Acts of terrorism directed against nations participating in U.S. President Bush's "coalition of the willing" increased public pressure on these governments to withdraw from the Iraqi occupation. Widening divisions in the coalition and the difficulties of writing a constitution and turning over power to an Iraqi interim government made the United States and Britain more receptive to the possibility of a wider U.N. role in Iraq.

1. *Identify two successful U.N. peacekeeping efforts.*

2. *Explain why the U.S-led invasion of Iraq was a failure for the United Nations.*

Problems With Peacekeeping. One of the problems of peace-keeping forces is that people expect them to be more than peace-keepers. Ideally, the peacekeepers move in only after warring factions have settled their differences. Then their job is straight-forward. They make sure that all sides in a dispute observe peace settlements or truces. They run free elections and ensure that relief supplies reach civilians. But in places like Somalia and Rwanda, peacekeepers not only found themselves in the midst of ongoing wars but also sometimes took part in the fighting.

A new peacekeeping mission was launched in East Timor (Timor-Leste) in mid-2006. Australia and other nations sent troops to deal with a wave of gang violence in Dili, the capital city. The kid-napping of two Israeli soldiers by Hezbollah, a terrorist organization based in Lebanon, resulted in an Israeli invasion of that country in July 2006. The U.N. responded with a cease-fire plan that

Members Only

required an international military force to aid the Lebanese army to stabilize the area by separating Israeli and Hezbollah troops.

Peacekeeping operations do not come cheap. The yearly cost of U.N. peacekeeping operations rose to $4.75 billion by 2006. Like the expenses of the regular budget, peacekeeping expenses are paid from assessments on U.N. member nations, but using a different formula. After the United States withheld payment for several years, the U.N. agreed in 2000 to lower the U.S. peacekeeping assessment from 31 to 26.5 percent by the end of 2002, and later to 25 percent. The United States had become the U.N.'s biggest debtor, owing more than $1 billion. Stabilizing the U.N.'s financial situation has been a key issue facing its members.

Debate has also focused on how the United Nations makes its decisions. Although U.N. membership has grown from 53 countries in 1945 to 192 today, most peacekeeping decisions are made by the 15-member Security Council. Each of the council's five permanent members—the United States, Russia (which inherited the seat of the Soviet Union), Britain, France, and China—has veto power. They are the nations that won World War II and established the world order of the cold war period. Plans for broadening the membership of the Security Council were proposed in 2005 by the African Union, the Group of Four (Brazil, Germany, India, and Japan), and other nations. The G-4 plan called for a 25-member Security Council. Discussion of these plans continues.

Ban Ki-Moon of South Korea became secretary general of the United Nations in December 2006. He pledged to rebuild faith in an organization that has been tarnished by scandal and divided by disputes between rich nations and poor nations. He began by establishing new requirements for hundreds of U.N. jobs.

1. *Explain how the role of the United Nations changed after the cold war.*

2. *List three reasons why critics of the U.N. doubt its ability to achieve international security or world peace.*

3. *Determine the error in each of the following sentences and rewrite each as a correct sentence.*

    a. *From 1945 to 1990, the U.N. prevented cold war military conflicts.*
    b. *U.N. military forces were successful in Afghanistan and Iraq.*
    c. *Financial support has not been a problem for U.N. peacekeepers.*
    d. *The present method of representation on the Security Council is satisfactory to all U.N. members.*

NATO Reorganization

In November 2002, at the North Atlantic Treaty Organization (NATO) Summit Conference in Prague, Secretary General George Robertson dealt with three main and pressing issues. First was the enlargement of NATO by the admission of seven eastern European nations in 2004 (Bulgaria, Estonia, Latvia, Lithuania, Romania, Slovakia, and Slovenia). In addition to this increase in the number of NATO member nations to 26, the alliance was extended geographically to Russia's border. Earlier in 2002, a NATO-Russia council had been formed to discuss peacekeeping, nuclear weapons, terrorism, and other security matters. As a follow-up, building closer relations between the alliance and Russia was the second major issue at the summit conference. The third issue was the development of a NATO Rapid Reaction Force, which could be readily deployed anywhere in the world. This updating of the alliance's mission meant that NATO would no longer confine itself to Europe; rather, it would respond to the growing threat of global terrorism and the danger of the disruption of the flow of oil supplies from the Middle East to Europe.

Lord Robertson described the Prague summit as part of a process of fundamental transformation of NATO. In this new conception, the alliance was to become more flexible, more rapidly deployable, and more able to maintain a strong political role. To achieve this goal, the Rapid Reaction Force would be structured for response to nuclear, radiological, and biological attacks. New mobile headquarters were being planned as part of a streamlined command structure.

NATO was created in 1949 in order to defend Western Europe and North America from attack by the Soviet Union and its Warsaw Pact allies in Eastern Europe. This threat was ended by the fall of the Soviet Union and the end of the cold war. The Prague summit continued the post–cold war reorganization of NATO, which had begun at the 1991 Rome summit. At that time, NATO leaders abandoned the strategy of massing forces in Germany to meet a threat from the Communist East. In its place, they adopted a more flexible military strategy, based on smaller but more modern forces, backed by highly mobile reserves. NATO also began to focus on the Mediterranean as an area in which future challenges to security are likely to occur. A dialogue developed between NATO authorities and Egypt, Israel, Jordan, Mauritania, Morocco, and Tunisia. It was recognized that political, social, and economic pressures in the non-NATO countries have the potential to create problems for the alliance.

Since its founding in 1949, NATO's top civilian post has been held by a European, while a U.S. general has served as the alliance's military commander. Dutch Foreign Minister Jaap de Hoop Scheffer became secretary general in 2004. He has been noted for his strong commitment to the modernization of the alliance, as well as for his strong support of the U.S.-led invasion and occupation of Iraq.

General John Craddock, an American, has held the position of Supreme Allied Commander, Europe, since February 2007. Among his chief goals have been development of the NATO Rapid Reaction Force and administration of military operations in Afghanistan.

♦ *Why was reorganization of NATO, as presented during the 2002 Prague summit conference, made necessary by developments in the post–cold war era?*

NATO Membership and Mission

Like the United Nations, NATO expanded over the years. Its 12 original members were joined by Greece and Turkey and then by West Germany and Spain. (Reunified Germany replaced West Germany in 1990.) The admission of West Germany led to some concerns. Because of its Nazi past, many people, in Germany and elsewhere, feared a military role for Germany outside its own borders. West Germany's 1949 constitution, adopted while the country was under Allied occupation, limited the scope of military operations. Later amendments restricted the German military to a single goal: protecting German territory. Thus, during the Persian Gulf War, Germany took no direct part in the invasion of Iraq. In 1994, Germany's highest court ruled that the constitution did not bar German troops from serving in international military actions abroad. Thereafter, Germany took a more active part in such operations. In 1995, Germany sent 4,000 ground troops as part of NATO's peacekeeping mission in Bosnia.

After the end of the cold war, the expansion of NATO became an even more troublesome issue. Many of the former Soviet satellites wanted to join the organization. But NATO members were not ready to let them all in. For starters, the newly democratic countries of Eastern Europe had weak military forces lacking standard NATO training and equipment. If they joined NATO, all NATO members would be obligated to go to their defense in case they came under attack. Moreover, Russia adamantly opposed any extension of NATO into Eastern Europe. It saw such an extension as a potential threat to its own security.

On the other hand, NATO leaders believed that some sort of link to NATO was necessary to promote stability in Eastern Europe. In 1994, they came up with a sort of "junior membership," inviting interested countries to cooperate with NATO in what was called a Partnership for Peace. The idea was to promote increased political and military cooperation (joint exercises, for example) without the burdens or opportunities of full membership. After first rejecting the idea, Russia signed on in 1995. It was one of 26 NATO "partners," stretching from Poland to Kazakhstan.

In 1999, three new members—Hungary, Poland, and the Czech Republic—joined NATO. The largest expansion was the 2004 admission of seven new members (see page 169). To train their military forces to NATO standards, an academy was set up for senior noncommissioned officers—especially those from eastern European nations. It is like the previously established academy for NATO officers. As NATO became more multinational, U.S. forces in Europe were reduced by two-thirds.

As NATO's membership changed, so did its mission. A milestone was the intervention in Bosnia. In 1994, two U.S. fighter planes assigned to NATO shot down four Serbian warplanes violating the "no-fly" zone over Bosnia. This first military strike in NATO history signaled that it was no longer acting only as a defense force against enemy attack but also as a police force. NATO's armed intervention was also crucial in Kosovo in 1999 and since.

In 2003, NATO accepted its first peacekeeping mission beyond Europe, in Afghanistan. This reflected a new commitment to protect members from terrorism and other security threats. Afghanistan's Taliban regime sheltered Al Qaeda's leadership, responsible for the September 11, 2001, terrorist attacks in the United States. Opposition fighters and U.S. forces overthrew the Taliban in late 2001. The International Security Assistance Force (ISAF) has involved NATO in helping the Afghan Transitional Authority move toward elections, the rule of law, and the country's reconstruction. In December 2006, ISAF forces numbered 32,000 troops from 37 nations.

The 2003 U.S.-British invasion of Iraq caused sharp division in NATO. France and Germany opposed it. Britain, Italy, Spain, and the eastern European members supported it. At the Istanbul summit in 2004, however, NATO leaders agreed to train the security forces of Iraq's new interim government.

A summit conference of NATO leaders was held in Riga, the capital of Latvia, in November 2006. The focus was a U.S.-led effort to reduce restrictions on the use in combat in Afghanistan of troops from certain member nations. France, Germany, Italy, and Spain agreed to the use of their troops in more emergency situations, such as saving the lives of NATO troops under extreme attack. They continued to stress, however, that their troops will not be joining U.S., British, Canadian, and Dutch troops fighting the Taliban and Al Qaeda in troubled areas of southern and eastern Afghanistan. Spain offered the use of helicopters, in short supply in Afghanistan, in exceptional circumstances to help evacuate wounded NATO soldiers.

At the Riga conference, it was announced that Serbia, Bosnia, and Montenegro would be offered Partnerships for Peace as a first step toward NATO membership.

1. *Summarize the decisions made about NATO since 1991.*

2. *Explain why you AGREE or DISAGREE with the following:*

   a. *After the cold war, NATO should have been disbanded.*

b. *NATO, as reorganized, is better able to keep the peace.*
c. *Germany should not play a larger military role in NATO.*
d. *NATO's 21st-century peacekeeping will focus on Europe.*

Beyond Europe: Peacekeeping by Regional Bodies

Organization of American States. During the crisis over Haiti in the 1990s, the Organization of American States (OAS) played a major role. In 1991, two days after a military coup ousted the elected president, Jean-Bertrand Aristide, the OAS began applying economic sanctions. Soon afterward, the organization stiffened the sanctions. It ordered a cutoff of almost all trade between Haiti and Western Hemisphere nations. With the OAS leading the way, the United Nations later applied sanctions of its own against Haiti. Eventually, the sanctions caused great hardship in Haiti and helped to weaken the military government. The Haitian junta stepped down in October 1994 under threat of a U.S. invasion.

Haiti was the first test of an OAS policy adopted earlier in 1991 to strengthen democracy in the Western Hemisphere. Ever since its creation 43 years before, the OAS had worked to promote democracy. Its work bore fruit in the 1980s, as several Latin American military regimes gave way to elected governments. Never before had democracy been so widespread in the Americas. OAS leaders wanted to make sure the weak new democracies did not slide back into military rule. So, in June 1991, the OAS authorized its foreign ministers to "adopt any measures deemed appropriate" to restore constitutional rule in any member country that experienced a military coup. In October 1991, the OAS leaders used that authority to place an embargo on Haiti.

The OAS was formed in Bogotá, Colombia, in 1948, at the urging of the United States. Its headquarters are in Washington, D.C. The purposes of the OAS are to prevent military conflict within the Western Hemisphere, to protect the independence of the nations of the Americas from outside aggressors, and to improve the social and political systems of its member states. All 35 nations in the Americas, including Cuba, belong to the OAS. (Cuba, however, was suspended from OAS activities in 1962.)

The success of the OAS has depended on U.S. support for its policies and goals. During the cold war, U.S. efforts to transform the organization into an anti-Communist alliance aroused Latin American resentment. Also resented were actions taken by the United States to contain communism in Cuba and to oppose leftist governments or movements in Guatemala, the Dominican Republic, Chile, El Salvador, and Nicaragua. Actions such as the U.S. invasion of the island of Grenada in 1983 and the intervention in Panama in 1989 completely ignored the OAS charter and reduced the effectiveness of the organization. In addition, many Latin Americans resented the U.S. position during the Falkland Islands War of 1982. U.S. leaders did nothing to prevent British military forces from entering the Western Hemisphere to fight Argentina over the disputed islands.

After the cold war, U.S. policy shifted in favor of stronger cooperation with the OAS. President George H. Bush made the encouragement of democracy and human rights the focus of this policy. To further improve the security and unity of the hemisphere, he negotiated a free trade agreement with Mexico and Canada, the North American Free Trade Agreement (NAFTA). President Clinton continued these policies. The United States consulted with the OAS about its actions in the Haiti crisis. And it supported OAS policies in Peru when, in 1992, President Fujimori suspended constitutional government there. The OAS sent a mission to Peru and monitored elections that restored a measure of democracy to the country.

President George W. Bush began his administration in 2001 by declaring his intention to focus U.S. foreign policy on relations with Latin America. This was prevented by the 9/11/01 terrorist attacks on the United States and the wars in Afghanistan and Iraq. In March 2007, Bush went on a five-nation tour of Latin America aimed at improving relations between the United States and a region in which democracy is yielding to the kind of anti-American populism of leaders such as Hugo Chávez of Venezuela. While Bush attempted to promote free trade, Latin Americans expressed anger at Bush's failure to keep his promise to legalize illegal immigrants and guest workers in the United States.

The success of the OAS depends upon the support of the United States. Some OAS members, however, have described the United States as an imperialist power and a negative world influence.

◆ *Describe the relationship between the United States and the Organization of American States.*

African Union. The Organization of African Unity (OAU) decided in July 2001 to transform itself into the African Union. It is modeled on the European Union, with close trade ties and a number of common institutions. Those institutions may eventually include an African parliament, a court of justice, and a central bank.

The OAU was born in May 1963, at a time when colonialism was crumbling and many African nations were gaining independence. The original 32 member states sought to coordinate cultural, scientific, political, and economic policies; end colonialism in Africa; and defend their independence. By 2001, membership had risen to 53 nations. The central headquarters of the OAU were in Addis Ababa, Ethiopia, as are those of the African Union.

The OAU was long seen as weak. It failed to address problems such as human rights violations by dictators, for fear of splitting the organization. And it avoided discussion of many controversial issues. This silence was due to a key principle of the OAU— not to interfere in member nations' internal affairs.

Nevertheless, the OAU had its successes. It helped to finance the work of the African National Congress to end apartheid and white-minority rule in South Africa. It also played a key role in ending white colonialism in Namibia and Zimbabwe. In 2000, it helped to arrange a peace treaty between Ethiopia and Eritrea.

However, the OAU was unable to make peace between the warring factions in Somalia, Sudan, or Angola. It did respond to the request of Western Saharans for independence from Morocco by admitting the Sahrawi Arab Democratic Republic to OAU membership in 1984. Morocco reacted by withdrawing from the OAU.

Although the OAU settled some African conflicts, it was always financially weak. It could not compel members to pay their dues. It had no armed forces or other means of enforcing its decisions. Still, it was the only African organization with even a limited capability to address the massive problems of the continent.

In 2007, the African Union sent Ugandan troops to Somalia. The AU peacekeepers were intended to replace Ethiopian troops in Mogadishu, the capital. The Ethiopians had been supporting the legitimate government of Somalia against Islamist rebels.

Arab League. The Arab League, founded with British encouragement in March 1945, started with seven members. Eventually, its membership grew to 22 countries. In 1979, the league moved its headquarters from Cairo to Tunis after expelling Egypt for violating Arab solidarity and making peace with Israel. The league readmitted Egypt in 1988, returning its headquarters to Cairo.

The league encourages cultural, economic, and communication ties among members. It mediates disputes between Arab nations and represents them in certain international negotiations. It also has coordinated a military, diplomatic, and economic offensive against Israel, with whom several of the league members have been at war since 1948. A controversial decision was the Arab League's creation of a committee in October 2000 to support a renewed Palestinian *intifada,* or uprising, against Israel after a breakdown of Middle East peace negotiations.

Immediately after Iraq invaded Kuwait in 1990, Egypt and Saudi Arabia sponsored a resolution authorizing the military forces of the Arab League to cooperate with U.S. and British troops in the Persian Gulf War. A minority of league members objected to this decision. Although a majority of Arab League members supported the U.S.-led coalition that drove Iraqi forces out of Kuwait, postwar divisions within the league limited its effectiveness as a peacemaker.

The March 2003 invasion of Iraq by U.S. and British forces and the 2006 conflict between Israel and the Hezbollah forces in Lebanon were opposed by the Arab League. In March 2007, an Arab League document called the Arab Peace Initiative received international attention as a possible agenda for a new effort to achieve peace between Israel and the Palestinians. The plan originated with Saudi Arabia's King Abdullah and was adopted by all Arab League members in 2002. It offers Israel peace and normal relations in return for release by Israel of the territories occupied in the 1967 war and accepting a "just" settlement for the Palestinian refugees.

Association of Southeast Asian Nations. The Association of Southeast Asian Nations (ASEAN) was formed in 1967. Its current members are Brunei, Cambodia, Indonesia, Laos, Malaysia, Myanmar, the Philippines, Singapore, Thailand, and Vietnam. The major purpose of ASEAN is to promote economic, social, and cultural cooperation among the states of the region. It has requested Japan to increase investment in its member countries and to make Japanese markets more open to them. ASEAN has also played a peacekeeping role. In 1992–1993, for example, the organization helped resettle Cambodian refugees returning to their country after its disastrous civil war. In the 21st century, some ASEAN members have benefited from Chinese investment in industrial development and improvements in transportation, communication, and agriculture. Eager to expand its influence in southeast Asia, China's money is offered without accompanying demands for improvements in human rights, environmental restrictions, or changes in taxation or public spending. Such requirements typically accompany financial aid from the International Monetary Fund (IMF) or other Western sources.

1. *List three regional organizations and explain how effective each one has been at peacekeeping.*

2. *Complete the following sentences:*
   a. *After the cold war, the United States changed its policy in the Western Hemisphere by _____ .*
   b. *Peacekeeping in Africa in the 1990s has been made difficult by _____ .*
   c. *In response to Iraq's 1990 invasion of Kuwait, the Arab League _____ .*

The International Trade in Weapons

In early 2007, Ivan Safronov, defense correspondent for a leading Russian newspaper, allegedly committed suicide by jumping out the fifth-floor window of an apartment block. The retired colonel turned journalist had been an irritant to the Russian army because he often exposed their secret weapons deals. Before he died, Safranov was investigating the sale of Russian arms and military jets via Belarus to Syria and Iran. Russia's Federal Security Service (FSB) had warned him not to publish the story.

The United States has dominated the global weapons market in the developing world. In 2005, however, Russia surpassed it as the leader in weapons sales to developing nations. Russian deals in 2005 included selling $700 million in surface-to-air missiles to Iran and eight aerial refueling tankers to China. Russia has also sold to China fighter aircraft, destroyers with antiship missiles, and diesel submarines. These purchases have been part of China's effort to transform its huge land-based ground force into a more mobile, diversified, high-tech military one.

While the world's leaders often denounce the trade in arms, they also encourage it. For years, U.S. administrations have actively assisted U.S. corporations in winning arms contracts from allied nations. After the cold war ended, with the U.S. government scaling back its own arms purchases, efforts to boost U.S. arms sales abroad took on a new urgency. U.S. arms manufacturers had to lay off workers, cut back research, and consolidate operations. In order to keep the arms industry from collapsing, government officials stepped up the promotion of sales to other countries.

In October 2006, it became known that the Pentagon runs a little publicized giveaway and bargain sale program to dispose of its unwanted weapons. The Pentagon also uses the Excess Defense Articles program to reward friends and allies of the United States.

Pakistan and Jordan acquired, in 2006, a number of used F-16 Falcon jets. Afghanistan received 75 used armored personnel carriers. The coast guard of Yemen obtained a small fleet of 30-year-old sea rescue lifeboats. The Pentagon program disposed of $1.56 billion worth of a wide range of military weapons and equipment. The program was expected to expand in 2007.

Helicopters, torpedoes, airplanes, launching craft, cargo trucks, radar systems, missiles, ammunition, uniforms, and other weapons and equipment worth $8 billion were given away or sold at very low prices between 2000 and 2005 to countries that cannot afford brand new equipment. Recent recipients have been the Philippines, Morocco, and the Dominican Republic.

Critics of the Excess Defense Articles program have said it contributes to a global arms race. U.S. military contractors fear that the used weapons may compete with new products they are trying to sell overseas.

The major nations do try to put limits on the sale of certain weapons, especially such modern ones as missiles. They also try to control sales of technology that might have military applications. Two main agreements help to coordinate those controls. The Missile Technology Control Regime (MTCR) was started in 1987 by the United States, Canada, France, Germany, Italy, Japan, and the United Kingdom. Several other nations have signed on since. The MTCR seeks to restrict exports of all but the shortest-range ballistic and cruise missiles. A separate agreement deals with exports in general, especially exports of military technology and machinery that serve military purposes. This agreement targets sales to such "troublesome" states as Iraq, Iran, North Korea, and Libya.

Although China did not sign the MTCR, it did agree to cooperate with the controls. Nevertheless, Beijing sold sensitive missile technology to Pakistan. China also purchased advanced military technology from Israel. In its efforts to prod China into cooperation, the United States has from time to time cut off China's purchases of high-tech American goods.

Other limitations in the sales of arms have been decreed by the United Nations. For example, the U.N. placed an embargo on arms sales to the former Yugoslavia, hoping to limit the fighting in Croatia and Bosnia. Supporters of Bosnia criticized the embargo as one-sided, saying it hurt the Bosnian government forces more than it hurt the Bosnian Serbs. More recently, the U.N. placed an arms embargo on Ethiopia and Eritrea when those two African nations fought a prolonged war.

♦ *State the contradiction in U.S. policy governing weapons sales.*

In the developing world, the leading buyer of weapons systems in the 21st century has been India, followed by Saudi Arabia and China. Iran has purchased SA-15 Gauntlet surface to air missile systems from Russia, in addition to SU-24 bombers, MiG-29 fighter aircraft, and T-72 battle tanks.

North Korea shipped ballistic missiles to other nations from 2001 to 2005—the only nation to have done so. Transfers of these weapons are prohibited under international agreements to control the trade of ballistic missiles.

By 2003, North Korea had developed missiles that can reach the western United States. In the same year, North Korea announced its intention to build nuclear weapons. In response, China organized a series of diplomatic negotiations involving itself, North Korea, Japan, the United States, and South Korea. The purpose of the talks has been to persuade North Korea to dismantle its nuclear weapons program in return for more food and energy assistance. Nevertheless, North Korea conducted a

Arms for Sale

small nuclear test explosion in 2006. A tentative agreement was reached in February 2007 that required North Korea to close its main facility to produce plutonium. It also allowed nuclear inspectors to return in exchange for shipments of heavy fuel oil. North Korea also demanded that sanctions be lifted on its funds frozen in a bank in Macao since 2005.

In March 2007, the British Parliament voted to renew Britain's nuclear deterrent by creating a new generation of nuclear submarines to carry U.S.-supplied Trident missiles. Many Britons opposed this measure, claiming that it would maintain the "balance of terror" and fuel the development of new nuclear weapons systems around the world.

1. *Explain how the international arms trade has increased the difficulty of global peacekeeping.*

2. *Indicate which statements are true and which are false. Correct each false statement.*
   a. *The United States tries to block weapons sales to Iran.*
   b. *Russia and China were among the nations that set up the Missile Technology Control Regime (MTCR).*
   c. *North Korea's army of more than one million soldiers worries both South Korea and Japan.*
   d. *China was among the customers for Israeli armaments.*
   e. *A U.N. arms embargo prevented the United States from selling weapons to the government of Bosnia.*

Chapter 8 Review

A. *Choose the item that best completes each sentence.*

1. *Following the end of the cold war, U.N. peacekeeping efforts were expanded to include   (a) internal conflicts, such as civil wars   (b) the defense of entire continents   (c) the restructuring of the governments of member nations.*

2. *In 2007, a U.N. cease-fire plan resulted in the withdrawal of Israeli troops from   (a) Syria   (b) Iraq   (c) Lebanon.*

3. *Critics of the peacekeeping efforts of the United Nations in recent years raised doubts about   (a) the training and funding of troops sent on peacekeeping missions   (b) the domination of the Security Council by the United States, Britain, and France   (c) both of these.*

4. After the cold war, nations that wanted seats on the Security Council included (a) Brazil and Germany (b) Armenia and Azerbaijan (c) Bosnia and Macedonia (d) Iraq and Iran.

5. At the Prague conference of 2002, the NATO allies dealt with (a) an invasion of Russia (b) development of a Rapid Reaction Force (c) rejection of new members from Eastern Europe.

6. NATO's 1994 intervention in Bosnia was the first time the organization (a) was commanded by a U.S. general (b) carried out a military strike (c) expanded beyond its original membership.

7. The regional organization that led the way for U.N. efforts to bring an end to the crisis in Haiti was the (a) Organization of African Unity (b) Arab League (c) Organization of American States.

8. The regional organization that supported the U.N. effort to liberate Kuwait from Iraq, in 1991, was the (a) Organization of African Unity (b) Arab League (c) Organization of American States.

9. Major suppliers of weapons that are traded on the world market include (a) Venezuela and Colombia (b) Russia and the United States (c) Japan and Vietnam.

10. Two nations that the United States wants to prevent from acquiring modern weapons are (a) Saudi Arabia and Kuwait (b) Italy and Canada (c) Iran and North Korea.

B. Reread "The United Nations After the Cold War," on pages 165–168. Then write a sentence or two to define or identify each of the following.

1. former Yugoslavia

2. Muhammad Farah Aydid

3. "no-fly" zone

4. Security Council

C. Reread "The International Trade in Weapons, " on pages 177–180. Then complete each of the following sentences:

1. To help keep the peace, the United States and other powers have attempted to limit _____ .

2. After the cold war, the U.S. government urgently supported arms sales by U.S. companies in order to _____ .

3. In 2005, Russia surpassed the United States as _____ .

4. Many nations have acquired used weapons at little or no cost from _____ .

5. Neighboring nations worry about North Korea because _____ .

D. Use information in the chapter to explain why you AGREE or DISAGREE with the following statements:

1. The United States should support global peacekeeping efforts by giving more financial and military support to the United Nations.

2. Regional organizations such as NATO should be authorized to use force to halt all internal disputes and conflicts between nations.

Chapter 9

Human Rights: Issues and Problems

In October 2001, a small foreign man named Purna was video-taping New York street scenes to take home to his family in Nepal. He did not know that an office of the Federal Bureau of Investigation (FBI) was located in one of the buildings he was taping. Purna, a Buddhist who spoke no English, was arrested by the FBI. Although he was not suspected of anything other than the videotaping, he was placed in solitary confinement in a federal detention center in Brooklyn. Swallowed by the U.S. government's new maximum security system of secret detention and secret hearings, Purna spent three months in solitary confinement before a Legal Aid lawyer was able to obtain his release and have him sent home to Nepal.

The released prisoner had spent his time in a six-by-nine-foot cell kept lighted 24 hours a day. Purna had been stripped naked and handled roughly. A subsequent investigation by the U.S. Department of Justice revealed a pattern of abuse of prisoners in this federal detention center. These included prisoners being strip-searched, slammed into walls, and subjected to secret video-tapings of conversations with lawyers.

Purna's only offense was that his tourist visa had expired. Following the September 11, 2001 terrorist attacks on the United States, however, the Justice Department instructed immigration judges to handle all "special interest" cases in closed courtrooms, without visitors or family, and with little access to lawyers. Visa violators could be held indefinitely.

Human rights advocates in the United States and around the world have questioned the denial of basic civil liberties as a means of increasing national security and fighting terrorism. These doubts were increased with the passage in October 2001 of the Uniting and Strengthening America by Providing Appropriate Tools Required to Intercept and Obstruct Terrorism Act of 2001. This law is more commonly known as the USA Patriot Act. It provides the federal government with greatly expanded police powers, including detention of suspects without trial or access to a lawyer, searches of homes and offices without warrants, and investigation of bank accounts, e-mails, credit card accounts, and drug prescriptions. Supporters of the law claim that the government must have these powers to protect citizens from terrorists. Critics fear that the expansion of police powers in the name of security will destroy individual freedom and human rights. In March 2006, the Patriot Act was renewed but with modest new curbs on the government's power to probe library, bank, and other records. Congressional critics of the act insisted on the new limits after learning that in December 2005, President Bush had authorized the National Security Agency to secretly wiretap U.S. residents without warrants.

The same concerns have been applied to the detention of prisoners captured in Afghanistan and Iraq and held at the U.S. naval base in Guantánamo Bay, Cuba. In 2004, the U.S. Supreme Court limited the federal government's ability to detain people indefinitely. Bush administration lawyers had argued that in wartime the president has the right to hold enemy combatants for the duration of the war. Human rights groups and other critics of the government's policy complained that the approximately 590 prisoners had been given no opportunity to challenge their detentions in court.

In mid-2004, the world was shocked by reports of the abuse of Iraqi prisoners by U.S. Army personnel at the Abu Ghraib prison in Iraq after the American-led invasion and occupation. Torture, humiliation, and resulting deaths were blamed on serious defects in training, organization, and policy regarding military detention operations in Iraq and Afghanistan.

America's problems with human rights in the Middle East and at home have been related to crises in other countries. Groups concerned with improving human rights have worked with the office of the U.N. high commissioner for human rights. That office was regarded by many as being ineffective. In 2007, it was replaced by a Human Rights Council.

Human Rights: The Historical Background

The idea that the way governments treat their own citizens should matter to the rest of the world gained acceptance after World War II. As the world became aware of the atrocities committed by Nazi Germany, a concern for human rights became a mandate for the founders of the United Nations. The U.N. Charter, adopted in 1945, stated that the organization "shall promote . . . universal respect for, and observance of, human rights and fundamental freedoms for all without distinction as to race, sex, language, or religion." In 1948, the U.N. explained what was meant by "human rights" in the Universal Declaration of Human Rights. This statement of commitment was adopted by the U.N. General Assembly, with no votes against. However, the Soviet Union, the East European nations, South Africa, and Saudi Arabia abstained from voting on the declaration. In subsequent years, the nations of the world further committed themselves to respect human rights through a number of international agreements. These included the European Convention on Human Rights (1950), the International Covenant on Civil and Political Rights (1966), the American Convention on Human Rights (1969), the Helsinki Accords (1975), and the African Charter on People's and Human Rights (1981).

Citizens in many countries formed nongovernmental organizations to seek compliance with the provisions of those agreements. NGOs became a force in shaping international public opinion by speaking out against nations that violated human rights. Nevertheless, most governments did not react strongly to abuses of human rights by other governments until the 1980s.

During the 1980s, a number of governments joined in making human rights a goal of their foreign policies. The Scandinavian countries and the Netherlands began issuing reports on the human rights practices of governments to which they were giving economic aid. Canada and Australia made the promotion of human rights an important part of their participation in international affairs. The Council of Europe made Turkey's application for membership conditional on improving its human rights practices. The European Union made human rights practices an important part of its economic relations with several countries.

♦ *Explain how and why a concern for human rights developed after World War II.*

In the United States, President Ronald Reagan believed that free elections were a key human right. Thus, a focus on elections dominated U.S. policy on human rights during the 1980s. It led the United States to help remove from power anti-Communist dictators and military rulers to whom the Reagan administration had initially been friendly. For example, the U.S. played a role in ousting President Ferdinand Marcos from the Philippines in 1986 and in ending the dictatorship of Augusto Pinochet in Chile in 1989. Nonetheless, the United States continued to maintain close relations with other anti-Communist governments (in Paraguay, for example) that held no free elections and abused human rights.

This stress on human rights deterred many governments from crushing domestic critics protesting human rights violations and lack of democratic procedures. Fear of other nations' condemnation and loss of Western economic aid led to reforms in such countries as Argentina (1983) and Uruguay (1985). The human rights cause also led to revolts to (1) remove dictators in Haiti and the Philippines (1986) and (2) force democratic elections in South Korea (1987). Worldwide condemnation targeted China's violent repression of student demands for democratic reform (1989). And there was a peaceful transition from communism to multiparty democracy in neighboring Mongolia, as well as movement toward democracy in Nepal.

The rights revolution continued into the 21st century. In 2004, dozens of countries urged the U.S. Supreme Court to block the execution of murderers who kill before the age of 18. The petitioners condemned execution of juveniles as inhumane. International attention was captured by a human disaster in the western Darfur region of Sudan. To defeat a rebellion that began in early 2003, the Sudanese government encouraged Arab militias to attack local black Africans. Both the U.N. and the United States have protested the deaths of tens of thousands and the expulsion from their homes of more than a million people. In June 2004, Israel's Supreme Court ordered that country's Defense Ministry to alter the path of its West Bank separation barrier to make it less burdensome on the Palestinians. Intended to protect Israelis from terrorist attacks by separating them from West Bank Palestinians, the barrier has been condemned by human rights groups and by the International Court of Justice. In a 2004 report on human rights by the Ombudsperson Institute, the U.N. mission in Kosovo and local Albanian leaders were criticized for failing to provide even minimal protection of the rights and freedoms of the province's Serbian minority. Nearly one million people marched in Hong Kong, in July 2004, to criticize China's government and to demand democratic elections. In February 2007, the International Court of Justice, the U.N.'s highest court, called the massacre of Bosnian Muslims by Bosnian Serb forces in 1995 an act of genocide. Although Serbia was not itself found guilty of the crime, the ruling stressed that other large-scale killings and abuse of Bosnian Muslims had taken place with the financial and military support of Serbia during the 1990 war that broke up Yugoslavia.

1. *List three international agreements about human rights.*
2. *Evaluate U.S. policy on human rights during the 1980s.*
3. *Identify human rights victories in Latin America and Asia.*

War Crimes Trials

International interest in human rights focused not only on governments but also on individuals, especially people accused of war crimes. After World War II, special courts tried several German and Japanese leaders, convicted many, and sentenced those found guilty to prison or death. No further war crimes trials were held until the 1990s.

During the crisis in Bosnia, the United Nations set up an international war crimes tribunal for the former Yugoslavia in The Hague, Netherlands. In 1994 it set up another special court, in Arusha, Tanzania, to try people accused of atrocities in the Rwandan bloodbath. The International Criminal Court (ICC) was established in July 2002. Its function is to try individuals accused of genocide, war crimes, or other crimes against humanity. Its first arrest warrants were issued in 2005 in connection with war crimes in Uganda. In early 2007, ICC prosecutors were seeking the arrest of warlords from four African nations on charges ranging from conscripting children as soldiers to murder, torture, and sexual violence.

The United States has opposed the treaty that created the ICC, citing concerns that U.S. military personnel might be unjustly accused of war crimes and tried without the protection of rights guaranteed by the U.S. Constitution. Although the United States signed the ICC treaty in 2000, its ratification was prevented after the administration of President George W. Bush rejected the treaty. By November 2006, 102 nations had become ICC members.

The court's 18 judges are elected by the member nations. China, Japan, Russia, and the United States were not members in 2007.

The tribunals for Yugoslavia and Rwanda pursued many cases. Among those charged with war crimes by the court for Yugoslavia were two Bosnian Serb leaders, Radovan Karadzic and Ratko Mladic, and a Serbian leader, Slobadan Milosevic. All refused to give themselves up, but Serbia turned Milosevic over for trial. The Hague tribunal also tried, and sometimes convicted, lower level officials and soldiers. In 1998, the U.N. tribunal for Rwanda convicted a former Rwandan leader and sentenced him to life in prison. His was the first genocide conviction by an international court.

♦ *Explain why you AGREE or DISAGREE with the following statement: War crimes trials are an unfair punishment of the defeated by the victorious.*

Immigrants and Aliens in Europe

In recent years, world disorder has resulted in a dramatic increase in the number of people fleeing their homelands to avoid war or persecution. Turmoil in the former Yugoslav republics and in some Central Asian republics of the former Soviet Union, as well as in Iraq and in such African countries as Rwanda, Liberia, Sierra Leone, and Congo, created millions of refugees. The civil war in Bosnia and Croatia alone displaced 3½ million people.

© Peter Schrank, peter.schrank@ukonline.uk

Since the collapse of communism in Eastern Europe, millions of people have moved across Europe. While the western portion of the continent has been the favored destination of many migrants, both legal and illegal, more have chosen the United States and Russia. This has been due partly to ethnic Russians returning to the motherland after the breakup of the Soviet Union. Also, Tajiks, Georgians, Moldovans, and other non-Slav citizens of former Soviet republics have moved to Russia in search of work. Georgia, for example, lost a fifth of its population between 1989 and 2003.

The 21st-century expansion of the European Union has also contributed to the movement of migrants across the continent. In 2004, eight Eastern European countries, Cyprus, and Malta joined the EU. Britain, Ireland, and Sweden granted unlimited access to their job markets to Eastern Europeans. In the next two years, about 450,000 Eastern Europeans migrated to employment in Britain.

According to a 2007 World Bank report, millions of migrants have been inspired by the dream of hard work abroad leading to a better life at home. Remittances (money earned in a foreign country but sent to families in the home country) have been estimated by the World Bank at around $19 billion annually. In some countries, remittances matter more than foreign investment. For ten former communist countries—Moldova, Bosnia, Albania, Tajikistan, Serbia, Armenia, Kyrgyzstan, Georgia, Macedonia, and Hungary—remittances have provided 5 percent of national income. In this region, three-quarters of the remittance money has come from immigrants working in the European Union.

Reactions to Immigrants. Almost all of the new arrivals required economic support from their host nations. Since the influx of immigrants in the 1990s came at a time of economic downturn throughout Western Europe, high levels of unemployment and shortages of housing caused increased resentment of the new arrivals. Many West Europeans were alarmed by the arrival of so many poor newcomers who lacked technical skills and differed in language, culture, religion, and sometimes race. The result was an increase in *ultranationalism*—an extreme attachment to one's own country, often accompanied by feelings of superiority to foreigners. Ultranationalists aimed to restrict immigration. Sometimes they used violence to intimidate aliens.

The new arrivals benefited the Western European economies, mostly by filling the need for lower skilled workers. Nevertheless, there has been massive public hostility to immigration in Britain and other countries. It has been claimed that the new arrivals strain resources on hospitals, schools, and public services. In response, the British government announced in October 2006 that only the most skilled migrant workers from Bulgaria and Romania would be allowed into Britain. These two countries became the newest EU members in January 2007. Also, lower skilled migrants from outside the EU were banned from entering Britain.

In 2005, France experienced three weeks of rioting and car burning in rough *banlieue* neighborhoods across the country. This was repeated on a smaller scale in 2006. *Banlieues* are poor suburbs inhabited mainly by immigrants and the children of immigrants, largely of North African and black African origin. Many are Muslim. Islam is the second largest religion in France. However, the riots were not caused by Islamic extremism. They were a protest against unemployment among the young and a lack of social mobility. France has always had a strong sense of national identity. Its doctrine of integrating immigrants and molding them into French citizens has not succeeded with the most recent arrivals—Algerians, Moroccans, Malians, Ivorians, and Senegalese—and their children. Racial discrimination on a large scale has produced a large jobless, multiethnic underclass. The lack of nonwhite faces in the upper levels of French society has resulted in tensions that explode into violence.

The *banlieue* riots increased French concerns with crime and security. Jean-Marie Le Pen, leader of the far right National Front Party, has made opposition to immigration his platform. In August 2006, Foreign Minister Nicolas Sarkozy ordered the deportation of illegal immigrants.

♦ *Explain the benefits and problems connected with 21st century immigration in Western Europe.*

Most European nations have taken steps to restrict illegal immigrants. They introduced rigorous checks to identify and expel foreign students and residents who took jobs illegally. They set up new ways to monitor short-term visitors. Among those most affected have been refugees from war-torn countries such as Iraq and Afghanistan.

The Dutch government decided to deport 26,000 asylum seekers from such countries as Yugoslavia, Iraq, Iran, and Afghanistan by 2006. Many of them claimed to be in danger of imprisonment or execution if returned home. The Dutch government did not believe them; officials stated that many requesting political asylum were actually seeking economic and social opportunities and, therefore, did not qualify for asylum. Subsequently, a newly elected parliament voted to freeze the deportation of rejected asylum seekers. However, immigration has remained Holland's hottest political issue.

In Russia, ethnic nationalism and opposition to non-Slavic immigrants, mostly from former Soviet republics of the Caucasus and Central Asia, had resulted in approximately one racist murder a week by early 2007. However, concern about the declining birthrate has led to President Vladimir Putin's statements about attracting more ethnic Russians to return from the other former Soviet states. More practically, new rules designed to make it easier for foreigners to work legally in Russia were introduced in 2007. The federal migration service has estimated that 8 to 12 million people were working in Russia illegally.

In mid-2004, European business and political leaders held an international conference in Marrakech, Morocco. Their main concern was declining European birthrates. Demographic projections show that many European countries will lose population at a rapid rate in several generations. (This will not happen in the United States, owing to immigration.) The Russian population is shrinking by around 750,000 per year. This decline is a result of the catastrophic death rate—by violence, heart disease, tuberculosis, and AIDS—among working-age men.

The European birthrate is too low to provide sufficient numbers of future workers. An obvious solution would be to welcome immigrants, especially from North African and other Arab countries that do not have declining birthrates. Europeans, however, fear that immigrants will prove to be terrorists, welfare recipients, or workers taking jobs when unemployment is already high.

By 2006, the number of immigrants entering Germany had declined sharply, while the number of Germans leaving the country had increased. Political and business leaders, once concerned about too many immigrants, began to worry about the number of young Germans leaving for greater economic and educational opportunities in the United States, Britain, Switzerland, and elsewhere. An unemployment rate of 10 percent and the slowest economic growth in the European Union contributed to a "brain drain" of doctors, engineers, and other professionals. In response,

German universities and local authorities created "welcome centers" to attract skilled foreigners, helping them get residence permits, find homes, and enroll in language classes.

1. *Explain why immigration became a major political issue in Europe in the late 20th and early 21st centuries.*

2. *Tell which of the following statements are* true *and which are* false. *Rewrite incorrect statements to make them true.*

   a. *The number of illegal aliens in Western Europe in recent years exceeded the number of legal immigrants.*
   b. *Germany had more foreign residents than any other European country.*
   c. *Violence against foreigners occurred only in Germany.*
   d. *Many European nations passed laws to restrict immigration.*
   e. *Holland's decision to expel asylum seekers was opposed by most Dutch citizens.*

Ultranationalism

Ultranationalism—the belief that one's own nation is superior to all others—often goes hand in hand with racism. In many countries, ultranationalism has led to hatred of foreigners, especially immigrants and migrant workers.

In the early 1990s, newly unified Germany faced serious problems. High among them was the threat that neo-Nazis and other right-wingers posed to democracy. In 1992, officials of Chancellor Helmut Kohl's conservative government began branding the rightists as terrorists, to be treated seriously. Germany's federal prosecutor expressed the belief that the aim of the right-wingers was to reestablish a National Socialist (that is, Nazi) dictatorship.

Right-wing extremists stress the biological inequality of people, races, and the sexes. They advocate subordination of individual rights to those of the nation. They engage in acts of violence against asylum seekers and guest workers. They are often anti-Semitic. In Germany and other nations, ultranationalists deny the crimes of the Nazis, claiming that the Holocaust—the murder of six million Jews and three million other Europeans during World War II—did not happen, despite overwhelming evidence to the contrary. In the 21st century, anti-Semitism and violence against Jews have risen in Europe. In response, some European governments have made denial of the Holocaust a crime.

Sellers of Hate

Neo-Nazism is regarded as the form of ultranationalism that is most dangerous to democracy and human rights. Its characteristics vary but often include allegiance to Adolf Hitler (dictator of Germany from 1933–1945), use of the swastika and other Nazi insignia, anti-Semitism, racism, *xenophobia* (hatred of foreigners), *homophobia* (hatred of homosexuals), and belief in nationalism and militarism. In the 21st century, neo-Nazism has become a global phenomenon with organized groups in every Western nation, as well as strong cooperative networks and connections among groups internationally.

Euronationalism is a newer form of neo-Nazism that has appeared in recent years. Its members attempt to appear moderate and mainstream while promoting prejudice, especially against Muslims and nonwhite asylum seekers. This movement has appeared in the United States and Canada in the form of racial organizations that claim to shed legitimate scientific light on genetic racial differences.

The most prominent neo-Nazi groups in the United States have been the American Nazi Party and the Aryan Brotherhood. U.S.-based neo-Nazi and similar groups often have Web sites, occasionally hold public demonstrations, and maintain international ties to groups in Europe and elsewhere. However, they represent a small minority of the population and are hampered by federal laws that impose extra penalties for hate crimes.

Several British groups have been also described as neo-Nazi. They include the British Nationalist Party, which has been linked to violent attacks on Asian immigrants as well as on Britons of Indian and Pakistani descent, the White Nationalist Party, and Combat 18. A Belgian neo-Nazi organization (called Blood, Land, Honor, and Faithfulness) came to public notice in September 2006, when 17 of its members were arrested under antiterrorist laws and laws against racism and anti-Semitism. The suspects were accused of preparing terrorist attacks to destabilize Belgium.

Greek neo-Nazis have been tied to attacks on immigrants, homosexuals, and leftists. The Blue Army—a nationalist group of football fans—launched a series of riots targeting Albanian immigrants in September 2004.

In Russia, the post-Soviet era has seen the rise of a variety of extremist nationalist political movements. These organizations are characterized by severe xenophobia and anti-Semitism. Some wish to overthrow the government.

There are several neo-Nazi groups active in Germany. They attract a growing number of extremists who prefer to remain apart from far-right political parties. Instead, they build loose autonomous groups, which are called *Kameradschaften* (comrades' organizations). There are an estimated 160 *Kameradschaften* throughout present-day Germany. These organizations are eager to establish contact with international right-wing extremists, especially Combat 18, a British group known for militant violence. The favorite targets of the *Kameradschaften* are foreigners, especially Africans, Turks, and Jews. German law forbids the production of pro-Nazi materials. Such items are smuggled into the country from the United States, Scandinavia, the Czech Republic, Hungary, and Italy. German neo-Nazi Web sites depend mainly on Internet servers in the United States and Canada.

An upsurge in Turkish ultranationalist feeling became pronounced in early 2007. A 17-year-old-gunman shot and killed a Turkish-Armenian newspaper editor, Hrant Dink, because he "insulted the Turks." The murder was viewed as an example of xenophobic nationalism aimed at Turkey's non-Muslim minorities and the Kurds, as well as Turkish advocates of improved human rights for these groups. Nationalist military officers and politicians have encouraged Turks to believe that the Western powers (the U.S. and the EU) are attempting to empower the Kurds and non-Muslim minorities to break up the country. Students in Turkish schools are taught that they have no other friend than the Turks. Kemal Kerincsiz, lawyer and leader of the Turkish

Jurists Union, has launched law cases against pro-human rights Turkish intellectuals under a law that makes insulting Turkishness a criminal offense. Mr. Kerincsiz's goal has been to protect the Turkish nation from what he refers to as Western imperialism and global forces that wish to dismember and destroy Turkey. Also, Belma Akcura, an investigative journalist, was jailed for three months in 2006 for writing a book in which she accused Turkish army officers of secretly organizing new ultranationalist groups.

At the root of all this is resentment of reforms legislated in the past four years by the mildly Islamist government of Prime Minister Recep Tayyip Erdoğan. These reforms—aimed at eventually qualifying Turkey for EU membership—have provided more freedom for the Kurds, limitations on the army's powers, and more compromises with Greece over Cyprus (an island inhabited by Greeks and Turks and administered by both nations). These reforms have angered Turkish nationalists, who harass and make death threats to prominent writers and academics who are in favor of the reforms.

1. *Define ultranationalism.*
2. *Explain why neo-Nazism is regarded as a global phenomenon and a threat to democracy and human rights.*
3. *Identify each of the following:*
   a. *Aryan Brotherhood*
   b. *Combat 18*
   c. *Blue Army*

Immigrants and Aliens in the United States

The United States has long been considered a nation of immigrants and a haven for refugees. People from all corners of the globe populated and built America. For much of the nation's history, however, entry into the United States has been regulated by immigration *quotas* (numerical limits) that regulated the number of new arrivals from each country. During the 19th and early 20th centuries, quotas were designed to favor immigrants from Western Europe. In 1965, this discriminatory system was changed to provide applicants from all nations a chance to qualify for permanent residence. By 2007, regulations set an annual limit of 26,500 entry visas for each country.

Migrant Workers and Liberty

Courtesy Cagle Cartoons, Inc.

Recent law has given preference to people with family members who are U.S. citizens or who already reside legally in the United States. Also given preference are workers whose skills are in demand and refugees fleeing war or persecution. Under this system, an average of about 800,000 legal immigrants entered the country annually during the early 2000s. Among the latest arrivals, Asians, Latin Americans, and Africans outnumbered Europeans. Around the world, the number of people hoping to settle in the United States continually increases. In the early 2000s, millions of people were on lists awaiting admission. But many others did not wait. An estimated 300,000 illegal immigrants enter the United States or overstay their visas each year.

Many immigrants face discrimination when looking for work. It is illegal to hire an alien lacking proper immigration documents; employers who do so risk fines and other penalties. Some will not hire any job applicants who "look foreign." Others hire illegals but pay them low wages to do unhealthful or dangerous work. If undocumented workers protest, their bosses may report them to the Immigration and Naturalization Service (INS), which usually results in deportation.

In March 2007, President George W. Bush made a five-country

tour of Latin America. Throughout this tour, Bush received criticism from Latin American leaders for his failure to fulfill promises to improve the lives of immigrants to the U.S. President Óscar Berger of Guatemala, for example, complained about the forced deportations of Guatemalans who enter the U.S. illegally. Repeatedly, Bush was faced with anger over what was perceived as U.S. neglect of the region and frustration with its tougher border security policies in the wake of the 2001 terrorist attacks.

From President Felipe Calderón of Mexico, Bush received criticism of American plans to build a 700-mile fence along the Mexican-U.S. border. Calderón warned that the only way to stem illegal migration and ensure regional security was to raise the standard of living of the Mexican people. This would diminish the economic motivation for immigration to the U.S. Bush responded by repeating his past promise to push for passage of a new immigration law that would allow more guest workers and provide a path to citizenship for many Mexicans living in the U.S. illegally.

Of the 300 million people living in the U.S. in 2007, about 37 million were born in another country. Census figures show that at least one-third of the foreign born come from Mexico. Legal permanent residents are no longer the majority of newcomers. Among new arrivals, illegal immigrants who were smuggled across a border, or overstayed legal visas, outnumber legal immigrants. Approximately 56 percent of illegal immigrants in the United States today come from Mexico.

The smuggling of immigrants into the United States by criminal organizations had become common by the 1990s and continued in the 21st century. Those who pay the smugglers in full are free to seek work on their own. Those who do not pay may be subject to forced labor and physical mistreatment. Some of the immigrants are recruited by gangs for criminal activities. In one notorious case exposed in 1997, some 60 Mexicans were smuggled into New York City to sell trinkets on the street and in the subways. Because the newcomers were deaf, they were especially vulnerable to the demands of their "employers."

1. *Give two possible reasons for someone to immigrate illegally to the United States.*

2. *State some of the problems faced by illegal immigrants.*

By some estimates, more than 40 percent of America's population growth over the next decade will come from immigrants. For *demographers* (scientists who study the rise and fall of population levels and their effects) and economists, this means that the United States will avoid the declining birthrates and shrinking tax bases that are threatening the future of several European countries. Also, immigration has been seen to stimulate economic activity and growth. Immigrants have been called the "entrepreneurial spark plugs" of many American cities. Immigrant businesses have turned dying neighborhoods into centers of commercial activity in New York, Chicago, and other large cities. The recent flow of immigrants to suburbs and small towns may cause a shift of economic stimulation away from the large cities.

However, there are challenges. Immigrant businesspeople often face language barriers, difficulties getting credit, and problems connecting with government and nonprofit agencies that help businesses grow. In New York and other cities, immigrant-friendly mayors have encouraged programs to help small businesses. In 2005, at least 22 of the 100 fastest growing companies in Los Angeles were created by first-generation immigrants.

Reactions Against Immigration. Fear of the consequences of sustained immigration led to a surge of modern nativism. *Nativism*, as ultranationalism in the United States is known, is a belief in the superiority of the native-born. Nativism was also stimulated by other movements, such as zero population growth, environmentalism, and "English-first." Some Americans carried nativism to extremes. Skinheads, white supremacists, and others committed acts of violence against foreigners, much as Europe's neo-Nazis did.

The rise in immigration and reaction against it spurred a national debate. Some political leaders described the rise in immigration as a threat. They said immigrants were adding to the cost of education, health services, police, and other public functions. The influx of immigrants, they argued, unfairly burdened taxpayers, while contributing to unemployment and other social problems.

Politicians from both major parties proposed sweeping measures to limit immigration, legal or illegal. In 1994, voters in California adopted by a three-to-two margin an initiative called Proposition 187. It proposed to block illegal aliens from using public services, such as schools, colleges, and medical facilities, in California. Court challenges eventually blocked the law. On the federal level, in 1996, Congress eliminated welfare and Medicaid benefits for immigrants, even legal immigrants, in their first five years of residency. (Some benefits were later restored.) Also in 1996, Congress passed a law requiring the deportation of all immigrants convicted of certain crimes, even for convictions far in the past.

Anti-immigrant reactions grew in the early 21st century. U.S-born information technology (IT) workers were angered by Congress's votes (1998 and 2000) to issue more visas for skilled, college-educated immigrants. Congress was accused of responding to pressure from high-tech industry leaders to replace U.S. IT workers with lower paid immigrants. Technical workers' fears of job loss increased as high-tech industries exported service jobs to "call centers" in India and elsewhere in Asia.

Accusations of holding "un-American" opinions accompanied a January 2007 debate at a meeting of the city council of a Dallas suburb. A proposed ban on renting apartments to illegal immigrants was revised to allow landlords to rent to families with the head of household or a spouse who has legal residency or citizenship. Opponents of the revision referred to illegal immigration as an invasion. In February 2007, the executive of Suffolk Country, in New York State, outlined a plan to limit the influx of illegal immigrants. Claiming that the basic harmony and quality of life in the Long Island suburbs was threatened, his plan included a crackdown on day laborers and contractors and the assignment of federal immigration officials to the county jail.

Immigrants—both legal and illegal—have been blamed for their failure to learn English. By 2007, however, it was recognized that the demand for English language instruction greatly exceeded opportunities to obtain it. As immigrants increasingly settle away from large cities, many must wait months, or even years, to get into government-financed English classes. Such classes are often overcrowded and lack textbooks. A 2006 survey found that in 12 states, 60 percent of the free English programs had waiting lists ranging from a few months to as long as two years. In Massachusetts, the statewide waiting list had 16,000 names. The U.S. Department of Education counted 1.2 million adults enrolled in public English language programs in 2005.

One of the best-known opponents of immigration in the United States has been Pat Buchanan, an original host of the CNN show *Crossfire*. In his book *State of Emergency: The Third World Invasion and Conquest of America*, Buchanan argues that the wrong sort of people are getting into America. He cites Mexicans, rather then Europeans, as an example. Buchanan claims that Mexican immigrants are engaged in a recapturing of the lands of the Southwest lost in the Texas War of Independence of 1835–1836 and the Mexican War of 1846–1848.

Those who disagree with Mr. Buchanan have urged that the economics of immigration be handled by better laws. They argue that immigrant workers be given a path to citizenship, and those within the immigrant-dependent industries, such as agriculture and hotels, be provided with a realistic framework for legally employing undocumented immigrants.

1. *Explain why human rights organizations became alarmed by American attitudes toward immigration and asylum.*

2. *Explain why you AGREE or DISAGREE with the following statement: European and U.S. responses to immigration differed greatly in the late 20th and early 21st centuries.*

3. *Complete the following sentences:*
   a. *Under current U.S. law, 20,000 _____ .*
   b. *Illegal aliens are often mistreated by _____ .*
   c. *In 1994, California voters decided to _____ .*

The Struggle for Women's Rights

In March 2007, Prime Minister Shinzo Abe of Japan outraged women's groups and human rights advocates around the world by denying that the Japanese military had forced women to act as sex slaves during World War II (1937–1945). Historians have agreed that approximately 200,000 Asian women were forced into military-run brothels and were held against their will. Some of the surviving women testified before a committee of the U.S. House of Representatives and at an international conference in 2007.

Prime Minister Abe is a nationalist who has gained the support of Japanese conservatives by refusing to acknowledge the atrocities committed by Japanese military forces during World War II. This has drawn criticism from China, South Korea, and the Philippines. These countries, occupied by Japan during the war, have demanded that the era be treated with greater historical accuracy.

Although Abe later issued a limited apology to the "comfort women," as the victims were called, he did not meet demands that he clearly acknowledge what had been done to them during the war. Japan has rejected most compensation claims from victims. Instead a private fund established in 1995 by the Japanese government has provided a way for Tokyo to support former sex slaves without offering official government compensation. Many women rejected the payments, demanding government compensation and a parliament-approved apology.

At the Fourth World Conference on Women, held in Beijing in 1995, delegates found much to celebrate. Female literacy was on the rise, for example, and governments were paying greater attention than in the past to women's rights. But the delegates also found much to protest—from systematic rape during the wars in Bosnia and Rwanda to deeply entrenched social, economic, and legal discrimination against women. During the conference, the delegates drew up a "platform for action." They urged the governments they represented to use the document as a guideline for guaranteeing the "full enjoyment by women of their human rights."

One of the lessons of the Beijing conference, and of earlier U.N. conferences, was that women of very different cultures could unite to pursue common goals. Representatives of women's groups flocked to China from all over the world. The nongovernmental organizations held their own, separate conference in a Beijing suburb. They wanted to make themselves heard by government delegates at the official conference.

Of course, the women's groups didn't always agree. And often they emphasized different issues. In some Third World countries, key issues include the selling of women as slaves and the ritual mutilation of young women. In the United States, women's groups typically focus on such issues as reproductive rights and sex discrimination. Issues of sex discrimination include unequal employment and promotion opportunities, salary differences, and sexual harassment. Many issues were common to all the women's groups, however—from sex discrimination to domestic violence (the physical abuse of women within family situations).

Women World Leaders. In recent years, women's rights groups have been encouraged by women achieving leadership positions. At the start of 2004, 15 of the world's 191 nations were headed by women. But the proportion of women in national legislatures had dropped since the 1980s, largely because of the collapse of European communism. Communist nations had set quotas of up to 30 percent for women in office. In 2000, France adopted its own quotas. It required political parties to put forth equal numbers of female and male candidates for most elections.

President Mary Robinson of the Republic of Ireland, in office from 1990 to 1997, was one of Europe's most popular heads of state. On one occasion, a poll of Irish voters gave President Robinson a 93 percent approval rating, compared to the 28 percent rating of the Irish prime minister of the time. When Robinson left office, the presidency was won by another woman, Mary McAleese.

President Vaira Vike-Freiberga became Latvia's head of state in 1999. Tarja Halonen has been president of Finland since 2000. Previously, she served as minister of justice, health minister, and member of parliament.

Angela Merkel took office in November 2005 as the first female *chancellor* (head of government) of Germany. She is also the first former citizen of the German Democratic Republic (East Germany) to lead the reunited Germany, and the first woman to lead Germany since it became a modern nation state in 1871. As of 2007, Ms. Merkel is also the youngest German chancellor since World War II. Considered by *Forbes Magazine* to be the most powerful woman in the world, Ms. Merkel also held the rotating six-month presidency of the European Union in early 2007. In the same year, she became a member of the Council of Women World Leaders. Vital topics of her term in office have been health care reform, future energy development, and development of a new EU constitution.

In Asia and the South Pacific, a number of national leaders were women in 2004. Foremost among them were Prime Minister Khaleda Zia of Bangladesh, President Chandrika Kumaratunga of Sri Lanka, Prime Minister Helen Clark of New Zealand, Executive President Gloria Macapagal Arroyo of the Philippines, and Executive President Megawati Sukarnoputri of Indonesia.

Bangladesh is a mainly Muslim country. Zia served as prime minister of Bangladesh from 1991 to 1996 and again from October 2001. She promoted the education and economic self-sufficiency of women. Another woman, Sheik Hasina Wazed, led Bangladesh from 1996 to 2001.

Indonesia also has a large Muslim population. Sukarnoputri became leader of the country's Democratic Party in 1993, vice president in 2000, and president in 2001. She was defeated in the 2004 election.

In Sri Lanka, a majority of the people are Buddhists. Kumaratunga won a 1994 election that was called "the battle of the widows." Her rival was the widow of an opposition leader killed two weeks before the election by a suicide bomber. Kumaratunga's father served as Sri Lanka's prime minister in the 1950s and was assassinated in 1959, when she was 14. Her husband too was a political figure who was assassinated. Immediately after her election as president, Kumaratunga appointed her 78-year-old mother as prime minister. Another woman, Ratnasiri Wickremanayake, became prime minister in November 2005.

Women Leaders in the United States. In the United States, women experienced political gains with the appointments of Madeleine Albright as the first woman U.S. secretary of state, Condoleezza Rice as the first woman national security adviser, Janet Reno as the first woman U.S. attorney general, Elaine Chao as the first female Asian-American Cabinet member (Secretary of Labor), and Ruth Bader Ginsburg as the second woman Supreme Court justice. (Sandra Day O'Connor, appointed by President Reagan in 1981, was the first.) As a lawyer, Ruth Bader Ginsburg had earlier argued six women's rights cases before the Supreme Court, winning five of them.

The people of New York State elected Hillary Rodham Clinton to the U.S. Senate in November 2000. It was the first time a First Lady of the United States was elected to public office. In January 2007, Senator Clinton was campaigning for the Democratic Party nomination for president of the U.S. In January 2005, Condoleeza Rice became the sixty-sixth secretary of state. Pursuing what she called transformational diplomacy, Dr. Rice addressed vital global issues such as terrorism, the Iraq war, and efforts to negotiate peace between Israelis and Palestinians. The victory of the Democratic Party in the congressional elections of November 2006

Looking for the Big Jobs

enabled Nancy Pelosi to become Speaker of the House of Representatives in January 2007. She is the first woman to hold this powerful legislative post. Speaker Pelosi worked her way up through California's Democratic Party before entering Congress in 1987. She was named minority leader in 2002, becoming the first woman to lead a political party in the history of the U.S. Congress. As Speaker, Ms. Pelosi has led efforts to end U.S. involvement in the Iraq war.

The rise of women in the political arena has been regarded as indicative of significant change in the status of women in the United States in the 21st century.

Women in the Islamic nations and Africa did not make the political and economic gains that women in other societies did. However, beginning in 2004, a vigorous debate on women's rights began across the Middle East.

1. *Compare and contrast the agendas of women's groups in Third World countries and in industrialized countries.*

2. *Match each person in Column A with the correct identification from Column B.*

Column A	Column B
1. Mary McAleese	*a. U.S. secretary of state*
2. Khaleda Zia	*b. Speaker of the House of*
3. Helen Clark	*Representatives*
4. Hillary Clinton	*c. U.S. senator*
5. Condoleezza Rice	*d. president of Ireland*
6. Nancy Pelosi	*e. prime minister of New Zealand*
	f. prime minister of Bangladesh

Poverty and Health Care

For many people, the right to basic health care has become one of the most important of human rights. The availability and quality of health care have varied greatly in global regions and nations.

Between 1970 and 1998, life expectancy at birth in *developing countries*—countries with simple technology, low income for the majority of the people, and few or poorly developed resources—increased from 55 years to 65 years. Also, the number of children in these countries who die before their fifth birthday dropped by half. Those gains were made possible by the increased availability of basic public health services. Standard immunizations, for example, saved approximately 3 million lives each year. Although the gap between rich and poor countries did not narrow in terms of income, it did in the area of health.

Nevertheless, enormous health problems remain. Much of the money spent globally on health services each year is used ineffectively. Also, growing numbers of children and older people are creating new demands on health systems in developing countries.

Global threats to health identified by experts in recent years include drug-resistant forms of malaria and tuberculosis, growing consumption of tobacco in Third World nations, and acquired immune deficiency syndrome (AIDS).

♦ *List some of the major health problems in the world today.*

A Case Study in Public Health: AIDS Drugs and Their Costs. The AIDS epidemic has been wreaking havoc ever since the disease was first identified in 1980. At the start of 2001, an estimated 40 million people were sick with AIDS or were infected with HIV, the virus that causes AIDS. Seventy percent of the victims lived in sub-Saharan Africa. In some African countries, one out of every ten children had lost both parents to AIDS. And in South Africa, Botswana, and Zimbabwe, one out of every seven adults had HIV or AIDS.

HIV/AIDS was a serious threat not just to physical health but also to economic health. When poor people fell ill, they often lost their ability to earn a living—and the national economy lost part of its workforce. In the developed world, HIV and AIDS were treated with a series of drug "cocktails" (combinations of separate drugs) that could cost $10,000 a year or more. The drugs allowed people to live indefinitely with a condition that was otherwise almost always fatal. In Africa, though, few people could afford such expensive treatments—nor could public health services pay.

Why are anti-AIDS drugs so expensive? The cost of manufacturing such drugs is in fact only a small percentage of their selling price. Prices tend to be high because drug companies that have developed and received patents on these drugs enjoy a monopoly on their sale. (A *patent* is an exclusive right to profit from an invention or discovery.) During a 20-year period, patent owners can charge as much as the market will bear, with little fear of competition—at least in countries that respect their patents. Companies like GlaxoSmithKline, Merck, and Bristol-Meyers Squibb argue that the patent system benefits everyone because it provides income that drug companies can use to pay for research on new and better drugs. Without the profit incentive offered by patents, they say, few new drugs would come to market. Critics assert that 20 years is too long for a patent to last. They also argue that drug companies take unreasonably high profits from patented medicines—much more than can be justified by their research costs, which are often supplemented by government-financed research. Critics also argue that patent protection is a form of trade protectionism, like tariffs, and that it is especially harmful to people in developing nations.

In 1997, South Africa passed a law that authorized the government to "comparison shop" for *generic* (non-brand-name) versions of drugs, either licensing their manufacture in South Africa or buying them from low-cost manufacturers in countries like India and South Korea. Thirty-nine major drug companies sued to block South Africa's law, arguing that it violated their patent rights. The suit aroused the anger of health activists in many countries, who demonstrated against "corporate greed" and "price gouging."

Meanwhile, a price war broke out when an Indian company slashed prices on generic AIDS drugs. In response, some big drug companies also cut prices for developing countries. The cost per patient for one patented "cocktail" dropped from $10,000 per year to $1,000. The price cut was in line with a European Union proposal for a lower price scale for developing nations. But it did not match the $600 price for a generic Third World version.

In July 2004, the first clinical trial of generic AIDS drugs in a simple three-in-one pill found that they work as well as brand-name drugs. One Triomune pill twice a day helps patients take all of their medicine more effectively than the more common "cocktails." The trial results were praised by the Global Fund to Fight AIDS, Tuberculosis, and Malaria. This organization buys generic drugs approved by the World Health Organization, including Triomune. So do several African countries.

A $15 billion AIDS emergency fund was established by President Bush in 2003. However, the funding was to be used for costly brand-name drugs in treatment programs run by nongovernmental agencies. Among the 15 nations selected as recipients, 12 were African countries. Their governments protested against a U.S.-controlled program inconsistent with their own plans and preferences. Eventually, the American plan was made more collaborative. Money was directed into health clinics, laboratories, testing centers, AIDS treatment and prevention, and the care of orphans.

1. *What complaints did health activists make about patent protection and its effect on the price of anti-AIDS drugs?*

2. *What arguments did big drug companies make in favor of patent protection?*

Government-Aided Health Insurance. To secure for citizens their right to basic health care, several nations have developed government-funded and -regulated national health services. National health plans are common in most industrialized countries of the West, although lately, countries like Britain, Sweden, and Canada have been cutting back services. The United States has no comparable program, although Medicare and Medicaid provide government-backed health insurance for the elderly and some of the poor.

In the United States, most people receive medical and health services through insurance plans funded jointly by employers and employees. Coverage varies greatly, however, and health-related costs have risen rapidly. Millions of Americans have only limited access to medical services. The unemployed, the elderly, and others obtain basic services with difficulty, if at all. Congress rejected a plan proposed by President Clinton in 1993 that would have created a system to provide universal health care. At that time, there were more than 35 million uninsured Americans. By the early 21st century, this total had grown to more than 42 million.

1. *Explain why you AGREE or DISAGREE with the following statement: Access to basic health care is a fundamental human right.*

2. *What signs have there been that public health in developing countries has been improving?*

3. *Why have the prices of anti-AIDS drugs in developing nations begun to drop?*

4. *Tell which of the following statements are* true *and which are* false. *Rewrite incorrect statements to make them true.*

   a. Sweden is expanding its government health services.
   b. In the United States, most people have private health insurance.
   c. Medicare is a national health service for all Americans.

Chapter 9 Review

A. *Choose the item that best completes each sentence.*

1. *Human rights groups have criticized the USA Patriot Act of 2001 for   (a) jeopardizing individual freedoms and human rights   (b) limiting government police powers   (c) preventing the government from dealing effectively with terrorists.*

2. *Guantánamo Bay and Abu Ghraib have attracted the attention of human rights groups because prisoners there have been   (a) forced to work on illegal construction projects   (b) tortured and detained indefinitely   (c) made to pose for propaganda photographs.*

3. *A belief in the obligation of nations to guarantee human rights for their citizens began after World War II because (a) Western nations needed a justification for interference in the internal affairs of Third World nations   (b) the United States found human rights to be a useful way to embarrass the Soviet Union during the cold war   (c) governments and populations were shocked by the atrocities practiced by the Nazis during the World War II era.*

4. *During the 1980s, the United States   (a) identified human rights with free elections   (b) identified human rights with social and economic progress   (c) pursued human rights only in Communist nations.*

5. *The most highly favored destinations for 21st century migrant workers and other immigrants have been   (a) Turkey and Iran   (b) the U.S. and Russia   (c) Mexico and Brazil.*

6. *Resentment of immigrants in Western Europe in the 1990s was closely related to   (a) distrust of communism   (b) rising oil prices   (c) global economic difficulties and shortages of jobs and housing.*

7. *A major human rights problem in the United States in recent years has been   (a) the abuse of illegal aliens by criminal organizations   (b) the deportation of all newly arrived immigrants by the Immigration and Naturalization Service   (c) the passage of laws barring immigration from the Middle East, Africa, and Asia.*

8. *The "platform for action" of the Fourth World Conference on Women was adopted by   (a) government delegates   (b) nongovernmental organizations   (c) both of these.*

9. American women's rights organizations have focused on (a) assisting Third World women to immigrate to the United States (b) ending sex discrimination (c) helping women to escape discrimination in the United States by immigrating to other countries.

10. Global threats to health today include all of the following except (a) drug-resistant forms of tuberculosis (b) smallpox (c) HIV / AIDS.

B. Reread "Immigrants and Aliens in Europe," on pages 188–192. Then write an essay on immigration issues in Western Europe by answering the following questions:

1. Explain why you AGREE or DISAGREE with the argument that countries with declining birth rates should welcome immigrants.

2. Describe the reactions of ultranationalist groups to immigration in the late 20th and early 21st centuries.

3. Discuss the reasons for changing attitudes toward immigration in Germany.

C. Examine Figures 9.1 and 9.2 on page 210 and indicate which statements are true and which are false.

1. Between 1990 and 2005, fewer adults were infected with HIV.

2. In the 1985–2005 period, HIV infection in sub-Saharan Africa increased significantly.

3. Global HIV infection was less of a problem in 2000 than it was in 1995.

4. Among sub-Saharan adults, fewer cases of HIV infection were reported in 1985.

5. By 2005, the global HIV epidemic was under control.

D. Reread "The Struggle for Women's Rights," on pages 200–204, and "Poverty and Health Care," on pages 204–207. Then write one or two paragraphs on each of the following topics.

1. women as national leaders

2. health services in developing nations

Figure 9.1 Global HIV Epidemic, 1990–2005

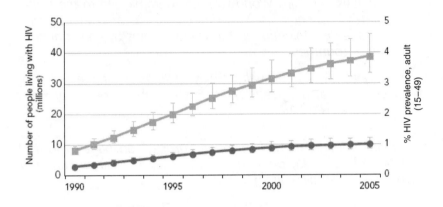

Figure 9.2 HIV Epidemic in Sub-Saharan Africa, 1985–2005

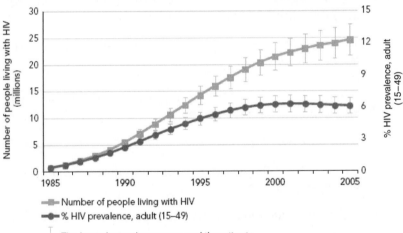

Chapter 10

Terrorism Threatens International Security

Terrorism has been defined as the use of unpredictable violence against society in general and innocent people in particular to express beliefs and achieve political goals. In modern times, terrorism has largely been an instrument of the weak (individuals or small groups of commandos) against the strong (ruling groups and governments). It is a weapon favored by extremists, whatever their beliefs.

After terrorists crashed hijacked airliners into the World Trade Center and the Pentagon in 2001, President George W. Bush declared all-out war on terrorism. The president said: "We will direct every resource at our command, every means of diplomacy, every tool of intelligence, every instrument of law enforcement, every financial influence and every necessary weapon of war to the disruption and defeat of the global terror network."

The toppling of the Taliban regime in Afghanistan in 2001 and the defeat of Saddam Hussein in Iraq in 2003 were regarded as victories in the war on terror. Western leaders believed that Al Qaeda was on the run, its leaders arrested or killed, and its ability to control operations damaged. By early 2007, however, it was apparent that from secure bases in Pakistan, Al Qaeda was rebuilding its command structure, directing a growing number of terrorist attacks on the West, and developing new alliances with other terrorist groups across the Middle East, North Africa, and Europe. Global terrorism was not on the run; it was on the march.

Terrorism: The Historical Background

As a political tool, terrorism was heavily used during the French Revolution (1789–1799). Radical revolutionaries, called Jacobins, began a reign of terror by sending supporters of the monarchy and other suspected political enemies to the guillotine for beheading. This kind of terrorism used the instruments of state power against political enemies. Similar methods were used by the Bolsheviks after they seized power in Russia in 1917. In the United States, groups like the Ku Klux Klan used terror as a means of enforcing white supremacy in the South after the Civil War.

The Post-World War II years. After the war, terrorism was used in a number of campaigns for national independence. Nationalists attacked officials and others associated with the British ruling colonial government in Kenya, Cyprus, and South Yemen. In Israel, Zionist leaders Menachem Begin and Yitzhak Shamir led two terrorist groups, Irgun and Stern, which assassinated British officials, and Arabs as well, in their drive to achieve independence for Israel. A long conflict, from 1954 to 1962, pitted Algerian nationalists against the French colonial regime. Anticolonialism of a different sort led to terrorism in Northern Ireland, where Catholic militants fought to end British rule and Protestant militants fought to continue it.

Groups within independent countries also used terror in their campaigns for political and social change. It was a common tactic of *separatists,* who sought to secede from national governments and set up their own homelands. In Spain, a Basque organization, the ETA, became active in the 1960s. Members assassinated the handpicked successor of dictator Francisco Franco in 1973. By the 1990s, ETA terrorism had claimed more than 500 lives. In the Philippines, the Moro National Liberation Front began a campaign to gain independence for Moros (Philippine Muslims) in the 1960s. Its acts of terror left 50,000 dead and drove 20,000 Moro refugees to Malaysia before factionalism weakened it.

Governments too used terrorist acts to advance their goals. In one famous incident, a Communist agent killed an anti-Communist Bulgarian dissident in a London subway by pricking his leg with a poison-tipped umbrella. During the 1960s, U.S. officials plotted ways of assassinating Cuban Premier Fidel Castro. They considered a range of methods, from poisons to explosives. They even went so far as to hire Mafia assassins. When news of such acts became public in the 1970s, Congress clamped tighter restrictions on U.S. intelligence agencies.

♦ *Identify each of the following:*

   a. Menachem Begin   c. separatists
   b. ETA

Guerrillas and Militants. In recent years, the term *terrorism* has been applied most often to acts of violence by guerrillas or militant organizations rather than to actions taken by governments. In the 1970s, the term *international terrorism* began to be used to describe acts of violence committed by political groups outside their own country. Another term that became common in this period was *state-sponsored terrorism.* It refers to acts of violence encouraged by governments or states for political purposes.

Terrorism erupted in many regions of the world in the 1970s. Rural guerrillas were especially active in Latin America. In Peru, Shining Path militants planned a worldwide Communist revolution based on the principles of Mao Zedong (Chapter 6). In both Argentina and Brazil, left-wing terrorists rebelled against military dictatorships. These in turn waged campaigns of terror against the guerrillas, in which thousands "disappeared" without a trace. In Colombia, persistent antigovernment radicals used terror in their agitation for land reform.

The industrialized nations of Europe also witnessed outbreaks of terrorism in the 1970s. In Germany, a left-wing group known as the Red Army Faction carried out bombings, arson, kidnappings, and assassinations in its campaign against the (West) German government. Evidence uncovered later indicated that the Red Army Faction was supported in part by the East German secret police. In Italy, numerous small revolutionary groups launched violent protests against the government. The best known of these, the Red Brigade, kidnapped and murdered Aldo Moro, a former prime minister, in 1978. In both Germany and Italy, concerted police action put an end to most radical terrorist activity by 1980.

In the United States, radical groups active in the 1960s and early 1970s worked mainly to force the United States out of Vietnam. Isolated acts of violence included the destruction of some university facilities and attacks on draft boards. In the late 1970s, the U.S. government made the fight against terrorism a major part of its foreign policy. Officials drew up a list of countries believed to support terrorism. The government set up special military units to prevent terrorist acts and to retaliate against terrorism when appropriate.

As terrorism continued in the 1980s, four main types of activity emerged: assassinations, bombings, seizures of hostages, and hijackings of airplanes and ships. These activities often caused the loss of innocent lives.

One of the most prominent victims of political assassination was Egypt's President Anwar Sadat, killed in 1981. The murder was attributed to Islamic religious extremists who disapproved of Sadat's ties with the United States and his peace treaty with Israel. India's Prime Minister Indira Gandhi was slain by her Sikh bodyguards in 1984. They were acting to avenge the deaths of several hundred Sikhs that occurred when soldiers under Gandhi's orders had stormed a Sikh temple in northern India. Gandhi's son Rajiv was killed in 1991, apparently the victim of Tamil separatists; two years later the president of Sri Lanka met a similar fate.

Bombings have resulted in hundreds of fatalities. In 1983, a terrorist on a suicide mission blew up the U.S. Marine headquarters in Lebanon, killing 241 Americans. After terrorists kidnapped, tortured, and killed the chief of the U.S. Central Intelligence Agency in Beirut, the CIA's director retaliated by ordering an attack on a Muslim cleric who headed a terrorist organization. The 1985 attack, using a truck bomb in a Beirut courtyard, killed 80 people but left the cleric unhurt. In 1988, a terrorist bomb blew up a U.S. passenger plane over Lockerbie, Scotland, killing 270. After years under international sanctions, Libya turned over two suspects; one, a Libyan intelligence agent, was convicted in 2001.

Hostages, like bombing victims, were usually innocent bystanders who happened to be in the wrong place at the wrong time. After the revolution that brought Islamic fundamentalists to power in Iran in 1979, Iranian militants seized the U.S. embassy and took some 50 Americans hostage. They demanded the return to Iran of the Shah. The former ruler had been sentenced to death by the new government. Even after the Shah died, in July 1980, the militants refused to release the hostages; they were finally freed in January 1981, after 444 days of captivity. During this period, several Americans and Europeans were kidnapped and held hostage for years by terrorists based in Lebanon.

A notable hijacking incident occurred in 1985. Four gunmen, reported to be members of a PLO splinter group, seized an Italian cruise ship, the *Achille Lauro,* in the eastern Mediterranean. The men demanded the release of Palestinians held prisoner by

Israel. Their demand was not met and eventually they surrendered, but not until they had killed a wheelchair-bound American.

In 1989, the Pentagon reported the existence of 52 terrorist groups in various parts of the world. In addition to the terroristic acts committed by the militant groups mentioned above, there were others, including violence by Armenians and Kurds against Turks and assaults by ultranationalist Germans against foreign workers (Chapter 9).

1. *Summarize five major examples of terrorism in the years between 1945 and 1990.*

2. *Match each victim of political assassination in Column A with his or her country in Column B.*

       Column A   Column B
   1. *Anwar Sadat*   a. *Italy*
   2. *Indira Gandhi*   b. *Egypt*
   3. *Aldo Moro*   c. *India*

3. *Complete the following sentences:*
   a. *The Red Army Faction was active in _____ .*
   b. *Beginning in 1979, some 50 Americans were held hostage in _____ .*
   c. *Gunmen who hijacked the* Achille Lauro *demanded _____ .*
   d. *Terrorism against foreign workers was committed by ultranationalists in _____ .*

Terrorist Attacks in the 1990s

Attacks Around the World. The Middle East was the scene of countless terrorist attacks in the 1990s. Many of them involved hostility between Arabs and Jews in Israel. Violence often took the form of suicide bombings by young Palestinians. These men belonged to such radical groups as Hamas and the Palestine Islamic Jihad. Fourteen such attacks by those two organizations between April 1994 and July 1997 killed more than 150 people. Dozens more suicide attacks came during the second Palestinian *intifada,* which began in September 2000 (see page 74).

In many Muslim countries, terror was a weapon used by both Islamic fundamentalists and governments. Nowhere was the resulting violence worse than in Algeria. It began in 1992, when the government canceled elections that the fundamentalists seemed certain to win. Extremist rebels such as the Armed Islamic Group (GIA) massacred thousands of innocent villagers. The government countered with mass arrests, imprisonment, and executions. Estimates of the dead vary from 60,000 to 100,000.

Algeria's troubles spread to France. In 1995 and 1996, several bombings in or near Paris subways killed ten people. The GIA claimed responsibility. France had been targeted because of its ties to the government of Algeria.

In Japan in 1995, extremists released a nerve gas called sarin in five Tokyo subway cars during rush hour. Twelve persons were killed and more than 5,000 injured. Japanese officials blamed the attack on a religious cult called Aum Shinrikyo. This group predicted massive destruction and the end of the world.

Russians became the victims of terrorist attacks in 1999. Nighttime bomb blasts in apartment buildings in Moscow and elsewhere killed 367 people. Russian authorities blamed Islamists and other militants from Chechnya. (See Chapter 2.)

In September 2004, the world was shocked by a brutal attack on a Russian school by Chechen rebels. When their demands for a Russian troop withdrawal from Chechnya and independence for the region were not met, bloodshed resulted. Fighting between the rebels and local militia left 300 dead, half of them children. Russian officials referred to the terrorists as "a new generation of fanatics."

♦ *How has the use of terror been linked to religion in the Middle East, Europe, and Asia?*

Attacks Against the United States. During the 1990s, the United States experienced several serious terrorist attacks. In February 1993 in New York City, a powerful truck bomb exploded in a garage under the World Trade Center. It caused extensive damage and six deaths. U.S. authorities blamed Islamists from the Middle East. They linked the bombing to a plot uncovered later in 1993 to blow up the United Nations headquarters in New York City and a tunnel linking the city and New Jersey, and to kill prominent political leaders. A key figure was an Egyptian fundamentalist Muslim leader, Sheik Omar Abdel Rahman, who lived in the United States. Four militant Islamists were convicted of the Trade Center bombing in 1994. The sheik and nine other defendants (including two U.S.-born Muslims) were found guilty in the case involving the broader plot in 1995. And in 1997, a jury convicted the accused mastermind of the Trade Center bombing. He was a Pakistani who wanted to punish the United States for its support of Israel.

A terrorist truck bomb in April 1995 blew up a federal office building in Oklahoma City. It killed 168 people, including 15 children at a day care center. At first, Islamists from the Middle East were suspected. But this time the bomber was an American, Timothy J. McVeigh. A former U.S. soldier, McVeigh had links to right-wing militias. These are groups of heavily armed U.S. militants who claim the United States is becoming a police state.

McVeigh apparently wanted to avenge two earlier incidents. In the first, in 1992, federal agents at Ruby Ridge, Idaho, attempted to arrest a white supremacist sought on a weapons charge. Shootouts killed the man's wife and son and a deputy marshal. In the second incident, in 1993, government forces stormed a compound near Waco, Texas. It was occupied by members of a religious cult, the Branch Davidians. In the resulting fire, some 80 Branch Davidians lost their lives. McVeigh was convicted in 1997 and executed in 2001.

In August 1998, car bombs exploded simultaneously at two U.S. embassies in Africa: in Nairobi, Kenya, and Dar es Salaam, Tanzania. The death toll came to 270. Twelve Americans were among the dead. U.S. authorities said that the mastermind behind the attacks was an exiled Saudi businessman, Osama bin Laden. They accused him of backing a prolonged campaign of anti-U.S. terrorism. Two weeks after the bombings, U.S. planes attacked bin Laden's camp in Afghanistan and a factory in Sudan that was suspected of making chemical weapons. The U.S.S. *Cole,* a Navy destroyer, was damaged by a terrorist bomb in Yemen in 2000.

♦ *Discuss the differences between the Oklahoma City bombing and the African embassy bombings.*

21st-Century Terrorism Sets the World on Edge

Terrorism reached a stunning new level of violence on the morning of September 11, 2001. Out of a sunny blue sky, two passenger airliners piloted by suicide hijackers plowed into the twin towers of the World Trade Center in New York City and exploded in flames. A third hijacked airliner crashed into the Pentagon in Arlington, Virginia, near Washington, D.C. A fourth plane came down in Pennsylvania woodland. An estimated 3,000 people died that morning in the crashes, the explosions, and the collapse of the Trade Center's 110-story towers.

"The Day the World Changed." When the first plane crashed into the north tower of the World Trade Center (or WTC) at 8:48 a.m., it appeared to be a horrible accident. Television cameras quickly carried live coverage showing the gaping hole around the 100th floor and black smoke that billowed out. Police, firefighters, and rescue crews rushed to the site. Office workers sought to flee down elevators and stairways.

Shortly after 9 a.m., TV viewers around the world watched in horror as the second plane smashed into the WTC's south tower. It sent a massive fireball out the opposite side. Within an hour the south tower collapsed. Thousands of office workers and rescuers were killed. An hour later, the north tower collapsed. Dust and smoke floated over lower Manhattan for weeks afterward. The search for bodies and the clearing of the rubble went on for many months.

The second strike at the WTC made it clear that the crashes were no accident. Further evidence came at 9:45 a.m. The third airliner struck the Pentagon, the five-story, five-sided building that houses the U.S. Department of Defense. The exploding plane destroyed about one-fifth of the building.

The planes that hit in New York had both left Boston that morning for cross-country flights to Los Angeles. The third plane was headed from Washington to San Francisco. Teams of four or five hijackers had seized the planes. They were armed with box cutters and small knives that escaped detection at airport security gates. Each team included trained pilots who took over the controls and flew the planes on suicide missions against their carefully chosen targets.

A fourth plane, from Newark, New Jersey, to Los Angeles, was also hijacked. Soon after it passed Pittsburgh it turned back toward the East Coast. But by this time, passengers with cell phones had learned of the attacks in New York and Washington. Risking their own lives to prevent any attack on a fourth target, several passengers rushed the hijackers. At 10:10 a.m. the plane crashed in a remote area southeast of Pittsburgh. There were no survivors. The final moments on the plane's cockpit voice recorder had the sounds of a frantic struggle in or near the cockpit.

The death toll on the four airplanes was 236, not including the hijackers. Another 125 people died at the Pentagon. But the greatest toll was at the World Trade Center. The dead or missing numbered 2,723 people from dozens of different nations. At least 343 firefighters and 60 police officers from New York and vicinity were lost.

The events of the day shocked and sickened Americans and people all over the world. President George W. Bush declared the attacks to be "acts of war." He vowed to strike back against all who had helped the hijackers. Americans who had previously felt safe behind two oceans and powerful armed forces suddenly felt at great risk. In its cover headline, a British newsmagazine summed it up: September 11 was "The Day the World Changed."

♦ *Why did the terrorist attacks of September 11, 2001, have such a dramatic impact on the United States?*

Who Did It—and Why? News media were cautious about placing blame. But U.S. officials soon named Osama bin Laden and his Al Qaeda organization as the main suspects.

Investigators traced the names on the four airliners' passenger lists. They concluded that 19 men of Arab origin had been the hijackers. Some had attended flight schools in Florida and other states, training to pilot passenger jets of various sizes. U.S. officials said the men were part of a worldwide terrorist conspiracy directed by bin Laden and associated Islamist extremists. Those extremists sought to impose their militant brand of Islam throughout the Middle East and in other countries with large Muslim populations. And they saw the United States as an obstacle in their way.

President Bush offered his own explanation of the terrorists' motives. In a speech to Congress, the president said: "They hate what we see right here in this chamber, a democratically elected government. Their leaders are self-appointed. They hate our freedoms, our freedom of religion, our freedom of speech, our freedom to vote and assemble and disagree with each other."

Experts offered further explanations. They said the United States was viewed as an enemy by many people in Third World countries. In the view of its critics, the United States boasted of its democratic ways while sending arms and money to support governments that oppressed their citizens. Many people in the Middle East—and not just Islamist militants—opposed U.S. policies. They objected to the U.S.'s strong support for Israel, its tough sanctions against Iraq (which were said to cause hunger and misery for the Iraqi people), and its frequent use of military force. At the same time, U.S. culture had a wide appeal in those same Middle Eastern countries. And "the American dream" had continued to attract a steady stream of immigrants to the United States from around the world.

Questions about the attackers' motives also focused on what they expected the United States to do in response. Did they want to provoke the United States into striking back blindly? Perhaps the terrorists hoped that U.S. military action would take a large toll in innocent lives, enrage the world's Muslims, and win new recruits for the Islamist cause. Many Americans worried about such a possibility. But polls showed strong public support for powerful and long-term military action against terrorists and their backers.

♦ *Identify each of the following:*
   a. Osama bin Laden
   b. Al Qaeda

Effects in the United States. The attacks of September 11 did more than kill people and destroy buildings. It badly damaged the economy of the United States (and the world). It undermined Americans' sense of security. And it sent waves of grief and anger through U.S. society.

The most immediate blow was to the airline industry. It faced massive insurance claims, a sharp rise in future insurance costs, and a sudden drop in passengers. For two days, U.S. authorities barred all planes from the skies. Tough new security measures were put into place. When flights resumed, many seats were empty. Thousands of jittery Americans canceled their travel plans. Ten days after the attack, Congress went to the industry's rescue. It passed a multibillion-dollar package of subsidies and loan guarantees.

The U.S. economy was already troubled by a drop in business activity and a sliding stock market. Stock markets stayed closed for almost a week after the attack. In part this was because several Wall Street firms with offices in the World Trade Center had lost many people. In part it was because disruptions to telephone and other services affected the nearby New York Stock Exchange. And in part it was to avoid the panicky selling of stocks. When stock markets did reopen, share prices plunged. The markets experienced the worst one-week percentage drop since the Great Depression of the 1930s. Share prices in other nations also fell amid fears of a global recession. Stock prices later regained some of the losses. Fears about the future still kept investors on edge.

In the United States and around the world, tens of thousands of workers lost their jobs. Airlines laid off thousands. So did hotels and other businesses related to travel and tourism. Many large corporations cut production and laid off workers. They were expecting sharp declines in business activity and in future profits. A few industries, however, saw business pick up. Defense industries prepared for new orders. Companies that provide security guards and other protective services had more work than they could handle.

U.S. officials planned major increases in spending as well as new tax cuts to help boost the economy. Before the attacks, Congress had been struggling to protect the federal budget surplus. But after the attacks, the emphasis was on hunting down the terrorists, tightening security within the United States, and reviving the economy.

♦ *What were the economic effects of the terrorist attacks of September 11, 2001?*

A Nation Aroused. In the days after September 11, television networks ran and reran the dramatic footage showing the attack on the World Trade Center. Americans responded with fervent displays of patriotism and an outpouring of charity. Flags appeared on homes, businesses, cars, and bicycles. People pinned flag emblems to their clothes. Many wore purple ribbons as a symbol of mourning and of national resolve. Contributions poured in to charities that aided victims of the attacks and their families.

People in other nations added their contributions and their expressions of sympathy. Almost all the world's governments joined in condemning the attacks as atrocities. (An exception was Iraq.) Palestinian leader Yasir Arafat denounced the attacks and donated blood for the victims. But some Palestinians did not share Arafat's attitude. A brief tape showing a group of Palestinians celebrating the attacks ran over and over on U.S. television. U.S. reporters found many people in Middle Eastern countries who condemned the attacks but were critical of the United States.

Fighting Terrorism at Home. The Bush administration immediately asked for and received from Congress more money and expanded authority to fight the terrorist threat within the United States. There were fears that terrorists might stage a chemical, biological, or nuclear attack. President Bush created a new

Department of Homeland Security to coordinate federal efforts to protect Americans against terrorism.

Congress granted new powers to agencies like the FBI to tap the phones and monitor the computers of suspected terrorists. It also gave immigration officials expanded powers over immigrants suspected of terrorism. Groups of both left and right warned against reducing civil liberties in the name of fighting terrorism.

In the days and weeks following the attacks, authorities arrested more than a thousand people. Many were aliens or U.S. citizens of Middle Eastern heritage. Some were suspected of playing an active part in terrorism. Others were held as possible witnesses.

As outrage about the murderous attacks built among the U.S. public, Muslims and people of Middle Eastern and South Asian origin came under wide suspicion. Security agents stopped them for questioning at airline check-in counters and boarding gates. Several airline pilots refused to take off until people of Middle Eastern origin were removed from the planes. Angry Americans attacked several Muslim houses of worship. And a few revenge seekers murdered people they assumed to be Muslim.

A September 11th commission, led by former New Jersey governor Thomas Kean, investigated the security problems that made the attacks possible and proposed measures necessary to prevent future disasters. The commission's 567-page report, published in July 2004, placed blame for major intelligence and security failures on both the Clinton and Bush administrations. President Bush ordered an immediate study of the report to rapidly implement the commission's recommendations.

1. *Describe the efforts taken to increase homeland security.*

2. *What was done to respond to Americans' demand to know why the September 11th attacks had not been prevented?*

Fighting Terrorism Abroad. President Bush put the nation on a war footing. He called up National Guard units. Warships and attack planes were sent to the Persian Gulf and Southwest Asia. And the president assembled a coalition of partners. (The first President Bush had done the same before the Persian Gulf War.) Bush said the United States would go after "every terrorist group of global reach" wherever it could be found. The United States would go after nations that harbored the terrorists. "Every nation in every region now has a decision to make," the president added. "Either you are with us or you are with the terrorists." U.S. and

British forces invaded Afghanistan to remove the Taliban government sheltering bin Laden and to destroy Al Qaeda bases there.

The United Nations Security Council strongly condemned the assaults on New York and Washington. Within weeks, it passed a resolution requiring all member countries to cooperate in a campaign against terrorists. The resolution also obliged members to deny money and protection to terrorists and their organizations. The council gave those requirements binding force by invoking Chapter Seven of the U.N. Charter. The U.N. did not directly authorize a military response. But U.S. officials said they considered the resolution to be a go-ahead for U.S. military action.

The United States' "war on terrorism" received strong backing from its allies in the NATO alliance and in Latin America. Russia pledged to share intelligence and give other support. Central Asian nations bordering Afghanistan offered help and bases. Middle Eastern governments gave more tentative support, They feared a backlash from their own people. Saudi Arabia, for example, denied the use of its territory for attacks on Muslim nations.

Under strong pressure from the United States, Pakistan allowed American forces to make use of its territory as a staging area for the military campaign against neighboring Afghanistan. Pakistan's military ruler, General Pervez Musharraf, agreed to help the United States. In return, Pakistan was to receive financial assistance. In addition, U.S. trade sanctions against Pakistan were lifted. The sanctions had been imposed in 1998 when both Pakistan and India had tested nuclear weapons. The United States also dropped sanctions against India when that country backed the antiterrorist campaign.

♦ *Why did the "war on terrorism" begin with military attacks on Afghanistan?*

In March 2003, U.S. and British forces invaded Iraq. Their mission was to destroy weapons of mass destruction (WMDs) and free the Iraqis from the dictatorship of Saddam Hussein. No WMDs were found. Nor was it proven that Saddam was funding Al Qaeda, as President Bush had asserted. Following the rapid defeat of his forces and the collapse of his regime, Saddam vanished. He was captured in December 2003 and eventually placed on trial before an Iraqi court for war crimes. The former dictator was hanged in 2006. The Americans and British began a long-term effort to rebuild Iraq. Ambushes, suicide bombings, and terrorist executions claimed the lives of Iraqis, Americans, and others, as Islamic terrorists and hostile Iraqis continued to attack the U.S.-led coalition. A new Iraqi government was chosen in a national election in which there was broad Iraqi participation in December 2005. Nuri al-Maliki, a Shiite, eventually became prime minister. However, the Iraqis had voted along ethnic lines. This produced an impasse that has limited the government's effectiveness. The outnumbered Sunnis have felt locked out of a new Iraq dominated by Shiites. As a result, ethnic fighting between rival militias increased. By 2007, Iraq was in the midst of civil war with daily terrorist attacks from suicide bombers and others claiming Iraqi and American lives.

1. *What action did the United Nations take in response to the terrorist attack on the World Trade Center and the Pentagon?*

2. *What did Pakistan stand to gain by siding with the United States? What risk did it take in doing so?*

3. *What were the results of the U.S.-British invasion, defeat, and occupation of Iraq?*

Case Studies in Terrorism

1. The PLO

When Israel was established in 1948, warfare broke out between the new state and its Arab neighbors. Thousands of Palestinians lost their homes and fled the country. Many lived in refugee camps in Jordan. (See Chapter 4.) Various pro-Palestinian groups sprang up. Some relied on terrorism to dramatize the Palestinians' cause. In 1964, an umbrella group, the Palestine Liberation Organization (PLO), was formed to unite many of these separate groups. Its purpose was to destroy Israel and gain political control of Palestine.

During the Six-Day War of June 1967, Israel defeated the armies of Egypt, Syria, and Jordan. Conquest of the West Bank region and the Gaza Strip brought 1½ million Palestinians under Israeli rule. The PLO responded with a campaign of bombings inside Israel.

In February 1969, Yasir Arafat was elected chairman of the PLO. Arafat was the head of Fatah, the largest Palestinian guerrilla group. He brought Fatah and many other groups together under the Palestinian Armed Struggle Command. These groups attacked all those they considered to be enemies of their cause.

Such "enemies" included moderate Palestinians who favored a political solution to the Arab-Israeli conflict.

In 1972, PLO-backed terrorists killed 28 people and injured 72 at Lod International Airport in Tel Aviv. In the same year, the PLO's radical Black September Faction sent a terrorist team to the summer Olympic Games in Munich, Germany. Storming the Olympic Village, they murdered 11 Israeli athletes.

The PLO also established a representative body to discuss policy. At a 1974 conference in Morocco, leaders from the Arab world declared the PLO to be "the sole legitimate representative of the Palestinian people." They pledged to support the PLO in the struggle against Israel. Also in 1974, the PLO was recognized as the formal representative of the Palestinian people. It was given a seat as a nonvoting observer at the United Nations.

A dramatic foiling of Palestinian terrorists occurred in 1976. Gunmen hijacked a French plane bound from Tel Aviv to Paris and diverted it to Entebbe airport in Uganda. The gunmen held its passengers hostage and demanded that Israel release the Palestinians it held in prison. The Israelis refused. They quickly mounted a commando raid that killed the militants and freed the hostages.

The PLO received a serious setback in 1982. It was driven out of its key bases in Lebanon by a massive invasion of Israeli forces. PLO guerrillas scattered to North Yemen, Algeria, Sudan, Iraq, and Tunisia. Yasir Arafat established a headquarters in Tunisia. He vowed to continue the struggle against Israel.

The killing continued. In 1982, the PLO turned on one of its own when killers shot a moderate Palestinian in a Portuguese hotel lobby. His crime had been advocating coexistence with Israel. In 1985, PLO-backed terrorists attacked the ticket counters of El Al (Israel's airline) at the Rome and Vienna airports. They murdered 18 people and injured 111 more.

♦ *Describe the growth of the PLO as a terrorist organization.*

By the late 1980s, there was little doubt that the PLO had been weakened. This had been caused by its retreat from Lebanon and the Israeli bombing of its headquarters in Tunisia in 1985. In 1987, an *intifada*, or uprising, of young Palestinians in Gaza and the West Bank began without PLO support. Also in 1987, Israeli commandos killed Abu Jihad. He was Arafat's deputy and the chief planner of the PLO's terror attacks.

In 1988, the PLO decided to change its tactics. Arafat promised that the PLO would no longer engage in terrorism. It accepted the right of Israel to exist. The goal of the PLO became the establishment of a Palestinian state in the West Bank and Gaza, alongside Israel. Several militant groups angrily withdrew support from the PLO. Two of the most extreme groups, Hamas and the Palestine Islamic Jihad, continued their terrorist attacks.

Perhaps the most important factor in weakening the PLO was Arafat's support for Iraq after its 1990 invasion of Kuwait. This cost the PLO the financial backing of Saudi Arabia and other Arab states. Before the Persian Gulf War, the PLO had been able to pay for medical services, education, and welfare for Palestinians in Gaza and the West Bank. Without the aid of wealthy Arab states, the PLO had to stop many of its services.

Mahmoud Abbas became chairman of the PLO after Arafat's death in November 2004. Drawing his main support from Fatah, Abbas became leader of the Palestinian Authority. A moderate and experienced negotiator, Abbas's rise increased hopes for a peaceful resolution to the Israeli-Palestinian conflict. Abbas, however, was opposed by Hamas—the Palestinian militant organization that continued terrorist attacks on Israel. In 2005, Palestinian elections placed Hamas in control of the government. Ismail Haniyeh became prime minister. Although Abbas remained president of the Palestinian Authority, his power was limited. Armed conflict began between Hamas and Fatah gunmen. In February 2007, after months of bloody clashes, the rival factions agreed to

form a unity government. However, fighting continued and Fatah was forced out of Gaza. President Abbas then established an emergency government on the West Bank.

1. *Explain how the development of the PLO, from 1964 to the present, reflected changes in the practice of terrorism in the Middle East.*

2. *PROVE or DISPROVE: In the 21st century, Hamas threatened the political power of the PLO and its claim as the "sole, legitimate representative of the Palestinian people."*

3. *For each year, state a development or event in the history of Middle Eastern terrorism: 1964, 1974, 1982, 1987, 1990, 1995, 1997, 1998, 2006.*

2. Hamas

Branded a terrorist organization by Israel, the United States, and the European Union, Hamas is seen by its supporters as a legimate fighting force defending Palestinians from a brutal Israeli military occupation. It is the largest Palestinian militant Islamist organization. Hamas was formed in 1987 at the beginning of the first *intifada*, or Palestinian uprising against Israel's occupation of the West Bank and Gaza.

Hamas's short-term goal has been to drive Israeli military forces from the occupied territories. To achieve this goal, it launched attacks on Israeli troops and settlers. It also has a long-term goal of establishing an Islamic state in all of historic Palestine. Most of the land claimed by Hamas lies within the borders of Israel.

Before taking control of the Palestinian government in 2006, Hamas was divided into two areas of operation. One dealt with social programs, such as building schools, hospitals, and religious institutions. The other dealt with military operations carried out by Hamas's Underground Brigades. It also had a political branch in exile, located in Jordan. After taking office in 1999, Jordan's King Abdullah II had Hamas' headquarters closed down and its senior personnel expelled to Qatar.

Hamas came to prominence as the main Palestinian opponent of the U.S.-sponsored peace process. Hamas' primary method of effecting this opposition has been by suicide bombings. In the late 20th and early 21st centuries, Hamas gained power and influence as Israel steadily destroyed the infrastructure of the Palestinian Authority, which has been dominated by Fatah, Hamas's rival organization.

Hamas has stated that it will never agree to a permanent cease-fire with Israel while that country occupies Palestinian territory. It has, however, offered a ten-year truce in return for complete Israeli withdrawal from the West Bank, Gaza, and east Jerusalem. Hamas also has insisted that Palestinians who left Israel in 1948, when the U.N. established Israel as a state, or their descendants, be allowed to return to their pre-1948 homes in Israel. The Israelis believe that agreement to this demand would threaten Israel's existence as a Jewish state.

Since being elected to office in 2006 by Palestinians who had lost faith in Fatah and the Palestinian Authority, Hamas has been subject to economic sanctions by Israel and other nations. These nations have demanded the establishment of a Palestinian government that recognizes Israel's right to exist and commits to past peace deals signed with Israel. Hamas has been unwilling to accept these demands.

In late 2006 and 2007, the violence between Hamas and Fatah caused the deaths of more Palestinians than have been killed by the Israeli army.

3. Osama bin Laden and Al Qaeda

The long and bitter war against Soviet occupation in Afghanistan gave birth to the organization called Al Qaeda. From the first, its top leader and financial backer was Osama bin Laden, a wealthy Saudi Arabian. At the age of 22, bin Laden had been deeply affected by the 1979 Islamic revolution in Iran. Many fundamentalist Muslims welcomed the Iranian revolution. They saw the revolution as the victory of Islamic traditions over Western-style modernization. Bin Laden seems to have shared this view. When Soviet troops poured into Afghanistan at the end of 1979, he vowed to resist the "infidels."

Osama bin Laden was one of 57 children of Mohammed bin Oud bin Laden. The father was a Yemeni who moved to Saudi Arabia in the 1930s. He used his early friendship with the Saudi royal family to acquire a prominent role in Saudi business life. He made a fortune in the construction industry. Upon his father's death in 1968, Osama bin Laden inherited tens of millions of dollars. While older brothers took over the family business, he earned a degree in civil engineering at a Saudi university.

In 1980, Osama bin Laden went to Pakistan. He used his inherited fortune to set up aid organizations for *mujahedeen* (Islamic guerrillas) fighting the Soviets in Afghanistan. He raised money from his wealthy friends. He provided construction equipment to build military bases and tunnels in guerrilla-controlled areas of Afghanistan. And he occasionally fought alongside the *mujahedeen*.

The guerrillas used Pakistan as a supply center and staging area for attacks on Soviet troops and their Afghan allies. At the time, the United States was giving strong support to various *mujahedeen* groups. It supplied money and weapons. In those days, U.S. officials viewed the militant Islamists as "freedom fighters" if they fought the Soviets.

Bin Laden and a number of close associates formed Al Qaeda, or "The Base," in about 1989, shortly before the Soviets left Afghanistan. These associates included men from many Islamic countries. Al Qaeda became a holy army. It was dedicated to Islamic revival and battling all those considered to be enemies of Islam. Its leaders included Islamic *mullahs*, or religious leaders. They followed a strict or pure form of Islam. They approved of terrorism against civilians in the service of a *jihad*, or holy war. Most Muslims do not share these beliefs.

♦ *Describe how Al Qaeda grew out of the battle against Soviet control of Afghanistan.*

After the Soviet departure, bin Laden and most of his supporters returned to their home countries. But the Gulf War of 1991 gave them a new mission. Bin Laden was angered at the way the Saudi government invited U.S. military forces onto its soil to launch a war on Iraqi forces, which had invaded Kuwait. He denounced the Saudi government for "betraying" Islam. According to bin Laden, Saudi leaders had allowed infidels into the holiest of Islamic countries. (Saudi Arabia is the birthplace of the prophet Muhammad. Islam's two holy cities, Mecca and Medina, are in Saudi Arabia. They attract thousands of pilgrims each year.) In bin Laden's eyes, Saudi leaders were traitors for backing a non-Muslim country (the United States) in a fight against Muslims (Iraqis). The Saudi government allowed no opposition. It put bin Laden under house arrest.

After fleeing Saudi Arabia in April 1991, bin Laden moved briefly to Afghanistan and then to Sudan, in North Africa. There and in Yemen, Al Qaeda set up training camps for urban and guerrilla warfare. Men from those camps were said to have been responsible for killing 18 U.S. servicemen in Somalia in 1993. That was also the year when a truck bomb exploded in the parking garage of the World Trade Center in New York, killing six people. U.S.

authorities said they found evidence linking that attack to Al Qaeda. Meanwhile, officials in Egypt and Algeria began blaming bin Laden for financing and training local Islamist militants.

Bin Laden renewed his attacks on the Saudi government when it allowed 5,000 "American crusader forces" (as bin Laden called them) to remain after the Gulf War ended. Saudi Arabia revoked bin Laden's citizenship in 1994. His family renounced him. In May 1996, under U.S. pressure, he and most of his supporters were expelled from Sudan.

Bin Laden moved his headquarters and training camps back to the mountains of Afghanistan and carried on. In September 1996, the Taliban gained control of Kabul, the Afghan capital. Its purist form of Islam was similar to that of Al Qaeda. Apparently, bin Laden used some of his wealth to finance the Taliban's activities.

In 1996 and again in 1998, bin Laden urged Muslims to wage *jihad* (war) against U.S. citizens wherever they might be found. "For more than seven years," he wrote in 1998, "the United States [has occupied] the lands of Islam in the holiest of its territories, overwhelming its rulers, humiliating its people, . . . and using its bases in the [Arabian] peninsula . . . to fight against the neighboring Islamic peoples." Bin Laden turned the charge of "terrorism" against the United States. He applied the term to the "starving" of Iraqi children through economic sanctions since 1991.

The U.S. blamed the bombings of its embassies in two East African nations in 1998 on bin Laden. The United Nations Security Council placed sanctions on the Taliban. It demanded that the Taliban hand over bin Laden for trial and stop providing sanctuary and training for international terrorist organizations.

Intelligence agencies of the United States and other nations have worked for years to find links between Al Qaeda and other terrorist organizations. U.S. officials believe that the bin Laden group has cooperated with such groups as the Iranian-backed Hezbollah, which is active in Palestine, Israel, and Lebanon. They say that Al Qaeda and groups like Hezbollah help train each other's agents in sabotage and terror, and that Al Qaeda often provides assistance for major terrorist operations.

After the terrorist attacks on New York and Washington in 2001, President Bush declared bin Laden to be the prime suspect. In response, U.S. and British forces invaded Afghanistan in late 2001. The Taliban government was removed, and Al Qaeda bases that the Taliban had sheltered were destroyed. A pro-Western government, led by Hamid Karzai, was established.

However, the fighting between NATO forces and a reorganized

Taliban and Al Qaeda bands continued. By 2007, Al Qaeda was rebuilding in the remote tribal areas of Pakistan's mountains. Under a new generation of leaders, Al Qaeda has become less hierarchical, with several planning centers working independently without constant contact with bin Laden.

From their bases in Pakistan, Al Qaeda's new leaders have directed significant terrorist operations, such as the July 2005 suicide bombing in London that killed 56 people, the summer 2006 plot to destroy multiple commercial airlines after takeoff from London, and the 2006 bombing of the Mumbai commuter train system in India.

1. *How did Osama bin Laden support the* mujahedeen *in Afghanistan?*

2. *Why did U.S. officials consider the* mujahedeen *at that time to be "freedom fighters"?*

3. *Which governments does Al Qaeda consider to be its chief enemies? Why?*

4. *Why do you think Western intelligence agencies were less concerned with hunting Osama bin Laden by 2007?*

Chapter 10 Review

A. *Choose the item that best completes each sentence.*

1. *Terrorism has been used by   (a) nationalists seeking independence   (b) separatists wishing to secede from national governments   (c) both of these.*

2. *A national leader assassinated by terrorists was   (a) Chancellor Helmut Kohl of Germany   (b) President F. W. De Klerk of South Africa   (c) Prime Minister Indira Gandhi of India.*

3. *The 1995 bombing of a building in Oklahoma City led to the arrest of   (a) members of the Afrikaner Resistance Movement   (b) followers of Sheik Omar Abdel Rahman   (c) a former U.S. soldier.*

4. *Until 1988, the goal of the PLO was   (a) to become the dominant power in the Middle East   (b) the destruction of Israel   (c) support of Islamic fundamentalism.*

5. *The U.S. government determined that the terrorists who flew airliners into the World Trade Center and the Pentagon were   (a) militant Islamists   (b) supporters of the American far right   (c) Iraqi secret agents.*

B. *Reread "Terrorist Attacks in the 1990s," on pages 215–217. Then indicate which statements are true and which are false.*

1. *The Armed Islamic Group has been blamed for massacres in Algeria.*

2. *European neo-Nazis bombed the World Trade Center and planned to bomb the United Nations in New York City.*

3. *Among those arrested by the FBI was Sheik Omar Abdel Rahman, a Muslim cleric.*

4. *The events of the 1990s proved that terrorists are no threat to American cities.*

5. *Terrorists showed they have the ability to strike even in the heart of a nation that is at peace.*

C. *Reread "21st-Century Terrorism Sets the World on Edge," on pages 217–224. Then write an essay on terrorism by answering the following questions:*

1. *Why were the terrorist attacks of September 11, 2001, carried out and by whom?*

2. *How did the United States respond to those attacks?*

3. *Why was the day of the attacks called "the day the world changed"?*

Unit II Review

A. *Use information from this unit to explain the problems of peacekeeping in each of the following areas:*

1. *former Yugoslavia*

2. *the Middle East*

3. *Africa*

4. *Asia*

B. *Review Chapter 8, "The Struggle to Keep the Peace," beginning on page 164. Then describe the background of each statement.*

1. Countries that contribute soldiers to U.N. peacekeeping missions run the risk of subjecting those soldiers to combat.

2. By 1999, Poland, Hungary, and the Czech Republic had been granted full NATO membership.

3. The Organization of American States supported efforts to restore Jean-Bertrand Aristide to power in Haiti.

4. The Organization of African Unity was unable to negotiate solutions to conflicts in Somalia, Sudan, and Angola.

5. The Arab League coordinated military, diplomatic, and economic actions against Israel.

C. Review Chapter 9, "Human Rights: Issues and Problems," beginning on page 183. Then write an essay of two or three paragraphs about ONE of the following:

1. The USA Patriot Act

2. Immigrants in Europe and America

3. Advances in Women's Rights

4. Is Basic Health Care a Human Right?

D. Review Chapter 10, "Terrorism Threatens International Security," beginning on page 211. Then PROVE or DISPROVE the following statements:

1. Terrorism is dangerous to world peace.

2. Terrorist attacks in the 1970s occurred solely in rural areas.

3. Since 1990, terrorism has been mainly a Middle Eastern problem.

4. Concerns about ethnicity and religion have been major causes of terrorism.

5. It is easier to fight terrorists than to fight an enemy nation.

Unit III

THE GLOBAL ECONOMY

Increasing globalization—*the interconnectedness of the whole world, especially in the realm of economics—characterizes the early 21st century. Nations are coming together in alliances to build economic strength. Business and trade operate globally, bound less and less by national boundaries. Globalization is aided by ever more sophisticated technology and scientific breakthroughs.*

The mix of technology and economic integration transforming the world has created unparalleled prosperity. In the early 21st century, the world has seen faster economic growth than at any time since the early 1970s. In China, each person now produces four times as much as in the early 1990s. Having joined the global labor force, millions of people in developing countries have the chance to escape poverty. This promises to improve the lot of humanity as a whole.

However, globalization produces winners and losers. Transferring production from the higher priced labor markets of the rich countries to developing nations where the work is done more cheaply has caused a shift in the labor market. It has created a job loss for many people, and increased the income gap between managers and workers. Since 2001, the average pay for American workers has increased little, with real wages growing less than half as fast as productivity. By contrast, the executives who attended the World Economic Forum in Switzerland in early 2007 have enjoyed a bonanza. The total pay of the typical top American manager increased from roughly 40 times the average for much of the past 20 years to 110 times the average in 2007. As corporate profits soar—while workers' wages and purchasing power do not—opposition to globalization grows. Workers who have lost their jobs to lower paid labor in developing countries want their government to be more protective. Economists warn that protectionism (government interference with the free flow of goods, services, and jobs) will damage the world economy.

The controversy over the benefits and disadvantages of globalization has emerged as the economic dilemma of the 21st century.

Chapter 11

Economic Organization: Global and Regional

The Group of Eight

Every year, the leaders of the world's major industrial nations meet to work out cooperative approaches to the problems of the global economy and to coordinate actions on other matters. The meetings began in 1975 with the leaders of Britain, Canada, France, Germany, Italy, Japan, and the United States. Thus the body was called the Group of Seven, or G-7. In 1997, at the 23rd annual meeting, Russia became a member and the body became known as the Group of Eight, or G-8.

A major focus of the G-7/G-8 has been issues raised by rapid changes in the way money moves around the world. On a weekday evening when people in San Francisco are getting ready for bed, businesses in Tokyo are well into their next workday. Before going to bed, a San Franciscan in pajamas can sit down at a computer, check the prices on the Tokyo stock market, and instruct a broker to buy shares in a Japanese company. Before dawn in San Francisco, the transaction will be completed. Likewise, someone in Japan or Hong Kong can place overnight orders on U.S. stock or currency markets. (Currency markets are where, for example, U.S. dollars are traded for Japanese yen.) Like your neighborhood convenience store, some of the world's financial markets stay open 24 hours a day.

All this means that a financial crisis in one country can make waves around the world in hours, if not minutes. Every 24 hours, $1 trillion changes hands on the world's currency markets. That total is four times greater than it was in the 1980s. A trillion dollars is a lot of money to be moving back and forth. Sometimes it moves too fast and turns a small crisis into a big one, or a big crisis into an even bigger one.

That's what happened in December 1994, when Mexico ran out of places to borrow money to meet its debt payments. News of Mexico's dilemma sent the value of the Mexican peso into a nosedive. Eager to sell before the price fell any lower, investors and banks that held Mexican pesos dumped them onto the currency market. But of course that just forced the price down even more. When institutions like the International Monetary Fund (IMF) could not raise enough money to rescue the Mexican government, the United States helped to arrange a multibillion-dollar loan. But that addressed only Mexico's immediate crisis, not a future one that might be just as bad, or worse.

At the next G-7 summit in Halifax, Nova Scotia, in June 1995, leaders tried to work out better ways of dealing with such crises. The G-7 leaders issued a statement that said, in part:

> The world economy has changed beyond all recognition over the last fifty years. The process of globalization, driven by technological change, has led to increased economic interdependence. . . . The prevention of crisis . . . requires an improved early-warning system, so that we can act more quickly to prevent or handle economic shocks.

The leaders proposed creating a new emergency source of funds so that the IMF could act quickly in any future crisis. During the early 1990s, the G-7 took on the task of rescuing the Russian economy. In pursuit of that goal, G-7 members contributed billions of dollars in aid to Russia. At other sessions, the G-7 put pressure on Japan and the United States to change some of their policies. The issue with Japan was trade. Japan was running up huge trade surpluses with Europe and North America. Other G-7 members urged it to buy more from those regions to restore a balance. The issue with the United States was its huge federal budget deficits. Other G-7 members pressed the United States to balance its budget.

The issues addressed by the G-8 reflect key global concerns. Foremost have been efforts to remove trade barriers and stimulate world trade, prevent recessions (or at least keep their effects from spreading), and reduce chronic unemployment. The G-8 also seeks to promote human rights, limit nuclear proliferation, deal with terrorism, and find solutions to political crises, such as those in the former Yugoslavia.

The July 2006 G-8 summit conference was held in St. Petersburg, Russia. In addition to focus on collective approaches to critical international issues—such as globalization, the wars in Iraq and Afghanistan, and the nuclear ambitions of North Korea and Iran—priority concerns of Russian President Vladimir Putin were discussed. These included global energy security, development of modern education systems, and the fight against infectious diseases. Putin offered to provide Western energy companies the opportunity to invest in Russian gas reserve development if the United States would drop its objections to Russia joining the World Trade Organization. The Russian president's emphasis on energy stemmed from Russia's position as the second largest oil producer in the world and one of the biggest natural gas providers, especially to eastern and central Europe. However, Russia needs help from Western nations to develop its huge reserves. Many Western governments have been wary because of the way Russia shut off gas supplies to Ukraine in the winter of 2005–2006 when Ukraine objected to Russia's price increases.

1. *Explain why you AGREE or DISAGREE: G-8 is needed to help solve problems in the world economy.*

2. *Research the G-8 in your school library. Investigate its strengths and weaknesses. List ways the group could solve problems more easily.*

The World Bank

Stimulating economic growth in developing nations by means of loans and advice is the function of the International Bank for Reconstruction and Development (IBRD), or World Bank. Created after World War II to promote European reconstruction, the World Bank became the largest single source of lending for development. Between 1947 and 2000, the funds loaned mainly to nations in Asia, Latin America, the Middle East, and Africa totaled $350 billion. Loans went mainly to higher income developing countries, which had the resources to pay the money back.

Four other organizations work with the World Bank. Collectively they are known as the World Bank Group.

- The International Development Association (IDA) was set up in 1960. It provides loans for up to 40 years, with a 10-year grace period and no interest, to the poorest countries. The IDA gets its capital from the World Bank and from periodic donations from wealthy countries.
- The International Finance Corporation (IFC), founded in 1956, has the mission of spreading private enterprise across the world. It assists developing countries in attracting investors. The IFC uses its own funds to mobilize the financing of projects by other investors and lenders.
- The Multilateral Investment Guarantee Agency (MIGA) was established in 1988. Its job is to stimulate the flow of foreign investment to developing nations by providing guarantees against political risk such as armed conflict and civil war, nationalization and expropriation, restrictions on currency transfer, and breaches of contract by host governments.
- The International Center for Settlement of Investment Disputes (ICSID) was founded in 1966. It provides facilities for conciliation and the arbitration of disputes between governments. The ICSID has no full-time conciliators or arbitrators but appoints them for each case. So far, the ICSID has settled more than 40 cases, most of them by arbitration.

The World Bank is owned by its 183 member nations. They provide its basic financing. All powers are held by the bank's board of governors, consisting of one governor from each member country. That body meets only once a year. Most of its authority is delegated to a 24-member board of executive directors who meet in permanent session at the bank's headquarters in Washington, D.C. Shares in the bank determine voting power. With 45 percent of the shares, the G-8 nations control the World Bank.

The United States has enjoyed a dominant role in the leadership of the World Bank. All presidents of the bank have been Americans selected by the U.S. president. That has not prevented the bank from making loans to nations regarded by the United States as unsuitable or for projects not favored by the United States. However, the bank has undertaken no major programs or initiatives without American approval.

Nominated by U.S. President George W. Bush, Paul Wolfowitz became head of the World Bank in 2005. A former deputy defense secretary, Wolfowitz had been a key planner of the American invasion of Iraq in 2003 and of U.S. foreign policy in Iraq. As World

Bank president, Wolfowitz drew international criticism by pursuing a strategy of using World Bank money to fight graft and corruption. Wolfowitz interrupted the flow of money to a number of countries and projects he found questionable. Included were a neonatal health project in India suspected of allowing harmful medicines to fall into the wrong hands, a plan to cancel the debts of the Republic of Congo while its president ran up an $80,000 hotel bill in New York, and a plan to lend money to Kenya after its top anti-corruption official had fled the country. Critics charged Wolfowitz of trying to force borrowing countries to follow the economic policies favored by the World Bank instead of pursuing the bank's mission of helping people in developing countries to live better lives. Wolfowitz resigned in 2007 following charges that he had violated World Bank's rules by helping a female friend to get a better paying job. On May 30, 2007, Robert B. Zoellick, a Goldman Sachs executive and former U.S. trade representative, was selected by President Bush as the next World Bank president.

1. *Describe the purpose of the World Bank.*

2. *PROVE or DISPROVE: The programs of the World Bank are totally controlled by the United States.*

3. *Examine the pie graph and answer the questions that follow.*

Figure 11.1 Total World Bank Lending by Region, Fiscal Year 2006

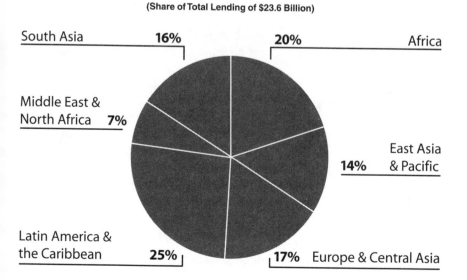

(Share of Total Lending of $23.6 Billion)

South Asia   **16%**   **20%**   Africa

Middle East & North Africa   **7%**

East Asia
14%   & Pacific

Latin America & the Caribbean   **25%**   **17%**   Europe & Central Asia

a. In fiscal year 2006, the region that received the most in World Bank loans was _____.

b. The region that received the least World Bank money was _____.

c. The region that received 20% of World Bank loans was _____.

d. Europe and Central Asia received _____ of World Bank loans.

e. In fiscal year 2006, the World Bank lent a total of _____.

The International Monetary Fund

The work of the International Monetary Fund (IMF) has been closely connected to that of the World Bank. Established in 1944, the IMF was designed to oversee the global rules governing money and to ensure orderly currency arrangements among the industrial nations. It also was intended to be a lender of last resort for rich and poor nations alike. Through the years, however, the role of the IMF has changed. Today, its primary mission is to assist weak economies in the Third World. Its aid comes with conditions, though, since the IMF requires that nations first open their economies to free market forces. Also, it insists on cutting budget deficits, which often means sharp cuts in social programs.

Strict Teacher

The strict conditions set by the IMF for loans and the closeness with which the conditions are monitored have created tensions between the IMF and the developing nations. To qualify for an IMF loan, a borrower must agree to IMF requirements for economic reform and restructuring. Failure to carry out such measures usually results in suspension of the loan.

The IMF's policies are highly controversial. Antiglobalization protesters call the IMF a tool of the industrial and capitalist nations. They say the IMF's insistence on strict free market policies exposes Third World economies to greedy international corporations, corruption, social unrest, and political instability. Supporters of the IMF agree that free market remedies can cause pain. However, they argue that developing nations benefit in the long run by building more competitive economies.

Periodic recessions in industrial and developing countries have left many nations unable to pay their debts. The task of financing debt-reduction schemes and managing the global debt crisis involved the IMF in many complex problems and resulted in record amounts owed to the IMF by debtor nations.

In recent years, the IMF has supervised economic reform programs in more than 50 countries. Among them were the emerging market economies of Eastern Europe and the former Soviet Union. The IMF guided the development of capitalism in those countries as they moved away from Communist-style central planning.

Like the World Bank, the IMF is controlled by the wealthy nations, especially the United States, France, Britain, Germany, Japan, and Saudi Arabia. Those and other nations provide the financial resources of the IMF in accordance with a quota assigned to each member country. Each member government is represented on the board of governors. The board delegates many of its powers to 24 executive directors in Washington. The managing director is usually a European.

In 2004, the IMF warned the United States that its large debt threatened the financial stability of the global economy. Starting in 2001, the United States had spent so much on security, the war on global terrorism, and invasions of Afghanistan and Iraq that a federal surplus became a federal deficit. The reduction of taxes by the Bush administration during this period increased the deficit. By 2007, the federal debt (the sum of the money borrowed by the government to pay for all the annual deficits) was more than $8.8 trillion. In other words, the U.S. government spends much more money than it has. It does this by borrowing from foreign lenders. As the debt grows, so do the interest charges. As a result, the United States owes a mushrooming debt to the rest of the world. Investors have less confidence in the American economy and pump less money into it. This limits economic growth in the United States and around the world. Experts have warned of danger if the U.S. debt is not better controlled.

In April 2007, the IMF predicted strong growth by the world economy at a rate of 4.9 percent in 2007 and 2008. However, the growth rate for the U.S. economy in the same period was projected at only 2.2 percent, the slowest since 2002. This slowdown was attributed to a slump in the American housing market.

The IMF urged policy makers to take advantage of the continuing strong performance of the global economy to confront longer term challenges, such as aging populations and rising opposition to globalization.

A plan to restructure the IMF was revealed in 2006 by Managing Director Rodrigo Rato. The intention was to give more influence to developing countries, including China, South Korea, Turkey, and Mexico. These countries received increases in their voting rights as part of a two-year reform designed to reflect the shifting balance of power in the global economy.

1. *List the purposes of the International Monetary Fund.*

2. *What conditions does the IMF attach to its assistance?*

World Trade Groups

From 1948 to 1995, the main international framework for organizing world trade was the General Agreement on Tariffs and Trade (GATT). It gave way in 1995 to a new body called the World Trade Organization (WTO).

General Agreement on Tariffs and Trade. GATT was created at a time when tariff barriers erected during the Great Depression of the 1930s were limiting world trade. It aimed to expand world trade by reducing such barriers. (*Tariffs* are taxes on imports.)

How did GATT work? First of all, it set rules governing certain aspects of global trade. For example, GATT required each member nation to treat all other members equally. This rule was known as the most-favored-nation clause. Under this clause, if Country A granted a trade benefit to Country B, it had to extend the same benefit automatically to all other member countries. In other words, each nation had the same benefits as the most-favored nation.

Second, GATT provided its 125 member nations with a forum for striking deals and settling disputes on trade. GATT specialized in conference diplomacy. It staged eight successive rounds of international trade negotiations. The first six rounds, held from the late 1940s through the 1960s, led to a dramatic decline in tariff barriers and a major increase in world trade. In the 1970s and 1980s, however, the industrial nations practiced a greater degree of protectionism. The causes of this trend were rising energy costs, periodic recessions, and increasing competition from newly industrialized nations. The United States, Japan, and other nations used tariffs and other means to protect endangered industries. Evasion of the most-favored-nation rule for a wide range of industries and products placed a growing amount of world trade beyond the authority of GATT.

The last and most far-reaching achievement of GATT was a seven-year period of trade negotiations known as the Uruguay Round. The Uruguay Round ended in 1994 with the signing of an agreement to lower tariffs on imports by an average of 40 percent. The 1994 pact was the first GATT agreement to cover such areas as agriculture, textiles, and financial services. The agreement was so full of details and footnotes that it filled the equivalent of four big-city phone books.

The Uruguay Round turned back the tide of protectionism. It also opened the subject of trade in services. Services represent the fastest growing area of world trade. They include banking, insurance, telecommunications, construction, aviation, shipping, tourism, advertising, and broadcasting. Setting up global rules for them is expected to go on for decades. Negotiators in the Uruguay Round failed to reach agreement on free trade rules involving movies, television programs, and music; civil aircraft; and shipping and financial services like stock brokerage and banking. Talks continued on those subjects.

The World Trade Organization. The purpose of the WTO is similar to that of GATT. The organization goes beyond GATT, however, by trying to open up trade in services (for example, banking and insurance) as well as trade in goods. Like GATT, the WTO offers each member the same benefits as the most-favored nation in order to make global trade freer for all. The WTO is more powerful than GATT was. It can order trade penalties against member nations found to have broken its rules.

The World Trade Organization opened with a staff of 450 people. Its headquarters are in Geneva, Switzerland. Most GATT members joined the new organization, but some key nations were not on the initial membership list. Both Russia and China, for example, were absent, although they applied for membership. China was approved in 2001. Russia engaged in negotiations aimed at being admitted to the WTO in 2008.

The WTO's principles are essentially the same as GATT's. Beyond the most-favored-nation clause, key principles are:

- **Encouraging development.** The WTO has looser rules for developing nations than for industrial nations.
- **Opening greater access to markets.** The WTO continues GATT's emphasis on negotiating lower tariffs. Most forms of quotas (specific limits or targets for imports or exports) are forbidden.
- **Promoting fair competition.** Dumping and subsidies are considered unfair forms of competition. *Dumping* is selling a product for less than its actual cost. *Subsidies* are government payments to aid certain enterprises. If a nation violates a rule against dumping or subsidies, other nations can impose special "compensating tariffs" on that nation's exports.
- **Protecting intellectual property rights such as patents and copyrights.**

In recent years the WTO (like the World Bank and the IMF) has come under sharp criticism for its role in globalization. Angry demonstrations disrupted the 1999 WTO meeting in Seattle, Washington, which failed to agree on plans for a new round of global trade negotiations. After that, demonstrators turned up regularly at WTO meetings to demand changes in WTO policies described as harmful to the environment and to workers' rights.

In September 2003, WTO talks that were intended primarily to bring relief to the developing nations collapsed in disarray. Disgruntled delegates representing nations in Africa, the Caribbean, and Asia walked out of the conference, which was being held in Cancún, Mexico. The main dispute was over the objections of Third World nations to subsidies being made to agriculture by Western governments.

In July 2006, the WTO's annual Doha (the capital city of Qatar) conference, which began in 2001, was suspended by Pascal Lamy, the organization's director-general. Six "core" negotiators—the United States, India, Brazil, the European Union, Japan, and Australia—failed to reach agreements on agriculture. The U.S. wanted cuts in import tariffs for farm products. This has been rejected by the EU, Japan, and India. They have demanded cuts in subsidies paid to farmers. The poorer nations have claimed that the billions of dollars in subsidies paid to American farmers enable them to dump artificially cheap exports, including cotton, into the global market. Developing nations have refused to allow their subsistence farmers to lose their livelihood in order to provide market access to agricultural products from the U.S. Efforts to revive the Doha talks continued in 2007.

In April 2007, U.S. Trade Representative Susan Schwab announced that the U.S. would take China to court at the WTO over suspected trade barriers, such as subsidies to support Chinese manufactured goods and piracy of books, music, videos, and other goods. This statement of intent by the U.S. was seen by trade experts as the appropriate way to resolve differences through the WTO.

1. *Why do you think the WTO is regarded as the U.N. of global economics?*

2. *Explain the difference between free trade and protectionism. Which does the WTO support? Why?*

3. *Describe the conflict that stalled the Doha conference in 2006.*

The European Union

So far, we have discussed organizations that are more or less global in scope. But the interdependence of nations has led to the rise of regional economic bodies as well. One of the oldest and most successful of these is the European Union (EU), which celebrated its 50th anniversary in 2007.

The foundation of the EU was set in Rome in 1957, when six nations organized a trading bloc. They called their creation the European Community (EC) or Common Market. The goal was to build economic cooperation among the region's industrial countries and form a single market. The EC expanded over the years to become a major world economic force. By 1986, it had 12 members—Belgium, Denmark, France, Germany, Greece, Ireland, Italy, Luxembourg, the Netherlands, Portugal, Spain, and the United Kingdom. In 1995, Austria, Sweden, and Finland joined. The addition of Estonia, Latvia, Lithuania, Poland, the Czech Republic, Slovakia, Hungary, Slovenia, Malta, and Cyprus in 2004, and Romania and Bulgaria in 2007, raised membership to 27.

Figure 11.2   European Economic Organizations

The EC became the European Union when its members signed a treaty in 1992 in the Dutch city of Maastricht. The Maastricht Treaty (or the Treaty on European Union) provided for an economic union, to be achieved by the removal of almost all barriers to the free movement across borders of people, goods, and services. The treaty also committed members to establish a single European currency by 1999, and to coordinate foreign and defense policies. Creation of a single market, with provision for admitting new member nations, was intended to continue the process of strengthening Western Europe economically, while creating more political unity. A key goal was increased ability to compete with the United States and Japan, the commercial rivals of the European nations.

Many viewed the treaty as an important step toward a united Europe. The treaty increased the powers of the European Commission, the executive branch in Brussels, Belgium. However, many Europeans feared such a development. They worried that a stronger European Union would undermine the governments of individual nations. Britain was the leader of go-slow forces that did not want the European Union to gain too much power.

Lively debates over the treaty delayed ratification in some

countries. A variety of problems complicated the national debates. Chief among them were economic recession and rising unemployment, growing intolerance of Third World immigrants, demands for greater trade protectionism, and polls showing low levels of popularity for many European leaders. Those problems made the pursuit of economic and political union more difficult. In the end, however, all member nations accepted the Maastricht Treaty.

◆ *List some of the obstacles to approval of the Maastricht Treaty.*

The decision to create a single European currency stirred strong feelings. Many Europeans were reluctant to see an end to national currencies like the British pound, the French franc, and the German mark. EU leaders named the new currency the "euro."

Putting a monetary union into effect took several years. Some nations did not qualify under strict rules on national debts and budget deficits. Two nations, Britain and Denmark, were unwilling to give up their historic national currencies. Finally, led by France and Germany, 11 of the 15 nations formed the European Monetary Union in 1998, with a twelfth joining in 2001. A European central bank, based in Frankfurt, Germany, was created to set a common monetary policy. Participating nations began calculating all banking and stock exchange transactions in euros on January 1, 1999. They agreed to begin using euro banknotes and coins in place of national currencies in 2002. The 10 new EU members that joined in 2004 are expected to use the euro. This will make the euro group the world's second largest monetary power, after the United States.

Many nations have applied to join the EU. The union had expected Norway to come in with the three countries that entered in 1995. But Norwegian voters rejected membership in a referendum. One of the EU's most persistent applicants has been Turkey, a predominantly Muslim country that straddles the border between Europe and Asia. Turkey first applied in 1987. For years the EU discouraged Turkey, saying that the country was not yet ready economically and was not democratic enough. However, in 1995, EU leaders agreed to let Turkey move closer to membership by entering a customs union. This allows free trade between Turkey and the EU. Turkey's application for full membership remained active.

The Treaty of Nice modified the EU's rules for expansion. Voters in Ireland rejected the treaty in 2001. That action complicated the EU's expansion plans. Ireland, however, later approved the treaty.

Whichever nations eventually join the EU, trade within Europe is likely to become freer. In January 1994, the EU and several neighboring nations formed a 19-nation European Economic Area (EEA). The EEA became the world's largest trading bloc. It sought to promote freer trade among its members without the commitment to political unity that was part of the EU.

The European Union has become more democratic over the years. On major issues, the final say still rests with the governments of individual nations, and the larger nations have the most power. But the people of EU countries have a voice too, through the European Parliament, which meets in Strasbourg, France.

The European Parliament is the legislative body of the EU. Its members are elected every five years. The number elected from each country depends on its population. In the legislative chamber, however, members are seated by party, not nationality. The Socialists and the European People's Party were the largest groups elected in 1999. But the 2004 election was marked by the lowest voter participation in history. Europeans seemed to have little interest in EU politics.

The parliament has authority over the budget of the EU. And it can pass laws that apply to all EU nations. A Council of Ministers, composed of ministers representing the governments of the member nations, must approve all laws and budgetary decisions. There is also a 20-member European Commission, which acts as the EU's executive branch. It carries out the decisions and laws of the council and the parliament. Under the Maastricht Treaty, the parliament gained the power to approve or reject candidates nominated by the council as members of the European Commission. The parliament must also approve the appointment of the commission's president.

Some Europeans feared that EU enlargement would make efficient decision making impossible unless the rules on how to cast votes were changed. Accordingly, the draft of an EU constitution was prepared by a convention. The constitutional treaty, however, was rejected by French and Dutch voters in the summer of 2005. Germany's Chancellor Angela Merkel used her rotating six-month presidency of the EU, which began in January 2007, to launch an effort to revive the stalled constitution and achieve passage by 2009.

In March 2007, Ms. Merkel hosted a conference of the leaders of the 27 EU member nations in Berlin. In addition to the constitution, the crisis in Darfur and global warming were discussed. Prior to the Berlin gathering, the 27 nations agreed to reduce their greenhouse gas emissions by up to 30 percent from 1990 levels by 2020 and to generate 20 percent of their energy from renewable sources.

1. *State the purpose of the European Union.*

2. *List the member nations of the EU.*

3. *Complete the following sentences:*
   a. *The Maastricht Treaty is also called the ____ .*
   b. *Among the difficult problems faced by the EU in recent years are ____ .*
   c. *The purpose of the proposed EU constitution was ____ .*
   d. *Several EU countries have adopted a common currency called the ____ .*
   e. *Three functions of the European Parliament are to ____ .*

4. *Jacques Delors of France was one of the EU leaders in the 1990s. Research Delors' life. Find out what role he played in the EU and why he was a controversial figure.*

5. *Research the euro. What is the current value of the euro in relation to the U.S. dollar?*

The Organization of Petroleum Exporting Countries (OPEC)

The Organization of Petroleum Exporting Countries (OPEC) was founded in 1960. By the 1970s, it included most major petroleum exporting countries except Russia and Mexico. OPEC was mostly concerned at first with gaining more profits for its members. To do this, it pressed foreign companies to give up control of oil production facilities to host countries, mainly in the Middle East and North Africa. As OPEC countries gained control of production, they also acquired the power to raise or lower oil prices.

Rapid price increases during and after 1974 led to higher profits for the OPEC nations. Higher prices provided the oil-producing nations an incentive to explore and develop new sources of oil. With new sources, the supply of oil increased. That drove down prices in the early 1980s. OPEC then used production quotas to limit the market supply and stabilize prices. Saudi Arabia, the largest and most influential oil producer, encouraged this policy.

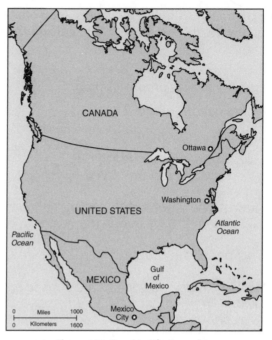

Figure 11.3   North America

Despite OPEC quotas, prices collapsed in 1998. After OPEC applied stricter controls in 1999, prices rose sharply.

Changes in the oil market and in the Middle East have begun to affect the status of OPEC. The capacity of OPEC members to expand oil production, for example, is now largely confined to the nations surrounding the Persian Gulf. Also, the discovery of new, non-OPEC oil sources and the substitution of alternatives to oil (gas, coal, nuclear energy) have weakened OPEC's power.

In April 2007, world attention focused on one OPEC member—Venezuela. President Hugo Chávez announced a plan to take control of several key oil projects from U.S. and European companies. This policy will force the world's largest energy companies, such as Exxon and Conoco Phillips, out of the Orinoco Belt (a region located near the Orinoco River in Venezuela). The heavy oil fields in this region have the potential to give Venezuela more oil reserves than Saudi Arabia. The U.S. Geological Survey has described the Orinoco Belt as the "largest single hydrocarbon accumulation in the world." Venezuela, therefore, has the most important energy resources outside the Middle East.

Chavez's oil policies are bad news for the United States, which imports 60 percent of its oil. The United States has been Venezuela's largest customer despite Chávez's threats to cut off all oil exports to America. Beyond OPEC policies designed to regulate global supplies and prices of oil, Chávez seeks to use Venezuela's oil fields to limit American influence around the world.

1. *State the purpose of OPEC and explain its importance as an organization.*

2. *Explain the difference between OPEC's purpose and the oil policy of Venezuela's president, Hugo Chávez.*

The North American Free Trade Agreement (NAFTA)

As Europe moves toward economic unity and the establishment of a single market, similar efforts have started in the Americas. In 1991, the governments of Canada, the United States, and Mexico negotiated the North American Free Trade Agreement (NAFTA). This agreement aims to eliminate, within 15 years, tariffs and other trade barriers between the three nations. The first tariff reductions went into effect in 1994. NAFTA will eventually create a single market of more than 380 million people.

In the United States, NAFTA stirred up a lively debate before Congress voted its approval in November 1993. Supporters said a North American free trade area was necessary if the region was to

Fair Trade?

compete with the European Union and other regional economic blocs. They argued that free trade under NAFTA would enable the United States, Mexico, and Canada to make their economies more efficient. In each nation, the most competitive industries would grow, because they would have access to larger markets. Supporters also argued that NAFTA would expand U.S. exports, create high-technology jobs in the United States, promote democratic reforms (and thus political stability) in Mexico, and reduce illegal immigration from Mexico to the United States. The administrations of Presidents George H. W. Bush and Bill Clinton both strongly supported NAFTA.

Opposition to the pact came from several different quarters. Labor unions argued that NAFTA would encourage U.S. companies to move their factories to Mexico, where wages were much lower. (In a notable image, third-party presidential candidate H. Ross Perot spoke of "the giant sucking sound" of American jobs going south.) Environmentalists took a different stance, arguing that Mexico would lure away U.S. industries by offering them an escape from compliance with U.S. antipollution laws. They also warned that Congress would be likely to weaken U.S. environmental laws in response. Still others said that the freedom of Congress to pass legislation on environmental and consumer issues might be impeded by the need to conform to NAFTA's free trade rules.

Changes were added to NAFTA to meet some of the critics' concerns. One change created a U.S. "safety net" to help people who lost jobs as a result of the agreement. The safety net extended unemployment benefits for up to a year and provided training for new jobs. Another change aimed to enforce compliance with environmental standards.

In both Canada and Mexico, similar debates took place. Critics claimed that NAFTA would expose the two countries to invasion by U.S. multinational companies and undermine their political sovereignty. In reply, NAFTA supporters argued that the pact would sharpen the competitive edge of all three North American countries. Without NAFTA, it was argued, the region could not stand up to the fierce competition from Europe, Japan, and the industrializing nations of the Third World.

◆ *Summarize the arguments made in the United States for and against NAFTA.*

Once NAFTA went into effect, the debate shifted to who had been right, supporters or critics. U.S. exports to both Canada and

Mexico increased sharply after 1994—but imports increased far more. The pre-NAFTA U.S. trade deficit with Canada more than doubled, and a small pre-NAFTA surplus in trade with Mexico turned into a deficit that reached $22.8 billion in 1999. NAFTA critics said such results signaled a shift in jobs to Canada and Mexico. Supporters of NAFTA, however, pointed to significant increases in total jobs in all three countries in the late 1990s—a sign, they said, that NAFTA was succeeding.

Almost before the ink was dry on the NAFTA accord, U.S. officials began talking about enlarging the free trade area. One proposal envisioned a Free Trade Area of the Americas (FTAA), a Western Hemisphere zone stretching from Canada to Chile and Argentina. Another proposal looked eastward by outlining a link of North American to European nations. Still another proposal suggested forming closer economic ties between the United States and Asian and Pacific nations.

U.S. leaders put the greatest emphasis on the Americas. The Central American Free Trade Agreement (CAFTA) was signed into law by U.S. President George W. Bush in August 2005. It allowed greater access for U.S. products in El Salvador, Guatemala, Honduras, Costa Rica, the Dominican Republic, and Nicaragua. Labor unions and environmental groups opposed the agreement. However, 80 percent of U.S. manufactured products and approximately 50 percent of U.S. farm products became immediately tariff free. Barriers to telecommunications, insurance, and financial services were eliminated or reduced.

1. *Explain why you AGREE or DISAGREE: The North American Free Trade Agreement has improved Americans' lives.*

2. *State one reason why Mexicans or Canadians might welcome NAFTA and one reason why they might fear it.*

3. *Indicate which of the following statements are true and which are false.*
   a. *NAFTA was first negotiated by the administration of U.S. President George H. W. Bush.*
   b. *Critics argued that NAFTA could have harmful effects on the environment.*
   c. *NAFTA economically links North America with Europe and Asia.*
   d. *Mexican workers earn lower average wages than U.S. workers.*
   e. *NAFTA gives Canadians increased access to Mexican and U.S. markets for their products.*

4. *Compare NAFTA to the EU. How are they similar? How are they different? How do both organizations reflect global economic trends in recent years?*

5. *What is the purpose of CAFTA?*

Chapter 11 Review

A. *Choose the item that best completes each sentence.*

1. *At the Halifax Conference of 1995, the Group of Seven agreed upon (a) tariff increases on selected products (b) greater protectionism for their industries (c) a new emergency source of funds for the IMF.*

2. *The G-7 became the G-8 when it was joined by (a) Italy (b) Russia (c) Japan.*

3. *During the Uruguay Round, GATT attempted to (a) increase the pace at which capitalism developed in formerly Communist nations (b) encourage social welfare programs in the least developed nations (c) increase global trade through liberalized trading rules.*

4. *A concern of the World Bank in recent years has been (a) reducing the influence of the United States in determining its policies (b) using World Bank money to fight graft and corruption (c) reducing tariffs among European nations.*

5. *A problem faced by the International Monetary Fund in recent years has been (a) the size of the U.S. federal debt (b) record amounts owed by debtor nations (c) preventing a Communist revival in Eastern Europe.*

6. *The purpose of the Maastricht Treaty was to achieve for the European Union (a) more economic unity, including a single currency and a European central bank (b) increased political unity, including increased powers for the European Parliament and the European Commission (c) both of these.*

7. *The countries that joined the European Union in 1995 were (a) Austria, Sweden, and Finland (b) Norway, Spain, and Denmark (c) Turkey, Hungary, and Poland.*

8. *The Organization of Petroleum Exporting Countries has faced competition in recent years from (a) non-OPEC oil suppliers (b) alternative energy sources (c) both of these.*

9. The North American Free Trade Agreement was designed to (a) create a single trading area for Canada, the United States, and Mexico   (b) protect U.S. industries from Canadian and Mexican competition   (c) enable the United States to control North American economic affairs.

10. Objections to NAFTA were raised by   (a) the Mexican government   (b) the U.S. government   (c) American environmental groups.

B. Reread "The European Union," on pages 247–251. Then write an essay on economic unity in Europe by answering the following questions:

1. What is meant by the term "single market"?

2. What is the Maastricht Treaty and what is its relationship to the EU?

3. Why is the European Union likely to add still more members?

C. Use information in Chapter 11 to explain the meaning of the following newspaper headlines:

NEEDY NATIONS RESIST IMF REQUIREMENTS

EUROPEANS PURSUE DREAM OF UNITY

ENVIRONMENTALISTS FIND FAULT WITH NAFTA

ANTIGLOBALIZATION PROTESTERS DISRUPT WTO MEETING

Chapter 12

Global Business and Trade

The growth of global economic organizations in recent years has mirrored significant economic developments all over the world. A new order is emerging, notable for far-reaching changes in Eastern Europe and the developing world. These changes in turn have affected the industrialized giants of the United States, Europe, and Asia. Experts have hoped that an increasingly interdependent world economy will improve the quality of life for people everywhere.

A New Economic Order

In the early 21st century, the volume of international trade stood at an all-time high. Its total just after World War II amounted to $57 billion; by the end of the century, this sum had reached a staggering $6,890 billion. Furthermore, the trading partners in this gigantic venture included many nations that had rarely, if ever, played an important role in world trade before.

One group of countries taking on a new importance were the nations of Eastern Europe—what had been the Soviet Union and its satellites. With the downfall of communism and the end of the cold war, these countries were developing free market economies. They were also *privatizing* by selling government-owned businesses to private investors, both domestic and foreign. They began expanding business connections with one another and building new ties to the more industrialized nations of the world.

Free market economies were also developing in the Third World. With more than 3 billion inhabitants hungry for a better life, this region began competing as never before with the industrialized nations. In many countries of Southeast Asia and Latin America, labor was plentiful and wages were low. Thus they attracted manufacturing jobs from industrialized nations, where production costs were high. In some industries, for example, Western workers earned five times as much as Taiwanese workers, ten times as much as Brazilian or Mexican workers. The new economic order also involved technology transfer from industrialized to developing nations. For instance, India was becoming a center for the manufacture of computer microchips.

A key aspect of the new economic order is the outsourcing of jobs from industrialized nations to less developed ones. In the information technology field (IT) and financial services fields, call centers have been established in India to provide technical support to computer users in North America and Europe. The increase in India's service and manufacturing jobs made its economy one of the fastest growing in the world in 2006.

♦ *Explain how a new world economic order began to develop in recent years.*

New Economic Order

Strategies for Coping With Change

Globalization made for a challenging economic climate. More than ever before, what happened in one part of the world was likely to have widespread consequences—not all of them good. Industrialized nations, in particular, faced tougher competition from abroad. Many developing countries offered a better combination of labor costs, productivity, and markets. Several U.S. manufacturers were able to shift thousands of jobs to Mexico. Another factor, related to the end of the cold war, was a drop in defense spending. More than a million U.S. defense jobs were lost.

Many industrial nations had relatively low rates of growth in the 1990s—averaging 2 to 3 percent a year. In France, unemployment rose. Japan, whose economy was weaker than it had been in the previous 40 years, experienced near-zero growth for several years.

To stay competitive, many firms *restructured*—that is, they reorganized their businesses to make them more efficient. This often meant *downsizing*—laying off large numbers of workers. Another tactic, *outsourcing*, involved having components of manufactured goods made by other companies, often in developing countries.

Another response to competition was increased privatization. France undertook to sell nearly two dozen state-owned companies, including Air France and Renault. Under private ownership, those companies restructured to become more competitive. The German government sold to private investors a significant portion of the giant state-owned telecommunications firm, Deutsche Telekom. The government kept a controlling 58 percent interest, however. The 1996 sale brought more than $13 billion.

Another response was deregulation. The United States cut back on government regulations affecting the financial services, airlines, telecommunications, and trucking industries. Similar efforts occurred in Europe.

An increasingly favored business tool was the *merger,* by which two or more companies combine into one. Related to it was the *acquisition* or *takeover,* in which one company buys another. In 2004, Japan's UFJ Holdings banking group proposed a merger with Mitsubishi Tokyo Financial Group, to create the world's largest bank. Sometimes, such a merger or takeover is challenged as a violation of antitrust laws to keep a single company from becoming too powerful. In 2000, WorldCom gave up a $115 billion deal to acquire Sprint after objections from the U.S. Justice Department and the European Union.

Still another tactic is to build more factories overseas. Nissan Motor's $800 million expansion of an auto plant in Mexico enabled it to produce cars not only for the Mexican market but also for export to Japan, Canada, and the rest of Latin America. In Mexico, lower production costs provide Nissan with an opportunity to increase profits.

Developing countries offer not only competition but also opportunity for industrialized nations. Emerging nations such as Malaysia are spending more money on roads, sewers, the environment, health care, and consumer goods. Over the next decade, Asia, excluding Japan, is expected to spend at least $1 trillion on telecommunications and power equipment. That investment will provide new market opportunities for the industrialized nations. Westinghouse Electric Corporation, for example, negotiated an agreement to modernize 400 power plants in China.

Consumer spending is also rising rapidly in the developing nations. Thanks to freer trade, U.S., European, and Japanese firms will have access to a growing global pool of consumers.

Globalization makes many workers in the industrialized world feel threatened. Some want their governments to restrict overseas competition by limiting imports. But free market economists believe that opening up trade helps to speed economic growth. Some go so far as to say that the survival of the industrialized

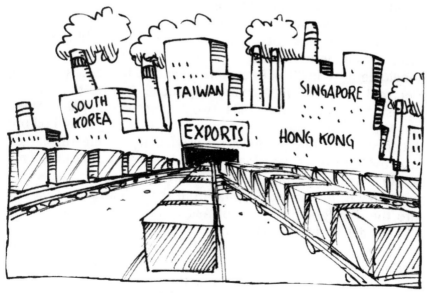

Asia: Boom or Bust?

nations depends on freer trade and freer markets. The nations that have enjoyed unchallenged economic power will have to learn to compete better in the changed marketplace created by globalization.

1. *Describe the efforts of the industrial countries to make their industries more competitive.*

2. *Complete the following sentences:*
    a. *Free market economists say that freer trade _____ .*
    b. *In the developing world, consumer spending is _____ .*
    c. *In the industrial nations, some workers want their governments to _____ .*

Giants of Global Industry and Trade

In the United States, Cingular Wireless purchased AT&T Wireless in February 2004. This $41 billion deal created the largest wireless telephone carrier in the United States. It is believed that this acquisition will slow the decline of cell phone call prices. Fierce competition had forced these prices down in the early 21st century. With 46 million customers, however, Cingular will have less need to compete as strongly as in previous years. The combined company will realize large savings by laying off thousands of workers in overlapping positions, starting in 2006.

Beyond the United States, foreign investors bought nearly half the shares in South Korea's top ten publicly traded *chaebols,* or conglomerates. In 2004, foreigners owned 60 percent of Samsung Electronics and 46.9 percent of Hyundai Motors, the nation's largest carmaker. Also in 2004, two Japanese companies, Mitsui and Mitsubishi, owned 45 percent of the Russian gas and oil producer Sakhalin Energy. As a result, Japan became the largest investor in Russia's resource-rich Far East region, with $820 million in investments. In general, the early 21st century has seen a large flow of investment capital from the industrialized nations into the developing nations of Asia, Latin America, Africa, the Middle East, and eastern Europe.

While globalization has opened new markets to rich companies, it has also given birth to a number of fast-growing new multinationals that are emerging from the poor world. Indian and Chinese firms have been giving their rich rivals increasing competition. In 2007, Indian firms, led by Hindalco and Tata Steel, bought 34 foreign companies for a combined $10.7 billion. Indian information technology (IT) services companies, such as Infosys, Tata Consultancy Services, and Wipro, have begun to threaten the market domination of older firms, even the mighty IBM. A Chinese multinational, Lenovo, bought IBM's personal computer business. PetroChina has become a force in Africa's oil development market. Russian multinationals have invested heavily in foreign firms and launched an effort to buy Alitalia, Italy's state airline, in 2007.

The growing strength of multinationals from the poor world has forced older rich firms to improve their operations. The restructuring of IBM's worldwide operations involves the placement of different activities wherever they are done best, without regard to geographical boundaries. In 2007, IBM had over 50,000 employees in India and plans a further expansion there. Although India has become IBM's second biggest operation outside the United States, the company has moved its head of procurement from New York to Shenzen in China.

IBM's approach is possible only because globalization is flourishing. Many of the barriers that in the past stopped cross-border business operations have disappeared. Increasingly, success for a multinational will depend on correctly determining which places best suit the firm's activities.

Economists believe that increased competition from poor multinationals will force a strengthening of rich firms. Consumers around the world, they believe, will benefit.

1. *Define multinational.*

2. *Explain the relationship between multinationals and globalization.*

Technology Boom, Technology Bust

In the 1990s, new-technology industries tended to do better than old-technology industries like steel and cars. For a time U.S. software giant Microsoft led all the world's companies, with a market value that topped $600 billion in 1999. (*Market value* is the total worth of a company's shares of stock.) As the U.S. economy soared in the late 1990s, technology companies were riding high.

The rise of the Internet had given birth to hundreds of so-called dot-com and high-tech companies. Small dot-coms found it amazingly easy to raise capital to build their businesses. They sold shares to the public by launching IPOs (*initial public offerings*, or first-time stock sales). The Nasdaq stock market, which specializes in technology stocks, became the hot place to invest. Eager investors snapped up stock offerings as soon as they hit the market, quickly bidding up the price of shares in new companies such as Netscape, Yahoo!, and eBay. Investors poured millions of dollars into companies that had never shown a profit and had no immediate hope of doing so.

The rising stock market made many investors rich (at least on paper) and fueled rapid growth for high-tech companies. But during the year 2000, an economic downturn began. Companies cut back on orders for new computers, software, and Internet advertising. They scrapped plans for new factories. Almost overnight the bubble burst, and tech stocks began to tumble in value—down to 50 percent, 30 percent, even as little as 1 percent of their peak prices. Many investors had big losses. Dozens of dot-coms slashed jobs and closed branches. Many went out of business. By the spring of 2001, even Microsoft had seen its stock price cut in half, whittling the company's market value down to $300 billion. And the downturn had affected old-technology companies as well, reducing their market value and leading to a new wave of downsizings.

The slide of U.S. share prices in the early 2000s touched off similar declines on stock markets in Tokyo, Singapore, London, and elsewhere. In the space of one year, global share prices dipped by nearly $10 trillion. Some economists posted warnings for the global economy as a whole. They warned that a U.S. downturn—combined with continued sluggishness in Japan—might pull down other nations' economies too. (The United States and Japan together accounted for 46 percent of total world output.) By 2004, however, technology share prices and those of other companies had revived. The U.S. Federal Reserve Board and central banks in other nations cautiously considered raising interest rates from their historic low levels. Improved corporate earnings reports and higher employment levels were seen as signs of global economic improvement.

1. *What are the dot-coms and how did their prospects change in the year 2000?*

2. *How did the fall in dot-com share prices affect the companies' (a) employees   (b) shareholders?*

Asia: Opportunity and Risk

In 1960, Asian nations accounted for less than 5 percent of the world's gross domestic product. By 2000, their share of global GDP had increased to 34 percent. In many Asian countries, annual growth rates were higher than in Western industrialized nations.

Southeast Asia has attracted special attention in recent years. For example, the world's largest real estate development is in Kuala Lumpur, the capital of Malaysia. It included the twin Petronas Towers, the world's tallest skyscrapers (until taller buildings could be completed elsewhere). The development featured a multistory shopping center, hotels, a theater, and condominiums. Thailand was the home of the conglomerate Charoen Pokphand (CP), which owned more than 250 companies in 20 countries and did $11 billion in yearly business.

Successes like these attracted considerable foreign investment, especially by Japanese. Observers spoke of the "Asian tigers"— Pacific Rim countries whose economies seemed to be outperforming those in the rest of the world. But a crisis developed late in 1997. First Thailand, then Indonesia, then South Korea faced financial ruin. Banks and other financial institutions had made hundreds of risky loans. Crony capitalism was at fault in many cases, with relatives and friends benefiting from unsound business practices. When a borrower could not repay—for instance, when a construction firm found that a grandiose office building could not rent to enough tenants—the business defaulted and faced bankruptcy. As this occurred more and more often, the banks themselves were threatened with failure. Public confidence declined, investors pulled back, and more failures loomed.

To prevent disaster, the IMF advanced funds to bail out troubled financial institutions. The crisis soon eased, and investors again showed confidence in Asian markets. Like NAFTA, the South Asian Free Trade Area was organized to remove barriers to trade between its members. By 2006, it linked India, Pakistan, Bangladesh, Bhutan, the Maldives, Nepal, and Sri Lanka.

Asia has emerged as the new global market for investment. Private investment firms committed $28.9 billion to Asian companies outside Japan in 2006, a 78 percent increase over 2005. Texas Pacific and its Asian investment arm, TPG Newbridge, were among the first to see opportunities in Asia. These firms invested about $1 billion in 2006, buying shares in hospitals in Singapore and Malaysia, a department store in Australia, a natural gas producer in

China, and finance companies in Taiwan and India. Other global investment firms have also sought opportunities in Asia. These include Kohlberg Kravis Roberts, the Carlyle Group, Bain Capital, and CVC Capital Partners.

Financial ties between Asia and the Middle East have been strengthening. By 2006, Chinese companies seeking investors were turning to Saudi Arabia and other oil-rich Middle East sources of petrodollars, rather than the traditional centers of capital in New York and London. American and British banks estimated that Middle East buyers will invest $20 billion to $30 billion in Asian businesses in 2007. As a result, Middle Eastern investment money moving to Europe and the U.S. will diminish.

Oil and gas from the Middle East are vital for China, Japan, and every fast-growing market in the Asia-Pacific region. And the Middle Eastern money generated by that oil wealth is searching for investments with high returns. From 2000 to 2005, trade between the Middle East and Asia more than doubled, reaching $240 billion in 2005.

1. *Why have foreigners invested heavily in Asia in recent years?*

2. *Why did several Asian countries briefly face economic collapse in the late 1990s?*

3. *How have financial relations between Asia and the Middle East developed in the 21st century?*

The Global Auto Industry

Beginning in 2005, American automobile manufacturers suffered heavy losses in sales and profitability. After losing $10.4 billion in 2005, General Motors struggled to restructure its giant operations. Progress was indicated by a loss of only $2 billion for 2006. GM's problems were partially caused by its production of large-sized vehicles at a time when many Americans were worried about rising oil prices, along with the hefty benefits paid to current and retired workers. To lower its operating costs, GM cut production and eliminated thousands of jobs. By July 2007, GM, Ford, and Chrysler sales had declined to 48.1 percent of the U.S. market. Foreign auto companies had 51.9 percent of sales in the U.S.

While GM's American operation has been ceding its historic market dominance to Japanese competitors like Toyota, its South Korean unit—GM Daewoo Auto and Technology—has been expanding rapidly. It produces popular vehicles for the Chinese market and pushes global sales of the Chevrolet and Buick brands. Despite South Korean hostility to foreign businesses, GM has won respect by hiring South Korean workers and by a 2006 purchase of a Daewoo plant that can produce 400,000 cars a year. In 2006, GM Daewoo surpassed Kia Motors as South Korea's second largest carmaker, after Hyundai. However, challenges loom. Toyota and Honda are powerful global competitors. Also, the rising value of the won (South Korea's currency) is lowering the competitiveness of all South Korean exports by making them more expensive for foreign customers. GM Daewoo, more than any other South Korean carmaker, depends on export sales.

The Ford Motor Company's sales continued to drop in 2006 and 2007. There was no expectation of a profit from North American operations before 2009. Despite good sales from its newer models, such as the Fusion sedan and the Edge, a crossover vehicle introduced in December 2006, Ford's recovery plan involved deep cuts in facilities and personnel. Titled the "Way Forward," the plan required Ford to close 16 factories and to eliminate 44,000 jobs, about one-third of its workforce, by 2012.

Ford also began to reduce the number of its dealers. In April 2007, there were 4,600 Ford and Lincoln-Mercury dealers in the U.S. The Toyota Motor Corporation, a main competitor, had 1,300 Toyota and Lexus dealers in the U.S.

The British-based carmaker Aston Martin was sold by Ford in 2007 as part of its downsizing. The buyer was a consortium of businesses that included two Kuwaiti investment firms. Automobile industry analysts speculated that Ford might be forced to sell other luxury vehicles it owned, such as Jaguar.

China's growing economic power has been extended into the global automobile industry in the 21st century. In March 2007, the Nanjing Automobile Corporation announced its intention to revive the famous British MG by producing it as a Chinese sports car. Economists viewed this as an example of the way Chinese industries have been reaching carefully into foreign markets, buying troubled companies with established brands, and using them to channel hundreds of billions of dollars into overseas investment. The Chinese government has seen the entire world, including developing countries in Africa and Latin America, as a field for investment, especially the purchasing of foreign companies.

European automakers have attempted to protect themselves from hostile takeovers. Germany's automobile industry is trying to avoid being in the same position as Britain's, where every notable name has been sold to foreign companies. Daimler Chrysler sold Chrysler to Cerebus Capital Management in May 2007. The sale was intended to strengthen Daimler and enable it to increase emphasis on Mercedes, its luxury car brand. Experts regarded it as an opportunity for Chrysler to reinvent itself, concentrating on improved manufacturing and vehicle quality. To protect Volkswagen, Porsche moved to increase the number of shares it owns in that firm. Within a five-year period, Volkswagen had eliminated 20,000 jobs. Porsche relies upon Volkswagen for the production of some of its sports utility vehicles. In addition to its stake in Volkswagen, Porsche owns Lamborghini and Bugatti.

♦ *PROVE OR DISPROVE: The U.S. automobile industry has had no difficulty in maintaining its domination of global markets in the 21st century.*

Empire of the Sun: The Toyota Way. Within a decade, Toyota grew into a vast international group and a global leader in the automobile industry. While its corporate headquarters has remained in Toyota City, Japan, the company has exported its manufacturing and management methods to 200,000 workers at 27 plants overseas. In 2007, only one-third of Toyota's workers were employed at 18 plants in Japan.

Global expansion has led to quality control problems. A surge in recalls was due partly to Toyota's failure to spread its insistence for craftsmanship among its non-Japanese factory workers and managers. In response, Toyota established an institute for teaching—the *Toyota Way*. This includes principles such as mutual ownership of problems, solving problems at the source—instead of behind desks—and a sense of crisis behind the company's constant desire to improve.

Toyota executives believe that the maintenance of the company's position as the most highly valued automaker in the world is dependent on its ability to transplant its culture to foreign markets.

♦ *Contrast Toyota's position in the global auto industry with that of General Motors and Ford.*

Economic Growth and the Quality of Life

Since 1990, the United Nations Development Program has been examining the extent to which global economic growth responds to human needs. It has asserted a need for measures to ensure that economic development benefits ordinary people, not just governments and powerful groups. In a report, it called for a "people-centered world order" in which security is redefined as security for people rather than for nations and is achieved through economic development. To reverse a trend in which economies expand without creating new jobs, the report recommends the conversion of defense industries to civilian production, more investment in education, deregulation of businesses, and aid to small enterprises.

In its human-development reports, the U.N. Development Program has rated nations according to their ability to raise living standards and otherwise improve the quality of life for their citizens. Each nation's rating is based upon such criteria as life expectancy, educational standards, and individual purchasing power. In a recent report, the United States was in third place, after Canada and Norway and just ahead of Australia and Iceland. However, the report noted a broad gap between the living standards of white Americans and Americans of other races.

Several developing countries scored higher on the human-development scale than did some more industrialized ones. Uruguay, for example, ranked above Poland. The lowest human-development scores were given to the poorest African nations. In Ethiopia, Burkina Faso, Niger, Sierra Leone, and other African countries, wealth is limited to a very few.

In the U.N. reports, a high per capita (per person) income or gross national product did not necessarily mean a high quality of life. The average Venezuelan, for example, earned more than the average Costa Rican. Costa Rica, however, received a higher human-development rating than Venezuela. This is because the average Costa Rican lives longer (because of such factors as cleaner water and better sanitation) than does the average Venezuelan.

Differences in quality of life between men and women were also noted. No country was credited with treating its female citizens as well as its males. Women in most nations, for example, had fewer job opportunities and lower earnings than men. In the developing countries, the greatest differences between men and women have been in the areas of employment, health care, nutrition, and education.

If nations all over the world can strengthen the link between economic growth and human development, they will improve the quality of life for their people.

1. *Define:*

   a. *people-centered world order*
   b. *human-development scale*

2. *List some of the factors that have been linked to quality of life in developing and industrialized nations.*

3. *Explain why some developing countries scored higher on the human-development scale than did some more industrialized countries.*

Chapter 12 Review

A. *Choose the item that best completes each sentence.*

1. *In the new economic order of recent years, new investment opportunities have developed especially in   (a) Western Europe and North America   (b) Eastern Europe and the developing world   (c) Africa and the Middle East.*

2. *Three nations of Eastern Europe that have been successful in moving toward market economies are   (a) Norway, Sweden, Denmark   (b) Serbia, Macedonia, Greece   (c) Poland, the Czech Republic, Slovakia.*

3. *To remain competitive, business firms in the industrialized nations tried   (a) restructuring   (b) outsourcing   (c) both of these.*

4. *The purchase of AT&T Wireless in 2004 was achieved by   (a) Vodafone   (b) British Telecom   (c) Cingular Wireless.*

5. *Foreign investors bought nearly half the shares in the top conglomerates of   (a) South Korea   (b) Indonesia   (c) Japan.*

6. *Thailand's Charoen Pokphand (CP) is an example of a   (a) conglomerate   (b) multinational   (c) both of these.*

7. *Financial ruin threatened Southeast Asia because of   (a) environmental regulations   (b) risky bank loans   (c) political instability.*

8. *A region that has attracted Western and Middle Eastern investors in 2006 and 2007 is   (a) Africa   (b) Latin America   (c) Asia.*

9. To compensate for the effects of NAFTA, a group of countries have made free trade agreements in   (a) Central America   (b) the Middle East   (c) Africa.

10. Reports issued by the U.N. Development Program focus on (a) transportation in industrialized nations   (b) how economic growth affects human needs   (c) national security concerns.

B. Reread "Strategies for Coping With Change" and "Giants of Global Industry and Trade," on pages 260–263. Then write an essay on the specific steps firms in industrialized countries are taking in order to remain competitive.

C. Reread the chapter introduction and "A New Economic Order," starting on page 258. Then read the statements below. Write a paragraph to explain how the four statements are related to the new economic order.

1. Businesses in the industrialized nations restructured to meet the increased competition in international markets.

2. American information technology workers were seriously affected by outsourcing.

3. The end of the cold war led to privatization and the development of free-market economies in Eastern Europe.

4. Manufacturing jobs have flowed from the more expensive labor markets of the developed nations to the less costly developing nations.

Chapter 13

Global Technology and Science

Smart Cards

Passengers on certain sections of the Paris Metro (subway) can sail through the turnstiles without reaching into their pockets for a token or a card. They carry a special *smart card* that stays in their pockets. The card contains a tiny built-in microchip. When the passenger buys the card, it is encoded with an amount of money to pay for subway fares. As the passenger passes through the turnstile, an electronic device reads the card and deducts the price of a fare. Every so often, the passenger pays more money, and the new value is recorded electronically on the card. New York City subway and bus riders can buy MetroCards that work the same way.

Similar cards have been introduced on U.S. highways, bridges, and tunnels. In the New York City metropolitan area and elsewhere, for example, the E-Zpass system allows drivers to avoid waiting in line to pay highway tolls. The driver simply attaches a small plastic tag to the vehicle's windshield. A radio receiver reads the tag and charges the price of the toll to the driver's E-Zpass account.

In June 2004, the U.S. Department of Agriculture announced a historic change in the food stamp program. Paper coupons had been replaced with electronic benefits and debit cards. In addition, many states now issue electronic benefits in place of welfare checks. Less abuse and faster payments to merchants have resulted.

Is old-fashioned money on the way out? Some experts claim

that the smart card is making cash obsolete. Central banks will need to print or mint less money. They'll no longer need to transport and secure so many coins and banknotes.

Another variation of the smart card contains a wealth of information about its holder. For instance, Gemplus, a French manufacturer, produces an "intelligent," nonforgeable identity card containing a microchip. The card carries a photograph of its owner, together with a range of personal details. The European Union has tested a health card capable of storing a person's medical history. Schools in France and in some U.S. cities are now using microchip cards that contain records of students' financial status, grades, and attendance.

Smart cards represent only one way that innovations in technology are affecting everyday life. Advances in computer technology, telecommunications, environmental protection, medical technology, transportation, and space exploration are doing much to shape our world in the 21st century.

♦ *Explain why you AGREE or DISAGREE with the following statement: Smart cards are an improvement over traditional money.*

The Continuing Computer Revolution

Compact electronic computing machines, able quickly to process and store information, have developed rapidly since the 1940s. The introduction of the microchip—storing thousands of transistors on a small silicon chip—in 1970 made it possible for computers to operate more quickly and store huge amounts of information, while taking up less space. By the 1990s, computers had become essential tools in every field of human activity.

Electronic Superhighways. The increasing commercial value of information has transformed the economies of the industrialized nations. By 1990, for example, the production and sale of information accounted for 50 percent of the gross domestic product of the United States. Today, approximately half of all workers in the United States have jobs in the information business. Information is the source of great wealth. And technology has made it possible for information of any kind to race along *electronic superhighways* at the speed of light.

Tiny strands of high-strength fiber optic cable can transport pulses of light. Sound and text are examples of data that can be reduced to pulses of light and transmitted via cable within or between computers. Fiber optics have been linked to digital

"Dennis, I would like to talk to you for a minute—off-line."

technology. Letters, numbers, sounds, and images are reduced to a sequence of zeros and ones. In computers, more data are processed faster. These developments help to propel the latest stage of the computer revolution, the development of interactive media.

Interactive media combine computer technology with telecommunications. They are providing consumers with new ways of obtaining and using information. New advances are announced almost daily. In 2007, for example, Google, an Internet search engine, began to expand its advertising sales operation into traditional media like newspapers, radio, and television. A partnership with Clear Channel Communications, the largest radio station owner in the United States, provided Google with access to 675 radio stations at all times of the day.

Among multimedia products are prerecorded optical discs that can be viewed on a personal computer equipped with a DVD-ROM or CD-ROM player. Another product is the V-chip, a microchip that can block out certain types of programs. With this chip, viewers can screen programs with objectionable content and monitor new channels. Since 2000, the Federal Communications Commission (FCC) in the United States has required all new television sets larger than 13 inches to contain a V-chip.

Corporations have been competing frantically to offer commercial services over the worldwide Internet. The *Internet*, the most familiar form of information superhighway, is a web of electronic connections open to public access. It links computers in far-flung locations into what amounts to one giant network. Individuals in their homes or cars can reach the Internet by using telephone signals. Businesses, universities, and increasing numbers of individuals connect to the Internet over higher speed direct lines. For years now, people have been using the Internet to exchange messages (electronic mail, or *e-mail*), to share files (including recorded music), and to search for all kinds of information. Political groups find that the Internet is a particularly efficient means of publishing their ideas. Hate groups use it to influence the public. Universities and research institutions, with government help, have started a new information superhighway called Internet2 that aims to be up to a thousand times faster than the regular Internet.

By 2003, Internet users were converting to high-speed access modes, such as cable modems, satellites, and, especially, the Digital Subscriber Line (DSL).

The World Wide Web has become well established as the

world's shopping mall. A growing number and variety of *Web sites* deliver text, sound, graphics, and opportunities to purchase products, access services, and gain information. In the 21st century, Web sites have become a common avenue of communication for governments, business companies, universities, and many other types of organizations. A commercial organization's Web site provides information about its purpose, its products, its services, and its personnel, as well as providing a highly efficient means for others to communicate with the organization by voice or e-mail.

Innovations. Advances in computer technology have led to many new products. Mid-20th-century scientists found that one small silicon chip could process (as a microprocessor) and store (as a memory chip) vast amounts of information. By the early 21st century, Intel—the world's leading producer of microprocessors—was making a chip that contained over 42 million transistors.

As a result of miniaturization, microprocessors have found an increasing number of applications. They are critical components in everything from smart cards and digital wristwatches to microwaves and videocassette recorders (VCRs).

One innovation of recent years is the small, handheld pocket computer that can use wireless technology to "talk" with telephones, faxes, and computers. This personal digital assistant (PDA) is also sometimes called a palmtop—as compared to the desktop, laptop, and notebook.

Another application of the microprocessor is the digital video disc (DVD). This device, a replacement for the VCR, is laser-based like a CD-ROM, but discs are capable of holding much more data—several movies, for example. Still another breakthrough in recent years has been digital photography, a marriage of computer chips with a traditional camera. Digital cameras capture photographs in digital form. Plasma TVs and TIVO (a device for recording television programs) also appeared in the 21st century.

Some innovations still lie in the realm of possibility. At Los Alamos National Laboratory in New Mexico and elsewhere, scientists have manipulated single atoms and molecules in an attempt to perfect an entirely new device—the *quantum computer*. Such a computer would harness quantum mechanics—the laws that apply only to subatomic particles, or particles smaller than a single atom. If theorists are correct, quantum computers would be capable of far more complex operations than current computers, and at un-heard-of speeds. They could break even the strongest codes and solve problems now deemed impossible to solve.

Supercomputers. Beyond the realm of personal computers and other consumer-oriented electronic devices is the world of super-computers. These are used by large industrial firms and government agencies for major research and development operations.

One of the world's most powerful supercomputers is ASCI White, built by IBM and located at the Lawrence Livermore National Laboratory in California. (*ASCI* stands for Accelerated Supercomputing Initiative.) ASCI White is the size of two basketball courts, has 8,192 processors, and can perform up to 12 trillion floating-point calculations per second. This amounts to some 2,000 calculations for every person in the world every second—seven times the speed of the fastest previous supercomputer. ASCI White is used for simulating, or imitating, nuclear explosions.

Another powerful supercomputer is located in Germany. It is the 112-processor Hitachi SR8000-F1, used for academic research. A supercomputer in Britain, the Fujitsu VPP5000/100, assists in weather research.

Since 2002, the fastest supercomputer in the world has been the Earth Simulator. Built by Japan's NEC, it is used for climate modeling.

Supercomputers that use *massively parallel processing* have been in great demand. By linking a number of small and relatively inexpensive standard workstation processors together, designers can make something far more powerful than earlier generations of supercomputers. Programmers no longer need to work through a problem by dealing with each equation in sequence. Instead, they can split the problem into small, independent parts, assign each to a different processor, and obtain a faster solution.

With a new design called *symmetric multiprocessing*, super-computers no longer have to be mammoth machines. In fact, a supercomputing project can be spread among hundreds of thousands of standard desktop computers linked over the Internet. "SETI at Home" does just that. This "Search for Extra-Terrestrial Intelligence" collects data about radio signals from space and distributes the information piece by piece to computers all over the world. Special software written for the project processes the data during a computer's spare time. This may be overnight, or when a computer user is on a coffee break, or even between keystrokes in a relatively undemanding task such as word processing. More than 2 million volunteers have helped with the SETI project.

1. *Define the following terms:*

   a. *interactive media*   d. *Internet*
   b. *information superhighway*   e. *World Wide Web*
   c. *fiber optics*   f. *supercomputers*

2. *Select one of the terms listed above. Write a paragraph explaining its importance in the continuing computer revolution.*

The Expanding World of Telecommunications

Consider this scenario: You're on a camping trip high in the Rockies or deep in the Amazon jungle. Back home, a crisis arises. Your parents need to reach you. They pick up a phone, dial your number, and in your lonely camp you get their call. A communications company sent the call via satellite, direct to your handheld phone.

Global Communications. Several companies have invested heavily in research and development to set up satellite-based communications systems that will make this scenario common. One early system, called Iridium, spent $5 billion putting 66 small satellites into low orbit, circling 100 miles above Earth. But too few customers signed up for the expensive service and in 1999, two years after launching its first satellite, Iridium filed for bankruptcy. It later resumed limited service under a new owner.

Another effort, called Teledesic, was started by Bill Gates of Microsoft, Craig McCaw, the cellular phone pioneer, and Boeing. This system planned to use about 300 satellites in low orbit to offer broadband data services to fixed locations.

These ventures are just a sampling of the corporate world's responses to the explosive growth in wireless communications. The field includes cellular telephones, two-way paging devices, handheld computers, and mobile fax machines. All such devices use radio waves to send and receive information.

An explosive growth in the field of wireless communications has taken place in the 21st century. The "smart phone," such as the Treo, Palm, Windows, and BlackBerry, combines the features of a cell phone with those of a computer. It provides Internet access, text messaging, and e-mail in addition to wireless telephone service. Originally used mainly by information technology and corporate managers, new devices like the BlackBerry Pearl and the Treo 700 series were introduced in 2006 to make smart phones more broadly popular. A2DP technology has made possible the addition of headsets, such as the Bluetooth and Pulsar 590A, to smart phones. Headsets enable hands-free utilization of cell phones, smart phones, and ipods (portable media players). Global Positioning System (GPS) additions can be connected to many smart phones. A keyboard that communicates wirelessly with the smart phone can also be added. The I-Tech Virtual Laser Keyboard is a small device that paints a keyboard on any surface in laser light.

In late June 2007, customers lined up at Apple stores to pay $500 to $600 for a new iPhone, a tiny hand-held computer equipped with a sensitive touch-screen. The sleek and thin phone includes a cellphone, video, iPod, e-mail terminal, web browser, camera, alarm clock, and organizer.

Around 2.8 billion mobile phones were in use in 2007. To

The iPod portable media player

enable cell phone owners to engage in impulse shopping, the Shop Text company introduced a system that lets people buy products instantly using text messages. This eliminates the need to go to a store or even visit a Web site. Any product for which a text code is available can be ordered by sending that code through the cell phone.

Text messaging is not the only way to use cell phones for purchases. In 2007, MasterCard began testing mobile payment in New York with Nokia phones that can be used to shop at selected stores, using a radio technology called near field communication. Other marketers have been experimenting with Bluetooth, GPS, and bar codes.

Text messaging, however, has become increasingly popular. About 35 percent of cell phone users were sending or receiving text messages in 2007. Among 18-to-24 year old young people, 76 percent use text messaging.

♦ *Identify the "smart phone" that most impresses you and explain the reasons for your selection.*

Computer-Displayed Newspapers and Books. Since the 1990s, the Internet has made newspapers and periodicals available on-line in many countries. In the United States, major newspapers offer all or part of their content on-line. Sometimes publishers simply repackage a paper's printed contents. But they may add special features such as news updates, interactive forums, and games.

Electronic books ("e-books") are now an alternative to paper books ("p-books"). Several models of reader consoles are available. They look like a tablet, a little bigger and thicker than a magazine. They have a backlit liquid crystal display (LCD) screen that can be read in the dark. Or you can download special software and read e-books on your handheld, laptop, or other computer. E-books have a number of advanced features. They allow readers to search for text electronically and to highlight and take notes on passages they like. Readers can also increase the type size, which is an advantage for people with limited vision.

But the p-book is not dead yet. Publishers have been developing print-on-demand systems with which they hope to avoid the high costs associated with unsold copies of books. With print-on-demand, books will never need to go out of print. Publishers can keep a digital copy of all their books and run off very small press runs—even a single copy at a time.

Cyber schools offer all of their courses online, with only limited use of print products. University instructors and, increasingly, secondary school teachers rely upon course packs (digitally reproduced materials coordinated with the course syllabus) and course publishing. Course publications enable the instructor to select portions from several data-based books for reproduction and binding into a single book. The resulting product follows the course syllabus closely. Distance learning enables students working at computers in different locations to receive the same instruction.

Banking Services. New developments have also changed the banking industry. In the 1990s, a few banks began providing some of their customers with a special telephone. The phone had a miniature version of an automated teller machine's display. It "talked" to the same data network that served ATMs. The phone could do anything an ATM could do, except give cash. Although the special telephone was inexpensive, this approach did not catch on. Now most online banking is done over the Internet. Thousands of banks in the United States and other countries offer Internet-based services that allow users to check their account information, pay bills, or apply for a loan 24 hours a day. Banks hope to save money by closing many of their traditional branches as more and more customers do their banking from home.

Technological change in the telecommunications field involves television, radio, compact discs, and every other means of communication. The effort to eliminate distance as an obstacle to communication is a key feature of the global economy in the 21st century.

1. *Explain why you AGREE or DISAGREE with the following statement: Reading the news online is a big improvement over reading a traditional newspaper.*

2. *Match the term or name listed in Column A with a description in Column B.*

Column A	Column B
1. Google	a. processes and stores information
2. silicon chip	
3. electronic superhighways	b. collects data and radio signals from space
4. quantum computer	c. Internet search engine
5. SETI	d. theoretical use of subatomic particles
	e. information transmitted at the speed of light

3. *Complete the following sentences:*

    a. *Smart phones provide* _____.
    b. *E-books are an alternative to* _____.
    c. *Online banking makes it possible to* _____.
    d. *The "computer revolution" was made possible by the invention of the* _____.

The Technology of Environmental Protection

In December 1997, the United Nations Conference on Climate Change brought together more than 5,000 representatives from some 150 countries. They met at Kyoto, Japan, to discuss *global warming*—the gradual heating up of Earth's atmosphere that many believe threatens the future of the planet. The meeting grew out of a U.N. Conference on Environment and Development, the so-called Earth Summit, that was held in Brazil in 1992.

Global Warming. The surface temperature of Earth has been rising since the late 1800s. Scientists believe that the chief reason for the change is the increasing amount of carbon dioxide in the atmo-

THE GREENHOUSE EFFECT

sphere. This gas is created with the burning of fossil fuels—chiefly coal, oil, and natural gas—on which the modern industrialized world depends.

Carbon dioxide, together with other gases such as methane and nitrous oxide, rises to form a sort of windowpane above Earth. The sun's radiation passes through the pane to warm Earth and is then reflected back upward. But some of the energy is trapped by the gases, making Earth's temperature rise. This is the so-called *greenhouse effect.*

The greenhouse effect is natural and necessary; without it, Earth would be too cold to sustain life. But environmentalists believe that it is at least partially to blame for global warming. There is disagreement, however, about what global warming might mean over the long run. Many experts fear that a temperature rise of only 2 or 3 degrees over the next century could have disastrous consequences, altering ocean currents and climate patterns, changing shorelines, and threatening the lives of humans, animals, and plants. The quantity of carbon dioxide in the atmosphere has risen significantly in recent years.

Delegates to the 1997 conference issued the Kyoto Protocol, the first international treaty to set binding limits on nations' emissions of carbon dioxide and five other greenhouse gases. The protocol called for the industrialized nations to reduce emissions 6–8 percent below 1990 levels by the year 2012. Developing countries were allowed to limit emissions voluntarily.

The United States is the world's largest single emitter of greenhouse gases. With only 4 percent of the globe's population, it is responsible for 25 percent of the greenhouse gases in the atmosphere. Cutting back on these emissions would require far-reaching changes, including the increased use of renewable energy (solar and wind power) and the development of more fuel-efficient cars.

The Kyoto Protocol had its critics. In the United States, especially, some feared that the emission limits would cripple economic growth. In March 2001, President George W. Bush rejected the Kyoto Protocol. In 2004, Russia approved it.

New Signs of Global Warming. In September 2006, NASA scientists reported that higher temperatures and a retreat of Arctic Ocean ice in 2004 and 2005 offered new evidence that greenhouse gases were changing the climate of the Arctic region. Since satellite observation of the region began in 1978, the amount of sea ice around the Arctic Ocean has steadily shrunk. In 2005, the most open water in a century was observed. Scientists regarded this as evidence of the growing danger of global warming for the whole world.

A 2006 British government report called for prompt action on the climate crisis, including more research. Without worldwide spending on research into low-carbon technologies, the report warned, coastal flooding in Europe and America, droughts in Africa, stronger hurricanes, and rising sea levels around the world could turn 200 million people into refugees.

The most promising technologies for limiting global warming are solar power, wind, ethanol and other farm-produced fuels, energy-efficient buildings, and environment-friendly automobiles.

♦ *Explain what causes the greenhouse effect and why it may be dangerous.*

Saving the Amazon Rain Forest. A crucial factor in global warming is the amount of forested land in the world. Trees absorb carbon dioxide and give off oxygen. As more and more land is cleared, there are fewer trees to perform this important conversion and thus more chance for greenhouse gases to accumulate.

The Amazon rain forest heads the list of areas that scientists and environmentalists want to protect. Its 5 million square kilometers are the largest continuous expanse of tropical rain forest remaining in the world. Although such forests cover only 7 percent of the planet's land surface, they contain approximately 50 percent of the plants and animals found on the globe. Of these, thousands of species face extinction each year as a result of forest destruction by loggers. (Trees are being cut down at the rate of 4,500 acres every hour.) Because Brazil has the highest number of species of plants and animals in the world, it is the center of efforts to stop global deforestation. However, Brazil has widespread poverty and an unequal distribution of wealth. Efforts to preserve the Amazon rain forest must be consistent with the human need for economic development. Scientists have been attempting to develop the methods and technology to accomplish both.

Economic development that preserves the environment and allows resources to be used over and over is called *sustainable development.* The patterns of sustainable development discovered in the Amazon may help to preserve threatened forest lands in other parts of the world.

♦ *Explain why environmentalists are so concerned about the Amazon rain forest.*

The Bloomberg Plan. On Earth Day in April 2007, Mayor Michael R. Bloomberg of New York City outlined a long-range plan to create the first environmentally sustainable 21st-century city. Among the mayor's proposals was a congestion charge for people who drive their cars into Manhattan, in order to reduce traffic and auto emissions. Improved energy efficiency in new buildings and the replacement of energy-consuming power plants would be pursued by a new agency with city, state, and private industry representatives. City sales taxes would be eliminated on energy-efficient hybrid vehicles. Mussels would be cultivated to suck pollution out of the city's rivers. One million trees would be planted over a ten-year period. To capture water runoff, incentives would

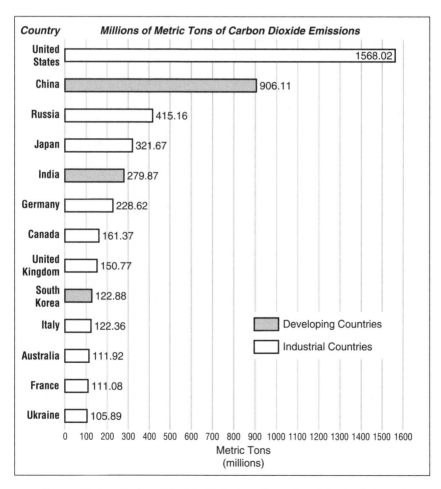

Figure 13.1   Carbon Dioxide Emissions From Fossil Fuels, Selected Countries, in 2002 (millions of metric tons)

be offered for larger and deeper sidewalk tree pits and green roofs. Incentives would also be offered to get heavy diesel trucks off the road. And the city would replace or modernize diesel-powered school buses.

Several other proposals were part of Mayor Bloomberg's vision. However, the congestion pricing for automobiles was the most likely to be opposed. Nevertheless, similar systems are in place in London and Singapore and have been shown to reduce congestion and improve air quality.

More Environmental Schemes. China is expected to become the world's biggest emitter of carbon gases before 2010. The Kyoto Protocol expires in 2012. A U.N. conference to set controls on global warming gases was held in Nairobi, Kenya, in November 2006. Its purpose was to set a timetable for determining new emissions targets for the five years that begin in 2012.

In 2006, California added to its tough air pollution standards an emissions trading scheme (ETS) with other states as part of its effort to control the output of greenhouse gases. The European Union had introduced an ETS in 2005. Such programs set targets for emissions and give emission allowances to industries and power plants. If companies wish to emit more than their allowances, they must buy extra allowances from other industries, states, or countries.

Diesel fuel—with just 3 percent of the sulfur content of older fuel—was made available for use in trucks and buses in late 2006. Like lead, previously removed from highway fuels, sulfur generates air pollution. Production of ethanol, a much cleaner fuel than gasoline and made from corn, reached five billion gallons in 2006. Biotechnology companies have begun research on genetically altering soybeans, beans, and prairie switch grass to produce ethanol and other biofuels. In 2007, a New Zealand company developed a method to produce ethanol from carbon monoxide gas, a previously untapped source.

1. *Reread "The Bloomberg Plan" on pages 285–286 and explain whether you would or would not be in favor of a "congestion charge."*

2. *Examine the graph (Figure 13.1) on page 285 and state which of the following are correct statements.*

   a. *The United States put more carbon dioxide into the atmosphere than the next five countries combined.*

b. The developing country with the highest level of carbon dioxide emissions was China.

c. The European country with the highest level of carbon dioxide emissions was Russia.

d. The graph tracks carbon dioxide given off by forest trees and other plants as well as by burning fossil fuels.

e. Eight of the top ten emitters of carbon dioxide are industrial countries.

3. Identify the major concerns of environmentalists in the 1990s and early 21st century.

Health and Medical Technology

Research, funding, and technological development in recent years have focused on AIDS, cancer, and other global threats to human life, on the disabled, and on genetic engineering.

At international AIDS conferences, the difficulties of achieving early detection of HIV, the virus that causes AIDS, have been a major topic of discussion. The ability of the virus to remain hidden in the blood cells for long periods of time increases the difficulty of treatment. Of the drugs produced to date, AZT, produced by the GlaxoSmithKline company, has received the most attention. AZT, however, appears to do little for patients who have the virus but have not developed symptoms. For people with AIDS, AZT has provided definite benefits. Researchers have recently begun to focus on instances of natural immunity to HIV. They hope to duplicate the protective process in people who do not have immunity.

A team of British doctors discovered a useful acid called ALA. This natural compound sensitizes cancer cells to light for a few hours. Used with ALA, a low-powered laser can destroy cancers near the surface of the skin without leaving a patient sensitive to sunlight for weeks. Research is continuing to determine correct drug dosages and laser intensities.

Lung cancer kills about one million people a year. The cancer must be detected while still small, before it spreads. Canadian researchers have experimented with photosensitive drugs that make tumors glow under ultraviolet (UV) light. While the drugs do not destroy cancer cells, the Canadians have discovered that all cells have a pale red glow in the presence of UV light. Healthy cells also emit green light. To help detect the difference, a group of doctors started a company called Xillix to build LIFE (lung-imaging fluorescent endoscope) machines. More than 130 such machines were in use in the early years of the 21st century.

To combat the memory loss caused by Alzheimer's disease, a California-based unit of the Elan Corporation of Ireland developed a vaccine. In mice, the vaccine both prevented and reversed an accumulation of protein deposits associated with the brain disorder. Tests then began on humans. Several drug companies are working on other drugs to combat the buildup of damaging deposits. Still another approach uses gene therapy. Doctors have taken skin cells, engineered them to produce a substance called *nerve growth factor*, and implanted them in a patient's brain. A lack of nerve growth factor is believed to contribute to Alzheimer's.

People With Disabilities. Beyond killer diseases, advances in technology have also led to assistance for the disabled. For those with hearing problems, a new type of hearing aid that is the equivalent of a contact lens has been developed by Resound Corporation, a California firm. The device uses a tiny magnet, called Earlens, that is placed directly on the eardrum. Held in place by a drop of oil, it amplifies the movements of the eardrum that produce the sensation of sound. The result is better-quality hearing. The eardrum magnet is activated by signals from a tiny receiver that can be worn on a necklace or pinned to an undergarment.

The development of virtual reality computer technology may help blind people use computers even when they cannot see the visual display. For some purposes, the monitor screen can be replaced by headphones giving a three-dimensional impression of the sounds in a room. British researchers are experimenting with the idea of using sound coming from a particular direction. Changing a menu into sounds requires changes to some basic program instructions. Research is still at an early stage. Another part of this European Union project is an attempt to develop a "sonic mouse." Sounds would indicate whether or not the user had clicked on the correct icon on the display. Another possibility is to use a speech synthesizer to read a menu aloud.

Genetic Engineering. A sheep born in 1997 made news all over the world. Her name was Dolly, and she was the first clone of an adult animal. *Cloning* is the process by which an organism is reproduced from only one parent, without fertilization. This means that the genetic structure of the clone is exactly the same as that of its parent. The Scottish scientists who cloned Dolly, and the scientific community as a whole, hope that cloning will lead to important medical advances. For example, it might create animals whose organs could be successfully transplanted into humans.

But Dolly created concern as well as admiration. Could human beings be cloned? If so, society would face problems of both safety and ethics. Scientists said that cloned animals often had genetic defects. Would cloning humans produce people with strange new diseases? Religious and political leaders also raised moral objections to "playing God" by cloning humans. Would cloning lead to a two-class society of ultrahumans and "naturals"? Legislation to ban human cloning has been proposed in the United States and several other countries. Nonetheless, in 2001 an international team of doctors announced plans to clone a human.

Begun in 1990, the Human Genome Project was finally brought to completion in 2003. Its mission was to map the human genome, the code of all human DNA. Scientists believe that this decoding will enable them to better understand the causes and treatment of disease. It is estimated that mutations, or errors in the coding of genes, are responsible for 3,000 to 4,000 hereditary diseases.

Scientists believe that stem cell research will lead to the elimination of certain diseases by engineering the necessary genes. Theoretically, genetic engineering could provide humans with desirable traits such as improved health, strength, and dexterity, while eliminating undesirable traits such as susceptibility to a variety of diseases. However, stem cell research is opposed by some. In August 2006, U.S. President Bush vetoed a bill that would have speeded stem cell research by funding research with new cell lines. Researchers have begun to view human embryonic cells as a research tool in a long-term program to study the mechanisms of disease.

By 2006, regenerative medicine, a practice that aims to replace or rebuild diseased or damaged tissue using the body's own healthy cells, had made significant progress. Scientists continue to work on tissue replacement projects for human hearts, livers, kidneys, and other body parts.

1. *Describe advances in medical technology that reduce the threat of AIDS and of lung cancer.*

2. *Why was the birth of a sheep named Dolly an important scientific advance?*

3. *Interview a doctor or another type of medical professional to get her or his reaction to recent developments in health and medical technology.*

Transportation Technology

Advances in technology made possible the Concorde, a supersonic airplane that traveled at up to twice the speed of sound; the hydrofoil boat, which skims the water on a pillow of air; the monorail train, a railroad that runs through a tunnel under the English Channel connecting Britain to the European continent; and continuing improvements in the safety and comfort of automobiles and the roads upon which they move. Recent research has focused especially on faster and safer air and road travel.

Commercial airline manufacturers in the United States and Europe have concentrated on making jumbo jets that travel at slightly less than the speed of sound, rather than on new supersonic models to replace the Concorde. The reason is simple: jumbo jets are far more profitable. When the Anglo-French Concorde went into service in 1976, its supporters called it the wave of the future. Instead, it proved to be a money loser. It used too much fuel (5,638 gallons an hour) and carried too few passengers (just 100, compared to 400 for Boeing's subsonic 747). In the end, only about 30 Concordes were ever built. British Airways and Air France retired the Concorde in 2003. The costs of maintaining the aging fleet were too great. As the 21st century opened, no company had any immediate plans for a new supersonic airliner. Instead, in 2007, the European giant Airbus Industries introduced the A380, a new jumbo jet for up to 800 passengers, while Boeing enlarged the 747.

For environmental and other reasons, American and Japanese auto manufacturers worked to develop a marketable electric car. In 1996, General Motors became the first automaker in the modern era to mass-produce an electric-powered vehicle, the EV1. Manufacturers also worked on "hybrid" cars that run on both gasoline (or diesel fuel) and electricity. The Honda Insight and the Toyota Prius went on sale in 2000. They featured high mileage and low emissions. U.S. companies introduced hybrids in 2003. "Flex-fuel" cars, using a mixture of gasoline and ethanol (alcohol), were sold in increasing numbers in 2003 and 2004.

The Big Three American auto manufacturers also examined ways to reduce auto weight in order to improve fuel economy. General Motors, Ford, and Chrysler sponsored joint research on aluminum, magnesium, and metal matrix composites. The use of such metals, along with more plastics, may make future cars lighter. In the mid-1990s, Ford designed two concept cars that relied heavily on light metals. The Synthesis 2010 used aluminum for every major component and was a half ton lighter than a Mercury Sable. An aluminized Sable was 400 pounds lighter.

"Smart" roads may prove to be the most effective way to make automobile travel safer and highways less congested. Smart roads depend upon sensors. The most basic is a wire strip across the road that works like a switch when a vehicle's wheels go over it. More sophisticated, and more durable, are magnetic induction loops buried in the road.

Sensors were first used to time and coordinate traffic lights. They can also count vehicles and determine the speed of the traffic. This information can be given to drivers. On many highways, the volume and speed of traffic are electronically monitored to give drivers instant warnings about traffic jams and accidents. These are displayed on electronic signs, which also advise on other things, such as when highway service stations are crowded.

Such information can now be transmitted directly to cars. In Britain, the Trafficmaster system keeps an eye on highway congestion. Its warnings, together with the speed of traffic, appear on maps on handheld or desktop computers and on small screens attached to the dashboards of those who subscribe to the system. By 2007, navigation systems, such as Global Positioning System (GPS), became a standard feature of new automobiles. For older cars, they are available as dashboard attachments. No driver need ever become lost or fail to find an alternative route if traffic conditions are adverse.

Sensing technology is used for law enforcement in automatic speed traps. It has also been introduced to monitor trucking. On one highway, road sensors automatically weigh trucks as they drive by to check on whether their loads are above the legal limit.

One unusual concept, a highway without drivers, was introduced in 1997. Using a combination of magnets, videocameras, and radar, this automated road—a stretch of 7.6 miles near San Diego—was created to test specially equipped vehicles without human drivers. General Motors, Lockheed Martin, and Carnegie-Mellon University formed a consortium that planned to use government grants to develop this program further.

◆ *Describe one technological improvement in each of the following areas:*

   a. air travel
   b. automobile design
   c. road safety

Space Exploration

The age of space exploration began in 1957, when the Soviets launched *Sputnik,* an orbiting space satellite. Advances in satellite technology resulted in improved television, radio, and telephone communications; more accurate weather forecasting; and important information about other planets. *Voyager 2*'s trip past Neptune in 1989 was one of the most important exploration missions.

During the 1960s, scientists labored to place people in space. In 1969, two American astronauts landed on the moon. In the 1970s and 1980s, however, the emphasis was on orbiting space stations. In those large spacecraft, astronaut-scientists have been able to conduct experiments in a gravity-free environment. The United States also invested heavily in reusable space shuttles. Those smaller craft are a blend of space capsule and airplane and are designed for repeated voyages.

Exploration of Mars has been a major objective. Previously, only the *Viking* Mars lander had visited the planet, in 1976. An American robot probe, *Mars Observer,* was designed to spend two to six years in Mars orbit. It was to map the planet in far greater detail than ever before. However, in 1993, the $1 billion probe failed to orbit Mars and was lost in space. The Russians also tried to reach Mars, losing two spacecraft in the process.

Success came in 1997, when NASA launched a vehicle named *Pathfinder.* After a seven-month journey, it landed on Mars on July 4. *Pathfinder* sent out a roving robotic explorer vehicle, *Sojourner,* which took pictures and scooped up samples from the planet's surface. Data was then transmitted to Earth in a steady stream, giving scientists unprecedented knowledge about the climate, atmosphere, and geology of Mars. The space vehicles functioned for about two months before being frozen in Mars' cold atmosphere. With initially better results, two new robotic rovers, named *Spirit* and *Opportunity,* began the exploration of the Martian surface in 2004.

These investigations of Mars were part of a new era of international coordination of space exploration. Cooperation among the European Space Agency, Russia, Japan, and the United States was made possible by the end of the cold war. Also, rising costs made a sharing of technologies attractive.

Jupiter has been another space target. *Galileo,* an American spacecraft launched in cooperation with Germany, carried cameras that showed the spectacular effects of Jupiter's collision with a flurry of comet fragments in 1994. The spacecraft *NEAR Shoemaker* orbited the asteroid Eros for a year, taking 160,000 pictures. Then in February 2001 it made a soft landing on the 21-mile-long, potato-shaped "space rock" and sent back further data.

In mid-2004, the *Cassini* spacecraft completed a 2.2-billion-mile journey to Saturn of nearly seven years. Orbiting the planet, it transmitted striking pictures of the planet's ice and rock rings.

The International Space Station (ISS) has been under construction since 1998. It is designed to house rotating teams of up to seven researchers from the United States and other nations. In June 2004, an American and a Russian astronaut conducted repairs to the exterior of the ISS while maneuvering in spacesuits. Space shuttles travel between the ISS and Earth. Regular shuttle flights, such as those of the *Discovery* and the *Atlantis* in 2006, were made in order to continue work on the ISS. Such flights continued in 2007, and more were planned for 2008. However, President Bush ordered the shutdown of the shuttle program by 2010. NASA will then begin the task of returning to the moon in a new generation of space vehicles.

The New Horizons spacecraft, launched by NASA in 2005, reached Jupiter in early 2007. The mission of the robot craft was to make 700 observations of Jupiter and its four largest moons. Upon completion, the New Horizons will move toward Pluto at 52,000 miles per hour. It is expected to reach that planet in 2015.

NASA's long-range program of placing telescopes in space launched the Hubble Space Telescope in 1990, the Compton Gamma Ray Observatory in 1991, and the Chandra X-ray Observatory in 1999. They enabled astronomers to discover the oldest known planet in 2004, a huge gaseous object nearly three times as old as Earth. Observations of galaxies far out in space and time have also revealed that expansion of the universe is accelerating. Influenced by a mysterious antigravitational force, galaxies are flying apart faster and faster.

By 2010, the number of operating Earth observing instruments on NASA satellites, most of which are past their planned lifetimes, is likely to drop by 40 percent. This will lessen the ability of scientists to observe the effects of global warming, such as retreating polar ice and shifting patterns of drought and rainfall. The diminished budget for replacing the aging sensors on the satellites has been linked to the priority given to the goals of President Bush. These include manned flights to Mars and establishing a permanent base on the moon.

1. *Explain why recent space exploration plans have included close cooperation among nations.*

2. *Complete the following sentences:*

   a. *The era of space exploration began in 1957, when _____ .*
   b. *Among the benefits gained from orbiting satellites have been _____ .*
   c. *Space stations make it possible for scientists to _____ .*
   d. *Two planets explored in 2004 were _____ and _____.*
   e. *A major international project of the 21st century is continued construction of _____ .*

Chapter 13 Review

A. *Choose the item that best completes each sentence.*

   1. *A consequence of the smart card revolution might be to use high-tech microchip cards to   (a) replace cash for most daily purchasing   (b) develop new accounting systems   (c) create new uses for plastic.*

   2. *A supercomputer in California is used for studying   (a) whale migration patterns   (b) atmospheric pollution   (c) nuclear bomb explosions.*

   3. *The term "interactive media" refers to   (a) computers that talk to their users   (b) integration of computer and telecommunications technologies   (c) replacement of computers by more advanced televisions.*

   4. *Among the advances in telecommunications technology in recent years were   (a) better cellular, digital, and satellite communications   (b) shortwave radio transmission   (c) the ability to transport objects to satellites orbiting in space.*

   5. *All of the following are advantages of e-books except   (a) they will last forever   (b) they can be read in the dark   (c) they allow a reader to conduct rapid searches to find a desired passage.*

   6. *The term "sustainable development" refers to   (a) logging and mining   (b) economic development that preserves the environment   (c) preserving endangered species.*

   7. *A major concern of environmentalists has been   (a) global warming   (b) deforestation   (c) both of these.*

8. Genetic engineering involves the manipulation of   (a) viruses (b) hormones   (c) DNA.

9. Smart roads use techniques such as electronic sensors, signs, and computerized cards to   (a) identify drivers for security purposes   (b) control pollution by checking on carbon emissions from vehicles   (c) provide drivers with information about speed limits, congestion, and service stations.

10. A major space project in the early 21st century involves (a) constructing a large space laboratory for international use (b) landing astronauts on Jupiter   (c) running shuttle flights to the moon.

B. Reread "The Expanding World of Telecommunications," on pages 278–281. Then answer the questions below.

1. Explain how the increased use of satellites has improved global communications in the 21st century.

2. List three examples of improvements in wireless technology.

3. Define interactive media and state an important benefit arising from it.

C. Reread "The Technology of Environmental Protection," on pages 282–286, and do the following:

1. Explain why the buildup of carbon dioxide in the atmosphere is an environmental problem.

2. Discuss the measures taken to reduce or prevent this problem.

Unit III Review

A. Study the list of nations below. Use information from Unit III to complete the sentences that follow.

Britain	Canada	Mexico	Bulgaria	Austria
Japan	United States	Russia	Sweden	Romania

1. A nation that has been struggling to introduce free market practices is _____ .

2. The nations that joined the European Union in 2007 are _____ and _____ .

3. A nation that experienced a drastic fall in the value of its currency in December 1994 is _____ .

4. An Asian nation that had a global trade surplus in the 1990s is _____ .

5. The nations that signed the North American Free Trade Agreement are _____ , _____ , and _____ .

B. Review Chapter 11 and do the following.

1. Describe the G-8 and how it operates.

2. State the changes brought to Europe by the Maastricht Treaty.

3. List arguments for and against NAFTA.

4. Tell why OPEC has trouble getting its members to agree on how much oil to produce.

C. Review Chapter 12 and answer the questions below.

1. Tell what is meant by the term "new economic order."

2. Give pros and cons of the new economic order.

3. Explain how changes in global trade and investment have contributed to unemployment in Europe.

4. Define multinationals and describe how they operate.

5. Describe the changes in the global auto industry in the 21st century.

D. Use information from Unit III to write a brief essay on ONE of the following topics:

European Economic Unity
Global Economic Development: The World Bank and
      the International Monetary Fund
The Computer Revolution

Unit IV

FACING THE FUTURE

Any attempt to describe world conditions in the years ahead must be in the form of questions. For example: Will the battle against terrorism shape the 21st century, as two world wars and the cold war did the 20th century? How will the globalization of economic life affect living standards in industrial and developing nations? How will the growing environmental crisis change our lives?

There can be no certain answers to those questions. However, examination of current trends and developments can provide us with insights into a possible future.

Chapter 14

The Challenge of Uncertainty

For a time in the 1990s, the world breathed more easily. The cold war was over. The conflicts that had made the world a place of anger and intrigue and stirred fears of all-out nuclear war seemed to be fading. To be sure, the entire world was not at peace. Cruel wars plagued the Balkans, Africa, and scattered corners of the world. But for the first time in a century, a more peaceful future seemed possible, even likely.

Then came the September 11, 2001, terrorist attacks on New York City and Washington. They were quickly followed by the U.S. invasions of Afghanistan and Iraq. Expectations of peace faded. The task of waging war moved front and center. Suddenly, it seemed a great deal harder to predict the future.

New Realities: The Search for Security

In responding to an act of terrorism, the United States found itself facing the same hard realities that many other nations had long endured. In countries such as Israel, Algeria, Northern Ireland, Spain, Kashmir, and Colombia, people had been living under the threat of terrorism for years. Governments there had used strong measures to protect the public. Metal detectors in shopping centers, frequent identity checks, military patrols, and similar measures were common. Not until after the September 2001 attacks did the United States begin seriously considering such measures for itself. Suddenly, strengthening public security became an urgent national goal.

The United States was now the world's only superpower. It had massive military forces armed with the latest nuclear weapons. But its power did not protect it from attack. Its defenses had not stopped terrorists from killing thousands of civilians in one carefully planned strike. Nor did those defenses prevent an outbreak of bioterrorism—the use by terrorists of disease-carrying microbes—that followed the start of U.S. attacks on Afghanistan in October 2001. Letters containing anthrax spores were mailed to television networks and government offices. Federal authorities moved quickly to stockpile antibiotics and other cures. Homeland defenses would have to be greatly expanded, U.S. leaders declared.

In the years ahead, we can expect the nation's domestic security to be the focus of close government attention. Shortly after the 2001 attacks on the United States, Congress passed the USA Patriot Act. This new law provided the government with greatly expanded police powers. Among other features, people under suspicion can be detained without access to an attorney or a trial; homes and offices may be searched without warrants; e-mails, bank accounts, and other personal records may be investigated. How will the rights of the innocent be protected? How successful will the nation be in balancing the need for security against the need to protect the constitutional rights upon which our liberties depend?

Dr. Martin Rees, a British cosmologist and astronomer, has predicted that civilization has only a 50 percent chance of surviving until 2100. He believes that by 2020, bioterror or bioerror will lead to one million casualties in a single event. By that year, Dr. Rees has warned, there will be thousands of people with the capability to cause a biological disaster. His concern is not only about organized terrorist groups such as Al Qaeda but also with deranged individuals like those who design computer viruses. Those who agree with Dr. Rees regard bioterrorism as the greatest threat to human existence in the world today. Although it is currently difficult for individuals or nongovernmental groups to obtain or manufacture biological weapons, the technology is getting cheaper and is becoming more available.

The biggest threat is of a nation deploying biological weapons. However, there has been a decline in the number of countries working on this technology. Nevertheless, the United States has poured money into defenses against biological weapons.

We can also expect a new look at domestic political and economic priorities. Increased military spending has put pressure on other areas of federal spending, including farm programs, social security and Medicare, and a "safety net" for poor people. By 2004, spending had created the largest federal deficit in U.S. history. Long-range damage to the U.S. economy and to the global economy is feared. Can the huge debts of the United States be paid off without weakening vital programs such as Social Security and Medicare?

1. *How have other nations dealt with the threat of terrorism?*

2. *State three ways in which the drive to promote U.S. domestic security may affect everyday lives.*

3. *Explain why you AGREE or DISAGREE with the idea that the United States will need to expand the role of the federal government.*

New Realities: Shifting Alliances and Alignments

The end of the cold war freed the world's nations to rethink their alliances and alignments. Nations began to seek new friendships across old barriers. The Persian Gulf War of 1991 was an example of such new alignments. A U.S.-led coalition of 13 countries undertook a U.N.-approved war that drove Iraqi forces out of Kuwait. Joining the coalition were both traditional U.S. allies like Britain and former opponents like Syria. The 21st-century "war on terrorism" carried the process further. Nations like Russia and Uzbekistan, once part of the former Soviet Union, offered the United States their cooperation. Twentieth-century political lines had become blurred. New partnerships were emerging.

Nations that face terrorist threats of their own will seek the support of the world community. The world will need to decide how to define terrorism. Should all fighters waging wars against government forces be considered terrorists? Many such fighters have carried out attacks that killed large numbers of civilians. They have used tactics such as assassination as well. Does that make them "terrorists"? Or should they be considered "freedom fighters" if their goal is to overthrow an unjust government? What about governments that use assassination and other terrorist tactics in trying to defeat rebel movements? Or governments that have the support of secret organizations that use such tactics? Should such governments be shunned by the world community?

Should they be subjected to sanctions? Should they be attacked by a U.N.-backed military force? Or should they be given money and assistance and encouraged to reform? There are so many questions that beg for answers.

During the cold war, the great divisions were: East and West, communism and capitalism, repression and democracy. What will they be in the 21st century? U.S. leaders envision a battle between freedom and terror. Some writers predict a clash of civilizations—wealthier Western nations with roots in Greece and Rome against poorer nations with different traditions. Others see a religious clash—Christians and Jews against Muslims. The United States hoped that its "war on terrorism" would not be seen as "war on Islam." Thus, U.S. and British leaders tried to build a broad coalition of nations. The 2003 invasion of Iraq, however, caused sharp rejections of U.S. leadership. France, Germany, Russia, and other nations sharply criticized the British-U.S. action. But Poland and other Eastern European countries supported it. By 2007, British troops were being withdrawn from Iraq, and demands from Iraqis and many Americans for a withdrawal of U.S. troops were increasing. Many considered the American-led effort to stabilize and democratize Iraq to be a failure. Furthermore, confidence in the ability of the U.S. to play a leadership role in the world had declined. Was the United States capable of fostering peace between Israel and the Palestinians, an essential building block of a general peace agreement in the Middle East?

1. *How did the "war on terrorism" reflect post–cold war changes in the world's system of alliances?*

2. *Under what circumstances, if any, in your opinion, would a government or group of fighters be justified in using violence in ways that might harm innocent civilians?*

3. *Why were U.S. leaders eager to win support from moderate Islamic nations for the "war on terrorism"?*

4. *Explain why you AGREE or DISAGREE with the description of the United States in the manifesto of Norway's governing Socialist Left Party as "the greatest threat to world peace."*

New Realities: Where Is the Global Economy Going?

Amid all the talk of fighting terrorism abroad and protecting security at home, the world's economic future was also clouded.

Even before September 11, 2001, the world economy was in trouble. Then came the terrorist attacks on the United States, dealing a sharp blow to many industries. Uncertainty about the future grew, not only in this country but around the world. A global economic downturn, or recession, seemed to be under way. But it could not last forever. Economic life goes in cycles, and even deep depression eventually gives way to recovery.

FALLOUT FROM THE NEW GLOBAL ECONOMY!

Perils of Globalization

© Carol*Simpson/Rothco

Regardless of the immediate future, some thinkers believe that economic issues will be a key to the rest of the 21st century. Status and power in the world community will depend not only upon a nation's military power but also upon its productivity and ability to compete.

The trend toward globalization—the increasing number of economic links among nations—is likely to continue. Multinational corporations have offices and factories all over the world. Money and investments move easily across international borders. Increasingly, so does trade. Most trade barriers have already been removed in North America and Europe, thanks to regional associations like the North American Free Trade Agreement and the European Union. With the admission of China and Taiwan early in the 21st century, the World Trade Organization expanded its scope to include almost all of the world's key nations. The rules of trade that the WTO enforces will help to promote more exchanges of goods and services. Thus, economic growth will be promoted.

Can the world's nations be persuaded to give up the national policies that hamper trade and distort economic life? One example is the subsidies that both the United States and the European Union provide to farmers. Another example is special help provided by governments to key industries, such as textiles and steel. The purpose is to keep out the goods of foreign competitors. And still another example is patent and copyright protection for the producers of everything from popular music and computer software to the latest drugs and "designer genes" of biotechnology. All such measures are forms of protectionism.

Many developing nations use these examples in arguing that the rules of international trade favor the wealthier nations. Either end special protections in industrial nations, they say, or adopt new rules that protect developing nations too. One proposal has been to forgive past debts of the poorer nations and let them start over with no debt to foreign lenders. Another has been to adopt special rules to boost the prices of raw materials like cocoa and coffee that many developing nations export. Prices on such exports have fallen in recent decades. The income of the nations selling them has also fallen.

For some people—in industrial and developing nations alike—globalization itself is an enemy. Critics argue that it harms local communities and industries. They say it takes away jobs from high-paid workers in industrial countries and gives them to low-paid workers in developing countries. Globalization is said to increase the profits mainly of large, multinational corporations. And it is said to undermine democracy by making those corporations richer and more powerful than some governments. By the start of the 21st century, antiglobalization protests had become part of the international scene. Protesters took to the streets at meetings of the World Bank and International Monetary Fund, and at gatherings of the Group of Eight leading industrial nations. Most of the protesters were peaceful. Some were political activists. Others were members of labor unions and religious groups. However, antiglobalization protests have often turned violent. Small groups of anarchists, who wish to destroy all governments, have turned up. They have attacked people and property and provoked vigorous police action. We can expect antiglobalization protests to continue, since the pain of globalization is very real.

Defenders of globalization argue that the gain is worth the pain. Job losses in industrial nations, they say, are offset by job gains in other parts of the world. And even though many of the newer jobs pay lower wages, economic growth is enhanced. This leads to more and better jobs. Moreover, say the defenders, globalization does not simply take jobs away from industrial nations. It adds new, higher paying jobs in industries that can take advantage of freer trade. Defenders of globalization see the search for profits as desirable, not shameful. They say the competition for profits

Copyright 2003 by Randy Glasbergen.
www.glasbergen.com

"Billy, you've been a fine son, but it's time for a change. I found a child overseas who can do it cheaper."

leads to higher efficiency, lower costs, and lower prices, which benefit everyone. Furthermore, supporters say globalization promotes democracy rather than reducing it. They argue that governments remain far more powerful than corporations. A 2007 research project by the Federal Reserve Bank of Dallas found that globalized nations (those more fully integrated into the global economy) pursued polices that achieve faster economic growth, lower inflation, higher incomes, and greater economic freedom. It was also found that nations more open to the world economy have more respect for the rule of law and protection of property rights and offer greater political stability than do less globalized nations.

1. *Explain why you AGREE or DISAGREE with the belief that the world in the rest of the 21st century will be shaped by economic issues.*

2. *What are some barriers to global free trade that industrial nations still maintain?*

3. *What arguments are made by opponents and defenders of globalization?*

New Realties: How Far Will Technology Take Us?

In 2007, scientists at IBM announced a new advance in the manufacture of semiconductors that could increase their speed and reduce their energy consumption. The new manufacturing process, to be used in 2009, will make possible a new generation of microprocessing chips.

The IBM advance has implications for wireless technology. In coming years, communication chips may be embedded in a host of everyday objects. Such chips, and the networks that link them together, may prove to be the most powerful form of wireless technology. Microprocessors have been built into everything in the past few decades. In the future, wireless communications may be expected to become part of all kinds of large and small objects. Machines will talk to other machines and be maintained and upgraded from a distance. Sensors on buildings and bridges will operate them and ensure that they are safe. Wireless systems on farms will control irrigation systems. The safety of medicines and foods will be certified by wireless tags. Tiny chips in people's bodies will send vital signs to doctors and clinics to maintain health. Carmakers are already using wireless communications to monitor vehicles so that they know when to replace parts before they fail.

The wireless communications revolution is about information, available anywhere at almost no cost. Without wires and cables, more information about more things will get to where it is most needed. The long-term concern about all of this is privacy. In a world in which wireless networks interconnect and information is widely shared, anyone can be monitored at any time. Electromagnetic radiation may become a danger to health.

New Realties: How Will the English Language Change the World?

As a response to globalization, business schools and universities around the world have been electing to make English their official language of instruction, rather than the language of the country in which the school is located. By 2007, for example, some South Korean universities were offering up to 30 percent of their courses in the English language. To accommodate an increasing number of international students, the Lille School of Management in France teaches half of its postgraduate programs in English. Candidates for a master's degree in business administration at the Instituto de Empressa in Spain may take their admission test in English and enroll in English-speaking courses.

The shift to learning English enables schools to better compete for students and the tuition payments that they bring. It makes it possible for students to come from anywhere in the world and to go everywhere after graduation.

Some university officials argue that the use of English is a natural consequence of globalization. Just as Latin was the language most used by scholars and diplomats during Europe's Middle Ages, English has become the international language of business, scientific research, and diplomacy in the 21st century. In the future, we may all live and work in an English-speaking world.

New Realities: A World in Flux

Nothing is simple. All is complex. That is one of the hard lessons the world learned during the 20th century. The rest of the 21st century will continue to teach that lesson. As the world faces the issues of war and peace, as it tries to find ways to shrink poverty and expand opportunity, people will face issues we cannot now predict or even imagine. But we can draw on our knowledge of the distant past and on the recent history discussed in this book for pointers and guidance. Year after year, "the world today" becomes "the world tomorrow." And there will be many more tomorrows to follow.

Chapter 14 Review

A. *Choose the item that best completes each sentence.*

1. *Methods that governments have adopted to fight terrorism include   (a) nuclear strikes   (b) metal detectors in shopping centers   (c) truck bombs.*

2. *One concern about stepped-up domestic security is that the government might   (a) run out of money   (b) ignore public opinion   (c) take away people's constitutional rights.*

3. *The mailing of anthrax spores to U.S. media and government offices was an example of   (a) chemical warfare   (b) massive retaliation   (c) bioterrorism.*

4. *Nations that offered support for the U.S.-led "war on terrorism" included   (a) Russia and Uzbekistan   (b) Syria and Britain   (c) Israel and Iraq.*

5. *The United States declared that its attack on terrorists was   (a) directed mainly at Muslims   (b) directed mainly at atheists   (c) not directed at Muslims.*

6. *Experts have claimed that the rest of the 21st century will be shaped by   (a) military conflicts   (b) economic issues   (c) competition for colonies.*

7. *One feature of globalization is that   (a) all barriers to trade have been removed   (b) democracy has spread to more nations   (c) economic ties among nations have increased.*

8. *One criticism of globalization is that it   (a) results in fewer jobs overall   (b) takes away jobs from workers in developed countries   (c) reduces businesses' profits.*

9. *One defense of globalization is that it leads to   (a) lower prices for consumers   (b) higher profits for multinational corporations   (c) more low-wage jobs in industrial countries.*

10. *Antiglobalization protesters often show up at meetings of the (a) United Nations   (b) World Bank   (c) World Health Organization.*

B. *Use information in Chapter 14 to explain the following possible future newspaper headlines:*

ARAB NATIONS DEBATE WHETHER TO BACK "WAR ON TERRORISM"

IMPROVED CHIP SPEEDS WIRELESS REVOLUTION

TAIWAN WELCOMES TRANSPLANTED U.S. FACTORIES

AMERICAN WORKERS SAY THEY ARE UNABLE TO COMPETE WITH LOW-PAID FOREIGN WORKERS

Unit IV Review

A. *Select ONE of the themes listed below. Use information from Unit IV to write an essay that answers the following questions:*

- ◆ *What do you think might happen regarding this theme in the near future?*
- ◆ *What recent events or developments indicate what the future might bring in this area?*

THEMES

1. *Strengthening security against terrorist attacks*

2. *The military response to international terrorism*

3. *Technological and linguistic change*

4. *The debate over globalization and its effects*

5. *Challenges for the United States in the years ahead*

B. *Use information from Unit IV to define the following terms:*

1. *"war on terrorism"*

2. *bioterrorism*

3. *globalization*

INDEX